Olympics in Conflict

In the second half of the twentieth century, the Olympics played an important role in the politics of the Cold War and was part of the conflicts between the Capitalist Block, the Socialist Block and Third World countries. The Games of the New Emerging Forces (GANEFO) is one of the best examples of the politicization of sport and the Olympics in the Cold War era. From the 1980s onward, the Olympics has facilitated communication and cooperation between nations in the post–Cold War era and contributed to the formation of a new world order. In August 2016, the Games of the XXXI Olympiad was held in Rio de Janeiro, making Brazil the first South American country to host the Summer Olympics. This was widely regarded as a new landmark event in the history of the modern Olympic movement. From the GANEFO to Rio, the Olympic Games have witnessed the shifting balance in international politics and world economy. This book aims at understanding the transformation of the Olympics over the past decades and tries to explain how the Olympic movement played its part in world politics, the world economy and international relations against the background of the rise of developing countries.

The chapters in this book were published as a special issue in *The International Journal of the History of Sport*.

Lu Zhouxiang is a Lecturer in Chinese Studies at the National University of Ireland Maynooth, Ireland. His main research interests are Chinese history, nationalism and China's sport policy and practice.

Fan Hong is a Professor in Asian Studies at Bangor University, Wales. Her main research interests are in the areas of sociology, politics, cross-cultural studies, sports studies and Asian studies.

Sport in the Global Society: Historical Perspectives

Edited by
Mark Dyreson, Pennsylvania State University, USA
Thierry Terret, University of Lyon, France
Rob Hess, Victoria University, Australia

Titles in the Series

The Sports Development of Hong Kong and Macau
New challenges after the handovers
Edited by Brian Bridges and Marcus P. Chu

Olympics in Conflict
From the games of the new emerging forces to the Rio Olympics
Edited by Lu Zhouxiang and Fan Hong

Methodology in Sports History
Edited by Wray Vamplew and Dave Day

Media, Culture, and the Meanings of Hockey
Constructing a Canadian hockey world, 1896-1907
By Stacy L. Lorenz

Olympic Perspectives
Edited by Stephan Wassong, Richard Baka and Janice Forsyth

Historicizing the Pan-American Games
Edited by Bruce Kidd and Cesar R. Torres

Sport and Violence: Rethinking Elias
Dominique Bodin and Luc Robène

Sport, War and Society in Australia and New Zealand
Edited by Martin Crotty and Robert Hess

Global Perspectives on Sport and Physical Cultures
Edited by Annette Hofmann, Gerald Gems and Maureen Smith

Games and Sporting Events in History
Organisations, performances and impact
Edited by Annette Hofmann, Gerald Gems and Maureen Smith

Brazilian Sports History
Edited by Maurício Drumond and Victor Andrade de Melo

Olympics in Conflict

From the Games of the New Emerging Forces to the Rio Olympics

Edited by
Lu Zhouxiang and Fan Hong

LONDON AND NEW YORK

First published 2018
by Routledge
2 Park Square, Milton Park, Abingdon, Oxon, OX14 4RN, UK

and by Routledge
711 Third Avenue, New York, NY 10017, USA

Routledge is an imprint of the Taylor & Francis Group, an informa business

© 2018 Taylor & Francis

All rights reserved. No part of this book may be reprinted or reproduced or utilised in any form or by any electronic, mechanical, or other means, now known or hereafter invented, including photocopying and recording, or in any information storage or retrieval system, without permission in writing from the publishers.

Trademark notice: Product or corporate names may be trademarks or registered trademarks, and are used only for identification and explanation without intent to infringe.

British Library Cataloguing in Publication Data
A catalogue record for this book is available from the British Library

ISBN13: 978-0-8153-9661-1

Typeset in MinionPro
by diacriTech, Chennai

Publisher's Note
The publisher accepts responsibility for any inconsistencies that may have arisen during the conversion of this book from journal articles to book chapters, namely the possible inclusion of journal terminology.

Disclaimer
Every effort has been made to contact copyright holders for their permission to reprint material in this book. The publishers would be grateful to hear from any copyright holder who is not here acknowledged and will undertake to rectify any errors or omissions in future editions of this book.

Contents

Citation Information		vii
Notes on Contributors		ix
Series Editors' Foreword		xi

Introduction   1
Lu Zhouxiang and Fan Hong

1   Independent Olympic Athletes and the Legitimacy of the International Olympic Committee in Resolving International Conflicts   2
Tiago Del Tedesco Guioti, Mauro Cardoso Simões and Eliana de Toledo

2   The Legacy of the Games of the New Emerging Forces and Indonesia's Relationship with the International Olympic Committee   19
Friederike Trotier

3   'The Sole Anti-Democratic Federation in the Entire Olympic Movement': Early International Association of Athletics Federations Development Initiatives Between Commercialization and Democratization, 1974–1987   39
Jörg Krieger

4   Sport in Singapore (1945–1948): From Rehabilitation to Olympic Status   59
Nick Aplin

5   Olympics, Media and Politics: The First Olympic Ideas in Brazilian Society During the Late Nineteenth and Early Twentieth Centuries   78
Fabio de Faria Peres, Victor Andrade de Melo and Jorge Knijnik

6   The Development of Social Media and its Impact on the Intercultural Exchange of the Olympic Movement, 2004–2012   93
Yinya Liu

CONTENTS

7 A Game for the Global North: The 2018 Winter Olympic Games in
   Pyeongchang and South Korean Cultural Politics   109
   Jung Woo Lee

8 The Development of the Olympic Narrative in Chinese Elite
   Sport Discourse from Its First Successful Olympic Bid to the
   Post-Beijing Games Era   125
   Richard Xiaoqian Hu and Ian Henry

9 Xi Jin-Ping's World Cup Dreams: From a Major Sports Country
   to a World Sports Power   147
   Tien-Chin Tan, Hsien-Che Huang, Alan Bairner and Yu-Wen Chen

   Index   163

Citation Information

The chapters in this book were originally published in *The International Journal of the History of Sport*, volume 33, issue 12 (June 2016). When citing this material, please use the original page numbering for each article, as follows:

Introduction
Introduction
Lu Zhouxiang and Fan Hong
The International Journal of the History of Sport, volume 33, issue 12 (June 2016)
pp. 1303

Chapter 1
Independent Olympic Athletes and the Legitimacy of the International Olympic Committee in Resolving International Conflicts
Tiago Del Tedesco Guioti, Mauro Cardoso Simões and Eliana de Toledo
The International Journal of the History of Sport, volume 33, issue 12 (June 2016)
pp. 1304–1320

Chapter 2
The Legacy of the Games of the New Emerging Forces and Indonesia's Relationship with the International Olympic Committee
Friederike Trotier
The International Journal of the History of Sport, volume 33, issue 12 (June 2016)
pp. 1321–1340

Chapter 3
'The Sole Anti-Democratic Federation in the Entire Olympic Movement': Early International Association of Athletics Federations Development Initiatives Between Commercialization and Democratization, 1974–1987
Jörg Krieger
The International Journal of the History of Sport, volume 33, issue 12 (June 2016)
pp. 1341–1360

CITATION INFORMATION

Chapter 4
Sport in Singapore (1945–1948): From Rehabilitation to Olympic Status
Nick Aplin
The International Journal of the History of Sport, volume 33, issue 12 (June 2016)
pp. 1361–1379

Chapter 5
Olympics, Media and Politics: The First Olympic Ideas in Brazilian Society During the Late Nineteenth and Early Twentieth Centuries
Fabio de Faria Peres, Victor Andrade de Melo and Jorge Knijnik
The International Journal of the History of Sport, volume 33, issue 12 (June 2016)
pp. 1380–1394

Chapter 6
The Development of Social Media and its Impact on the Intercultural Exchange of the Olympic Movement, 2004–2012
Yinya Liu
The International Journal of the History of Sport, volume 33, issue 12 (June 2016)
pp. 1395–1410

Chapter 7
A Game for the Global North: The 2018 Winter Olympic Games in Pyeongchang and South Korean Cultural Politics
Jung Woo Lee
The International Journal of the History of Sport, volume 33, issue 12 (June 2016)
pp. 1411–1426

Chapter 8
The Development of the Olympic Narrative in Chinese Elite Sport Discourse from Its First Successful Olympic Bid to the Post-Beijing Games Era
Richard Xiaoqian Hu and Ian Henry
The International Journal of the History of Sport, volume 33, issue 12 (June 2016)
pp. 1427–1448

Chapter 9
Xi Jin-Ping's World Cup Dreams: From a Major Sports Country to a World Sports Power
Tien-Chin Tan, Hsien-Che Huang, Alan Bairner and Yu-Wen Chen
The International Journal of the History of Sport, volume 33, issue 12 (June 2016)
pp. 1449–1465

For any permission-related enquiries please visit:
http://www.tandfonline.com/page/help/permissions

Notes on Contributors

Nick Aplin is a senior lecturer in the Physical Education and Sport Science Academic Group, National Institute of Education, Nanyang Technological University, Singapore. Research interests focus on games and sport in colonial and post-independence Singapore.

Alan Bairner is a professor at School of Sport, Exercise and Health Sciences, Loughborough University, UK. He has a long-standing research interest in the relationship between sport and politics with a particular focus on national identities and nationalism.

Yu-Wen Chen is a research assistant at the Department of Physical Education at National Taiwan Normal University, Taiwan. His research interests include sport policy, sport globalization and table tennis.

Fabio de Faria Peres is with the Graduate Program in Leisure Studies at the Federal University of Minas Gerais, Brazil.

Tiago Del Tedesco Guioti holds a bachelor's degree in Sports Science from the University of Campinas, Brazil, and a master's degree in Interdisciplinary Graduate in Humanities Applied Social Sciences at the same university.

Victor Andrade de Melo is a professor at the Graduate Program in Comparative History of Rio de Janeiro Federal University, Brazil.

Eliana de Toledo is a graduate in physical education from the University of Campinas, Brazil, and holds a master's degree in Physical Education, and a PhD in History, from the Pontifical Catholic University of São Paulo, Brazil.

Ian Henry is a professor of Leisure Management and Policy and Director of the Centre for Olympic Studies and Research in the School of Sport, Exercise and Health Sciences, Loughborough University, UK.

Fan Hong is a professor in Asian Studies at Bangor University, Wales. Her main research interests are in the areas of sociology, politics, cross-cultural studies, sports studies and Asian studies.

NOTES ON CONTRIBUTORS

Hsien-Che Huang is an assistant professor of the Physical Education Office at National Cheng Kung University, Taiwan. His current research interests include sport policy and social issues in sports.

Jorge Knijnik is with the Centre for Educational Research and the Institute for Culture and Society at Western Sydney University, Australia.

Jörg Krieger is a lecturer at the Institute of Sport History/Olympic Studies Centre of the German Sport University Cologne, Germany, and a research fellow within the Department of Sport and Movement Studies at the University of Johannesburg, South Africa.

Jung Woo Lee, PhD, is a lecturer at the University of Edinburgh, UK, and is a founding member of the Edinburgh Critical Studies in Sport (ECSS) Research Group at the same university. His research interests include semiotic reading of sporting signs and globalization of sport.

Yinya Liu is an assistant lecturer in Chinese Studies at the National University of Ireland Maynooth, Ireland. Her main research interests are Chinese philosophy, Chinese literature, cultural studies and philosophy in literature.

Mauro Cardoso Simões is a graduate in Philosophy from the Pontifical Catholic University of Campinas, Brazil.

Tien-Chin Tan is a professor of Sport Sociology and Policy at National Taiwan Normal University, Taiwan. His main research interests are sport globalization, sport migration, sport industry and public policy for sport in Taiwan and China.

Friederike Trotier is a lecturer and a PhD student at the Department of Southeast Asian Studies at Goethe University Frankfurt, Germany. Her main research interests are urban change, place marketing and sporting events in Indonesia and Southeast Asia.

Richard Xiaoqian Hu is an assistant professor in the Division of Sport Science and Physical Education of Tsinghua University, China. His research interests embrace areas relating to sport and leisure policies, governance and Olympic studies.

Lu Zhouxiang is a lecturer in Chinese Studies at the National University of Ireland Maynooth, Ireland. His main research interests are Chinese history, nationalism and China's sport policy and practice.

Series Editors' Foreword

Sport in the Global Society: Historical Perspectives explores the role of sport in cultures both around the world and across the timeframes of human history. In the world we currently inhabit, sport spans the globe. It captivates vast audiences. It defines, alters, and reinforces identities for individuals, communities, nations, and empires. Sport organises memories and perceptions, arouses passions and tensions, and reveals harmonies and cleavages. It builds and blurs social boundaries – animating discourses about class, gender, race, and ethnicity. Sport opens new vistas on the history of human cultures, intersecting with politics and economics, ideologies, and theologies. It reveals aesthetic tastes and energises consumer markets.

Our challenge is to explain how sport has developed into a global phenomenon. The series continues the tradition established by the original incarnation of *Sport in the Global Society* (and in 2010 divided into *Historical Perspectives* and *Contemporary Perspectives*) by promoting the academic study of one of the most significant and dynamic forces in shaping the historical landscapes of human cultures.

In the twenty-first century, a critical mass of scholars recognises the importance of sport in their analyses of human experiences and *Sport in the Global Society: Historical Perspectives* provides an international outlet for the world's leading investigators on these subjects. Building on previous work in the series and excavating new terrain, our series remains a consistent and coherent response to the attention the academic community demands for the serious study of sport.

Mark Dyreson
Thierry Terret
Rob Hess

Introduction

Lu Zhouxiang and Fan Hong

In the second half of the twentieth century the Olympics has played an important role in the politics of the Cold War and was part of the conflicts between the Capitalist Block, the Socialist Block and Third World countries. The Games of the New Emerging Forces (GANEFO) is one of the best examples of the politicization of sport and the Olympics in the Cold War era. From the 1980s onward, the Olympics has facilitated communication and cooperation between nations in the post-Cold War era and contributed to the formation of a new world order. In August 2016, the Games of the XXXI Olympiad were held in Rio de Janeiro, making Brazil the first South American country to host the Summer Olympics. This was widely regarded as a new landmark event in the history of the modern Olympic movement. From the GANEFO to Rio, the Olympic Games have witnessed the shifting balance in international politics and world economy.

This special issue aims at understanding the transformation of the Olympics over the past decades and tries to explain how the Olympic movement played its part in world politics, the world economy and international relations against the background of the rise of Third World countries. The collection is based on an international conference which took place at Maynooth University, Ireland between 20 and 21 May 2016. The theme of the conference was 'Olympics in Conflict: From GANEFO to the Rio Olympics'. It was a result of close collaboration between *The International Journal of the History of Sport* and Maynooth University. We wish to acknowledge the School of Modern Languages, Literatures and Cultures of Maynooth University for its organizational and financial support.

Disclosure Statement

No potential conflict of interest was reported by the authors.

Independent Olympic Athletes and the Legitimacy of the International Olympic Committee in Resolving International Conflicts

Tiago Del Tedesco Guioti [ID], Mauro Cardoso Simões and Eliana de Toledo

ABSTRACT
Over the last three centuries (nineteenth, twentieth, and twenty-first) humanity has been facing huge political and ideological conflicts, especially wars. For these reasons, it was seen how necessary it was to create global institutions that aimed to promote peace and reduce or stop conflicts of this magnitude. Therefore, an international institution had already brought on its premises the principles of international peace and reconciliation through sport: the International Olympic Committee (IOC). However, despite bringing together nations around peaceful ties in an international competition, the IOC and the Olympic Games event have always been affected by constant conflicts along their path in the twentieth century, emphasizing issues involving nationalities. Thereby, in a mediator posture of international conflicts and in an effort to reduce the subversions that surrounded it, the IOC, in the 1990s, created the delegation of Independent Olympic Athletes. Such a delegation consists of athletes who cannot represent their respective nationalities at the Olympics due to political factors and/or armament conflicts. This proposal of the IOC demonstrates its posture to avoid, minimize, and even cease ideological and political events that might interfere with the Olympics Games or the athletes participating in them.

Introduction

The current historic, economic–political and sociocultural context reveals the strength and hegemonic global power acquired by the International Olympic Committee (IOC). This institution, of great political empowerment inside and outside the sportive environment, has achieved global levels of importance not only for internationalist and for multiculturalist policies of the Olympic Movement, but also to the detriment arising out of globalization processes in the late twentieth century and early twenty-first century.

Although, at the moment of its creation, in 1894, the IOC was just an institution with internationalist bias at the turn of nineteenth to the twentieth century, when the historical context was full of wars, revolutions, political conflicts involving borders and territories, many of these national issues are of the modern age. This persisted until the arrival of a new economic and political order from the 1970s, where the market provided neoliberal ideas and an institutionalized power for global companies and corporations never seen before, hovering above nation states during the contemporary age.

In this way, due to hegemonic global power and their great institutional legitimacy in present days, the IOC has been conducting actions and creating resolutions by which it can minimize or even cease conflicts, involving their national members through dialogues with other international institutions such as the United Nations (UN). On assuming this position, the peaceful principles within the sports spectacle, the Olympic Games, including the creation of the Independent Olympic Athletes (IOA) delegation, are promoted.

Athletes who compete only in individual sports and who cannot represent their respective nationalities at the Olympic Games constitute this new Olympic delegation, as their National Olympic Committees (NOCs) had suffered punishments by the IOC due to political factors and/or armament conflicts. It becomes evident, with the emergence of those athletes without an official representative of a nationality, that the creation of a non-national Olympic delegation replaces national symbols, flags, and anthems, with symbols of a global international institution represented by the IOC.

Therefore, the IOA has been established as a creation of current historical context and one of the objects of this paper is to evidence a posture of the IOC in avoiding, minimizing, or ceasing political and ideological events that may affect the achievement of the Olympic Games, or the participation of athletes at the same. In that context, this paper aims to analyze how the creation of IOA at Olympic Games legitimizes the IOC as a global corporation and how that creation is also an alternative to minimize or contribute to the resolution of international conflicts.

The Constitution of the Independent Olympic Athletes

In order to legitimize its global hegemonic power and fulfill its role as a global corporation today, the IOC has its decisions based on political and sociocultural events surrounding the world historical context of globalization, differently from the context of the modern age where it was totally submissive and subservient to national political events. One of those forms to contextualize was the IOA delegation constitution.

It is important to state that this delegation can also be called Individual Olympic Athletes or Independent Olympic Participants (IOP). Nevertheless, it chooses the term Independent Olympic Athletes, since the three terms are concerned (i.e. have the same precedents, only changing their nomenclature). Moreover, the Olympic delegation of Athletes Olympic Refugees (ROA), created for the Olympic Games in Rio 2016, is not characterized as IOA even if representing the same symbols and having the same purpose, as such athletes are recognized as stateless persons (i.e. without a valid nationality, characterizing them as refugees). Already the IOA have a nationality that cannot be represented in the Olympic Games.

The advent of IOA relates to the argument that the political and social action of nation states has decreased and has passed to global corporations as they are also beginning to create non-national or global communities. In this way, the IOA are an Olympic delegation, such as any other, but without official representation of an NOC belonging to the IOC.[1] In other words, they are athletes who cannot represent their respective nationalities at the Olympic Games. It is exactly by not having a national representation that such a delegation is considered as an exception because it has an exclusive character, given that the predominant aspect of the IOC is precisely the encouragement of nationalities due to its internationalist policies.

Therefore, the argument for the legitimation of IOC global power comes about through the emergence of this aspect of non-official national representation at the Olympic Games, based as they were on political factors that threatened the existence of some NOCs, through civil wars and national independence processes. Because of the IOC's intervention on external political processes and the resolutions of military conflicts affected by some of its national members (for example, Yugoslavia, East Timor, South Sudan, and the Netherlands Antilles), it established itself as a global corporation, especially to promote and ensure one of its major principles, namely peace through sport.

It is important to consider the precedents that were necessary for the IOC creating or allowing the participation of athletes with no nationalities at the Olympic Games, an event that brings together about 206 national delegations.[2] Therefore, there are three precedents for this paper: the NOC, the Olympic truce idea, and relations and dialogues with the UN.

The IOC is ruled, in addition to its Executive members, by NOCs representing the members associated with it. In other words, for each recognized NOC there exists a nationality associated with the IOC,[3] and thereby the NOC means to be one of the three components of the Olympic Movement, together with the IOC and the International Sports Federations. Moreover, the mission of a NOC is to develop, promote, and protect the Olympic Movement in their respective nation states in accordance with the Olympic Charter.

Along the same line, Chappelet Mabbott suggests that NOCs 'are the territorial representatives of the IOC'.[4] When dealing with representation of a nationality, the existence of a NOC associated with the IOC is extremely important, especially when related to the exaltation of national symbols at the Olympic Games as well as to the constitution of the IOA, because the NOC has as its main objective to select, register, and send their athletes and teams to participate and therefore to represent the nationalities at an Olympic Games.[5]

Moreover, to understand the reason for the importance of NOCs, it is necessary to have the perception of how a NOC is recognized by the IOC. In that way, in the present day, the IOC recognizes at most one NOC for a State, possessing and accepting only a notion of a national state, referring to them as independent states recognized by the international community within the Olympic environment. In other words, in practice, those states which are recognized by the UN.[6]

However, this nation state conception, allied with the UN perception, occurred from the 1980s, because before that period, the recognition and above all, the nation state notion by the IOC, was given otherwise. Therefore, the IOC recognized the NOC to have around 10 territories, often islands, which had, to varying degrees, a dependency with other states.[7]

That conception has its roots in the slogan 'all games, all nations', which in principle is used to spread the Olympic spirit. In addition, it was another criterion used for recognition of an NOC, to possess the minimum number of five national sports federations (IFS), in which three of them represent a sport included in an Olympic Games program.[8]

While the IOC is formed and managed by NOCs and, above all, the Olympic Games continue to be an international sports competition with national representation, it is evident that the use of recognition or association with a NOC through the IOC is a political factor and a display of power to the world. It is for this reason that the difference about perceptions of what would be a nation state concept, allowed and still allows the Olympic governing body to have the highest number of UN associated members. In other words, they are 206 associate members against 193 members.[9] By way of explanation, the 13 extra members that the IOC has include Aruba, American Samoa, Bermuda, Cayman Islands, Cook Islands, Guam, Hong Kong, US Virgin Islands, British Virgin Islands, Palestine, Puerto Rico, Taiwan, and South Sudan.[10]

Although, for being a political institution, aware of changes in the political–economic and sociocultural dynamics of contemporary global society, for being influenced by international policies and for having an institutional power higher than national States, the IOC, in the same way that recognizes its members, can withdraw the recognition of a NOC for two major reasons.

The first is for a specific NOC which does not respect its obligations as specified in the Olympic Charter (for example, the loss of autonomy of their national government, corruption, and failure to comply with fundamental Olympic principles such as non-discrimination based on racial, ethnic, and religious grounds).[11] The second reason is that there are national representations that do not have a recognized NOC, because they are newly created states or because their respective NOCs have ceased to be recognized because there is no such national state.[12]

Therefore, it is in the impossibility, absence or suspension of a specific NOC (considering its importance to the national representation at the Olympic Games and concern to prevent these causalities and penalties affecting national members' athletes), that the IOC allows the participation of athletes with the designation IOA to attend the Olympic Games.

It is noteworthy that without an official representative of a nationality, the IOA participate and compete at the Olympic Games under the Olympic flag and in case they win a gold medal, the anthem to be played is the Olympic hymn.[13] That is, the most impressive symbols at the national level are replaced by symbols that represent an institution of international nature.

Moreover, although it does not represent any national symbol, the garb of the IOA is characterized by a uniform predominantly white. White is considered a neutral color, where the print of the Olympic flag and the printing of the acronym IOA can be observed, as well as the symbol of a great company of sports equipment responsible for making the same. This is evidence of the full inclusion of this delegation in the context of globalization.

Between the two reasons which determine the withdrawal of recognition of a NOC, which are decisive to create the IOA, one is a condition related to the emergence of another precedent for the IOA establishment supplanted by the IOC. The reason in question is international conflicts and/or political processes, especially those that came from military use.

Thus, the disposition of these processes rescued by the IOC during the 1990s, and supported beyond the recognition of NOCs, is the Olympic Truce. That truce idea was not created in the modern age and not even in the contemporary age, but it was one of the principles that guided the athletic practices at the Olympic Games of ancient Greece, where it was seen as an armistice to the peaceful conduct of Games in the Greek polis.[14] From that perception, the Olympic Truce idea reappears and has the same relevance as in classical antiquity due to the IOC coming across international conflicts that could remove the participation of athletes at the Games in the contemporary age.

However, as argued by Ramos,[15] the decision of the IOC to create the IOA, from 1992, broke the tradition of athletes representing their nations at the Olympics. At the same time, it has become a dangerous precedent, because in other situations, especially during boycotts, athletes were affected by these political processes and could ask the IOC to allow them to compete as independent athletes, as indeed happened, but the IOC refused. The reason of these refusals is not known, however, it is worth remembering that the historical context of the relevance of the concepts and national values were still strong and significant for refusing the creation of a non-national delegation.

The most relevant cases are the punishment of South Africa because of apartheid (1963–1993), the boycott resulting from the political processes of the Cold War in 1980 and 1984, as well as the case of China and Thailand in 1956 and 1976 and the boycott of the 1976 Games in Montreal by African states that had repudiated a friendly match between South Africa and New Zealand rugby teams in the period of apartheid sanctions.

In this way, the Olympic Truce ideal, resurgent during the contemporary age, has been the connecting link to the third major precedent to the establishment of the IOA: closer relationships between the IOC and the UN. Such relationships were due to forces promoting peace among its members in the post-Cold War period, a guiding principle to the creation of both institutions.[16] In this context, the relationship takes place through meetings, especially at the UN General Assembly, where the IOC President is invited to participate in subjects which include resolutions incumbent upon the IOC to decide, because it has a great artifice to attract the attention of the nation states on peace processes: sport through the Olympic Games.[17]

Starting from the 1990s, at the 48th UN General Assembly session, the Olympic Truce idea was adopted in UN resolutions every two years, one year before each Olympic Games event, referring to the winter and summer Olympic editions. In addition, this was the beginning of common activities between the IOC and UN.[18]

The first result of those negotiations with the UN was about the collapse of the former Republic of Yugoslavia. Yugoslavia had been banished from competing in the 1992 Olympic Games according to an IOC response to resolution number 757 of the National Council of UN Security, which established economic, diplomatic, cultural, and sports sanctions for genocide and civil war occurring against nations such as Croatia, Bosnia, and Herzegovina and Slovenia following the rupture of the Federal Republic of Yugoslavia in June 1991.[19] Living in a new age, the IOC members decided unanimously and in agreement with the UN, at the 99th Session of the IOC Executive Committee, to allow the participation of former Yugoslavia athletes as IOA, but only in individual sports.[20]

Therefore, introduced for the first time, the IOA delegation came under the IOC seal in collaboration with the UN, making sport, through an international sporting competition and the Olympic Truce, greater than global political and economic aspects. It is also pertinent to remember that the Yugoslavian NOC ceased to be recognized and it has been another reason for the establishment of that delegation at the 1992 Games.

Furthermore, this was not the only appearance of IOA in an Olympic Games. The IOA appeared again at the Olympic Games in Sydney in 2000. The case in question involved East Timor, which had just declared independence from its former colonial ruler Portugal, and Indonesia, after a long diplomatic negotiation process with UN support, of which its inhabitants voted for independence from Indonesia in August of 1999.[21] In that way, the IOC, again in accordance with the UN, allowed the East Timor athletes, who did not already have a recognized NOC, to be sent under their national representation to participate at the Olympics in the same manner as the 1992 delegation.

The last appearance of an IOA delegation analyzed for this paper was at the Olympic Games in London in 2012. Again, international conflicts had emerged and the IOC intervened, allowing the participation of South Sudan as IOA. South Sudan was a nation state created in 2011, to the detriment of peace agreements which ended the second civil war in Sudan.[22] Thus, with the creation of this new nation state there was no time for the constitution of a NOC recognized by the IOC,[23] as occurred with East Timor.

At the same Olympic Games there was also the unprecedented case of the Netherlands Antilles, and the withdrawal of recognition of its NOC because the Netherlands annexed the Netherlands Antilles to its government, after the island gave up their national autonomy and became a Dutch municipality from 2010.[24] This is due to the high level of dependence and proximity to cultural relations with the European nation state. From there, the IOC allowed the participation of athletes of that island as an IOA delegation aggregated with athletes from South Sudan.[25]

Therefore, the IOA constitution is a concrete fact and institutionalized by the IOC under the premises of NOC membership and obstruction of the NOC and the return of the Olympic Truce idea. We also saw agreements and dialogues constructed with the UN and the international community, which also made possible the constitution of the same. In other words, it is extremely important for the contribution of institutions and global corporations to create new forms of global identification and above all, the permission of participation of athletes without the aegis of the national symbols that were strong and remain strong even with the process of globalization.

Moreover, it is obvious that the premise of an IOA existence reflects the legitimacy of the power that the maximum Olympic entity has, in present days, because this new Olympic delegation is evidence of an attempt to resolve or minimize political processes such as the independence of East Timor and of South Sudan. Not to mention the dissolution of national sovereignty of the Netherlands Antilles, as well as international conflicts such as the civil war in Yugoslavia and many other cases outside the IOC.

Thus, the IOC rises to a level of global importance that equates or overlaps nation states including other global corporations that are so essential in the contemporary world. In that way, it is necessary to assess the history of the IOC to have an understanding of how it obtained such predominance legitimating it to perform actions, especially the creation of the IOA.

The IOC as an International Institution of the Modern Age

An institution or entity creates and establishes their principles according to a historical context in which it is located in the current political economic order and its sociocultural consequences, as well as in accordance with the principles and objectives of its founders and managers. With the IOC, it was not different given that it had its formation and the acquisition of an international power and global recognition in two specific historical contexts. The first one, of its construction and establishment, occurs in the nineteenth and twentieth century. The second one, of its recognition and obtaining a global hegemonic power, occurs in the late twentieth and early twenty-first centuries.

It is in this growing historical, economic and political context that the IOC is considered able to dialogue with their peers about the possible solutions and conflicts with the IOA. Thus, the analysis begins with the period of IOC construction, the time in question being the end of the nineteenth century that represented the advent of a new economic and political form of managing the world: The Industrial Revolution.

This revolution was characterized by the rising production of consumption goods that assisted capital accumulation, inspiring enrichment and structural strengthening of nation states under the influence of a free and expansionary economy.[26] Moreover, to obtain such an economy it was necessary that those modern nation states, created and strengthened as a result of the Industrial Revolution and other such as the French Revolution and the Democratic Revolutions of 1848, are based on the union of an economic ideology with a political ideology. In other words, the junction between economic liberalism and nationalism.[27]

Apart from providing the strengths and economic power acquired by modern states and a new form of social life, this period is also responsible for the institutionalization of athletic practices and games in systematic and regulated practices known as sport. It is important to note that the 'sport' name is a creation only from the modern age, given that its characteristics are configured and in line with the assumptions of social context mentioned above, as well as their goals, also created from a need for universal rules, such that each 'sport' could be played by different regions of the nation, and thereafter, among nations.[28]

In other words, the fun, festive and traditional games and athletic practices, practiced before the modern age, became sports through a process which resembles the invention of tradition proposed by Hobsbawm and Ranger in which 'new' traditions came about simply because of an inability to use or adapt old traditions to that context.[29]

Thereafter, through the influence of industrial revolutionary processes during the nineteenth century, modern sports have owned some principles similar to those of the Industrial Revolution, such as bureaucratic organization, transformation of social practices, and the principles of competition and performance. From this new structural logic, bureaucratic organization and its hierarchy and rationalization of traditional institutions made possible the creation of sports institutions such as sports clubs, confederations, federations, and committees (such as the IOC), to command the dissemination and sports development through associationalism and a rational order.[30]

Therefore, it is this rational way of managing the structures and institutions which resulted in the transformation of social practices in modern societies and thus sports were considered a civilizing process as well as educational institutions, because they provided a code of conduct and acceptable sensitivity,[31] bringing the citizenship process for members of a national modern and industrial society.

Others similar precepts are the principles of competition and performance that promoted and still promote modern and contemporary capitalist societies for their development, using sport as a metaphorical artifact of social and individual behavior to a higher production of goods and capital.[32] Finally, a similar principle between sport and modern capitalist societies which should be included here is 'social rising' because social groups are not, in the same way, strongly stratified as they were in the pre-modern period such as feudalism, where individuals were often born, lived, and died just a peasant. Now, in the modern age individuals have their classes imposed by an economic system, but they have a chance to rise socially if they accumulate goods and financial capital, causing a change in their livelihood patterns. In that sense, sport is useful as a driving force of 'social rising' from the mid twentieth century when sport became professional and, most of all, profitable.

Moreover, it is important to discuss English public schools, which were supported by aristocracies and the majority classes in order to develop educational and moral aspects of a civilizing process, as well as to affirm their high social status. Whereas, sport had an amateur and social distinction bias at the end of nineteenth century and the mid-twentieth century.[33] In other words, only those who attained a high purchasing power could practice it, pushing aside other disadvantaged classes.

Elias and Dunning point out that there are three aspects related to modern social life and sport that increase the meaning of sport, making us think about the relevance to the construction of IOC pillars. The first aspect concerns the development of sport as a pleasant excitement and as a disciplinary form of individual and social behavior. The second aspect is sport's transformation as one of the main means of collective identification, focusing on its political use by nation states due to the exaltation of national symbols such as flags and anthems. The third aspect is the emergence of sport as a decisive influence on people's lives, being responsible for sublimation and/or alienation of a society.[34]

With this appeal in the daily lives of citizens within nation states, sport has its meaning and relevance taken to a level that has increased the attention of sovereign state governments on sport as a possible tool of legitimation, providing for them a feeling of patriotism, and national representation.[35] In this way, inserted into the context of national economic expansion due to economic liberalism, conflicts over territories and border disputes by new national states, and by the thought that de Coubertin had about the contribution of sport to peace, attracting many people to share experiences and exalt the celebration of sports performance,[36] there was the need to create a neutral institution regarding nationalities that is, an international institution.

Therefore, the IOC was founded in 1894 at the Sorbonne in France, through a sports congress with the main objective to provide peace among nations because Coubertin had as a pedagogical and peaceful purpose, mutual respect between them resolving their disputes only by the use of reason, the laws of coexistence and sports celebration, and not the use of weapons.[37] Moreover, this resurgence not only had the influence of the historical context that longed for such an institution, but was also influenced by the Olympic Games held in the polis of ancient Greece, whose pacifying role had been inherited.[38]

In order to highlight the peaceful bias that has privileged such a creation, major stakeholders and those patrons responsible for promoting peace movements, arising prior to the creation of the IOC in the final decades of the nineteenth century, were, at the invitation of Coubertin, present at the Congress of Sorbonne. It is evident then, that the achievement of peace and the reduction of the risk of having wars has been aided by sports competitions involving athletes from various nations.[39]

Moreover, national representations through NOCs are those that manage the IOC constitution and control the entity. It was the 12 member nation states, most of them from Europe, who attended the initial meeting.[40]

All the national representations are extremely important to the creation and continuity of the IOC as an international institution, or even to be an international corporation, as well as to the understanding of the reasons for the creation of the IOA. We can see in the arguments of Chappelet and Mabbott that the IOC essence remains, as it was in the early years, an association of individuals/national members who must represent and promote IOC interests in their nation states and not the opposite.[41] In other words, the aim is to keep it as an international institution, the first institution with such characteristics as national interests were not allowed to overlap the majority interests of the precepts that this new institution established.[42]

Therefore, nothing could hover over the Olympic Movement, which was another form to accomplish the Olympic Games every four years from 1896. Ethical and moral principles are used within the IOC and each member must respect it. Conceptualizing the Olympic Movement, it can be seen as a life philosophy, exalting and combining in its balanced contingent the qualities of will and mind. By blending sport with culture and education, the Olympic Movement attempts to create a way of life based on the delight found in effort, the educational value of good example, and respect for universal fundamental ethical principles.[43]

With this point of view, it is clear that the Olympic movement is directed primarily to athletes, who compete in the Olympic Games, regardless of their nationality, but privileging them. Thus, Coubertin delineated some assignments for individuals who were considered able to participate in the Olympic Games.[44] The first of these assignments was the excitement associated with the nation, race, and national symbols that represented the athlete in Olympic ceremonies, in order to create an idea of sports religion, the *religio athletae*, among competitors.

The second assignment refers to that which Coubertin called the elite of the body of individual superiority. That is, only those able to compete and participate in the Olympic Games or be considered as Olympic, were the individuals who possessed a high sports education and were able to compete for world records.[45] For these athletes, therefore, was given the slogan: *Citius, Altius, Fortius* (faster, higher, and stronger) that should not be seen exclusively from a technical and sporting perspective, but also in terms of philosophy and techniques.[46] The third and final assignment made to competitors by Coubertin, within the Olympic Movement, is the union between body and spirit characterizing the element of beauty.[47]

Therefore, to be considered as an Olympic athlete, through the principles designed by Coubertin, the individual should bind, in an excellent way, physical abilities and intellectual development, as well as representing their nationality in order to create an environment of friendship and peace in the Olympic Games. These characteristics are also requirements for the IOA, with the only assignment that is not considered for their participation being national representation.

Furthermore, with some principles of this movement as mutual respect, fair play and sport considered beyond a physical exercise, the principle of internationalism is the most important for this paper's scope, by the preponderance of the IOC's claim to be an international institution, and the creation of peaceful ideas that culminated in the creation of the IOA. In that way, the internationalism, comes through nationalism, a crucial political ideology to legitimize the nation states, while the blend of different nations and their particular forms of life, creates an international and multicultural language that could serve as a placeholder for internationalism.[48]

It is therefore very important that participation and national representation at the Olympic Games is provided by the NOC because the national members are an essential pillar for the construction and maintenance of the internationalist policy of the IOC. Quanz, in his study of the formation of the IOC, argues that internationalism and the basic ideas of peace movements arose when nation states reached an internal maturity as civilized nations through constitutive laws.[49] Thus, external relations could now be organized on the same legal footing in the service of peace and prosperity through international law. And the sport and international competitions have been used as one of these forms of external relations since they have been institutionalized as a civilizing process in national modern societies, as well as creating codes of conduct and disciplinary manners, as asserted by Elias and Dunning.

Moreover, to strengthen internationalism, the IOC was based on two ideals needed to expand its global reach and foremost spread its principles across all continents of the world. They are the slogan 'all games, all nations', and the guideline 'sporting countries'.

The 'all games, all nations' idea was intended to spread sport and, above all, the Olympic spirit in various nation states,[50] while the Olympic guideline called 'sporting countries' was characterized as a proposal that sports geography does not coincide with political and territorial geography. In other words, nationalities which have a territory defined by borders but do not have any recognition as nation states, are defined territories by social and cultural productions that allow it to obtain national identities. Examples of 'sporting countries' are Palestine, Kosovo, Puerto Rico, Taiwan and Macau, and others. Thus, the IOC, as an international institution with aspirations to spread its ideals to any nationality without political and/or historical consideration, recognizes the NOC of these respective territories.[51]

Accordingly, with these peaceful ideals and internationalist policies, the IOC was established as an international institution and had a legitimacy to it decades before another major international institution, the UN. Established in 1945, after World War II (1939–1945), the UN holds essentially the same purpose as the IOC (that is, the promotion of peace among its members), and was fundamental in the creation of the IOA to unite their efforts for a peaceful world respecting the national peculiarities as explained in the section above.

To better represent their internationalist policies and their international action, the IOC itself created the Olympic flag, which also does refer to the Olympic principle of multiculturalism by uniting in five rings the five continents belonging to the globe. Advancing further, the purpose of the five rings was not merely to represent the continents and all nations, but from now they all belong to the Olympic Movement and they are willing to accept the fruitful rivalry that it implies. In other words, it created a truly international emblem.[52] It is also worth mentioning that this same flag is used as the official symbol, in addition to the Olympic hymn, of non-national Olympic delegations (i.e. of the IOA), reinforcing the idea of a symbol representative of internationalists and peace according to the IOC guidelines.

Moreover, it is pertinent to point out that the IOC legitimacy to be an international institution was given during a period in which nationalist ideologies prevailed as absolute power, causing several dark events throughout the twentieth century, such as the two world wars and many others military and non-military conflicts, such as the Cold War, which also had an impact on the Olympic Games and disrespects the principles contained in the Olympic Movement.

In that way, with nation states as holders of political and sociocultural economic power and legitimizers of an absolute power during the modern age, the IOC had only the legitimacy of spreading the Olympic Movement, promoting peace among its members, and ensuring and organizing the Olympic Games. So much that it was observed that the IOC had the same parameters to anticipate the creation of the IOA in the modern age, but as concerns the participation of a non-national delegation in the context of relevance and exaltation of national ideas, believing that this action was not present at the time (i.e. it was unthinkable).

On the other hand, the legitimacy of the IOC as a global hegemonic power increased according to economic and political strength acquired by institutions not regulated by national authorities in the contemporary age. It is this legitimacy and weakening of the relevance of national ideologies and feelings that allowed the IOC to create the IOA.

The IOC as a Global Corporation During the Contemporary Age

The strong nation states, used for an economic, political, social, and cultural conformity, no longer have the same strength and social supremacy they had before. It is this new political–economic and sociocultural perspective that worked the changes caused by globalization, resulting in the advent of the IOA for the legitimization of a global power credited to the IOC.

In this way, the IOC political outlook during the modern age and the international community perception about their actions changed when the flow of capital, the production and consumption of goods and services and above all, the regulation of national economies, ceased to belong only to national institutions or nation states, and now also belonging to major global financial corporations and multinationals, marking this whole process as globalization in a new age, in a new context, the contemporary age.

It is at this time, the late twentieth century and early twenty-first century, that international level corporations, such as the World Bank, the IMF, NATO, the IOC itself, and the UN, as well as the economic blocs of MERCOSUR and EU, and some others, have obtained relevance, space, and full autonomy for regulation and control of economic transactions, as well as to reveal a new form of global political governance and to demonstrate consequences for sociocultural aspects of contemporary societies. This global change in economic and political behaviors was due to the passage of liberal economic thought to neoliberalism. While the first thought preached the economic expansion by sovereignty and national autonomy of states allied with nationalism, neoliberalism preaches, in a few words, minimum state intervention in the direction of national economies. In other words, is the ideology that affirms the irrelevance of nation states during a time of globalization, a major cause of weakening of the same?[53]

Under the same point of view, Moraes points out the relevance of market supremacy through neoliberalism for allocating resources, distribution of goods, services, income and remuneration, in addition to making it intolerant, in the face of national public authority interventions at the thought that state actions inhibit the driving force behind progress, and affect global agents of competitiveness.[54] In other words, nowadays the markets, companies, and corporations that are observed away from the nation states' aegis, have greater autonomy in their direction and actions around the world.

Therefore, there is subordination of nation states to international agencies, on globalization, evidenced by the passage of national sovereignty economic power to global markets because, while liberalism was based on principles of national sovereignty, or at least took it as a parameter, neoliberalism passes over it, shifting the possibilities of sovereignty for organizations, corporations, and other entities globally.[55]

In that sense, with all thought developed regarding the transfer of power from nation states to institutional and global corporations, it can be observed that the IOC is one of those examples which began negotiating the Olympics as a consumer product of its tutelage, unfolding modern sport to sport spectacle, massifying sports without borders in the world, as well as the creating this new Olympic delegation without national symbols. Thus, the same entity put sport under the aegis of neoliberal policies, above the nation states, keeping the Olympic Games as one of the greatest sporting and sociocultural events worldwide.

For the IOC to reach this level the role of the mass media was very important. Broadcasting rights began to be paid by television channels in the 1960 Rome Olympics, but were still meagre amounts until the 1972 Olympic Games in Munich, due to the fact that the President of the IOC at the time, Avery Brundage (1952–1972) did not really believe in the potential of television and the IOC was not really equipped with a fully fledged administrative infrastructure capable of managing the organizational aspects of coping with the media at the Games.[56] After that period, the increasing amounts received by the IOC through new contracts and the appreciation of the Olympic brand is notorious, especially following the Barcelona Games in 1992.[57]

To better place this argument, some data in order to exemplify the revenues obtained by the IOC through the sale of broadcasting rights of the Olympic Games are provided. The data come from the study by Chappelet and Mabbott and shows that in the Olympics of 1960 in Rome the amount received by television networks was $1.1 million. In the Olympics of Athens in 2004, the value was $1,492,600 billion.[58] That is, over a period of 44 years, just with the broadcasting rights alone, the IOC had an increase of 1357% in its revenue. The same authors also provide a possible reason for this growth: in mid-2008 the sales value of slots for commercials involved around $600,000 for 30 seconds in the telecommunications networks.

Other relevant data are the evolution in contracts with the sponsoring companies. In the period of the Olympic Games in Seoul in 1988, the IOC had contracts with nine sponsoring companies altogether, with a value of $106,000,000. However, by the period of the Olympic Games of 2008 in Beijing, 20 years later, the IOC had 12 contracts with sponsors to the value of US$866 million. Thus, in relation to sponsorship, there was an increase of approximately 817% in revenues from the IOC in which, adding to the amount of other income (television and tickets), the income of the entity in the period 2005–2008 was $5 billion.

It is from this period that the maximum authority of the Olympic Games had its revenue increased to values arising from negotiations with television networks, the creation of an international marketing program by ticket sales, and business relationships with major sponsoring companies (such as beverage brands, sporting goods, and fast foods).[59]

However, for the legitimacy of the global hegemonic power achieved by these international corporations, it is pertinent to have a great impact, either in actions, or with the same consequences, within the sociocultural environment of globalization processes. For this, it is necessary to refute the thought that globalization refers only to economic and political processes. This is the positioning of Santos, who defines globalization as a range of social relations that result in the intensification of transnational interactions, whether interstate practices, global capitalist practices, or social and transnational cultures practices.[60] In other words, it is about a drastic rupture in ways of being, feeling, acting, thinking, and inventing. It is a heuristic event of great proportions, affecting not only convictions but also worldviews.[61]

The great reason for this process is broad in its directions as the characteristics of capitalism can be considered as part of a civilizing process. It can be observed, for example, that due to the strength, complexity, extent, and expansiveness of capitalism as a civilizing process, the most diverse organizational forms of productive and social life activities tend to be covered, subordinated, modified, or dissolved by this process.[62] In addition, if we really consider capitalism as a civilization artifact, the globalization process, thought of as capital internationalization, leads to current continuous change in societies in their ways of dealing with the world in their social and cultural spheres.

In addition, the creation of IOA means subsequent changes in ways of dealing with new sociocultural inserts, appropriating current ways of life according to the new forms of governance in the world, suggesting the establishment of new social groups corresponding with global sociocultural appeal.

Analyzing the current context and the high importance of international actors to the detriment of national officials to determine the patterns and ways of life, the IOC, taking the social significance of sport to a level never seen before, operates on issues, debates and decisions that involve the political–economic and sociocultural events from the international community. In other words, the IOC starts to act and have its opinion respected outside of its domestic scope, assuming the role of being one of the greatest and most influential global corporations today, next to the UN, for example.

Thus, the IOC is committed to attempting to resolve or minimize conflicts and political issues that are within its reach. And, one of the ways to solve conflicts or somehow relieve those who are in conflict that the IOC found was the creation of an exclusive delegation of the IOA. Importantly, this creation emerged in the historical context of a decline in national values and concomitantly in the pursuit of its hegemonic power, since it has become a global corporation. As for promotion of the institution of the IOA, the delegation without national representation is offered to athletes affected by sanctions and political processes without a mandatory character. That is, the IOC allows, in the etymological sense of the word, the participation of athletes in Olympic Games respecting the will and individuality of each athlete, as this delegation is considered an exception rather than the rule.

Conclusions

In fact, historical contexts are essential to an understanding of how to establish the operation, management, range, and role of institutions whether it be national or international. In the case of this paper, the IOC aims, in two different contexts of humanity, have varied mainly in relation to the current economic and political system.

Consequently, during the modern age with the prerogatives of economic liberalism and nationalism, which provided an absolute force for sovereignty and national autonomy to states and the institutionalization and universalization of modern sports, being an artifact for the processes of civilization and the creation of codes of conduct of national modern societies, the IOC was regarded as an international institution having as its premises the spread of the Olympic spirit, peace through sport, and the continuance of the Olympic Games. It is during this period that the IOC becomes condescending toward political events and military conflicts of the time, partly due to its subservience to national authorities and the fact that it had no legitimate power to resolve conflicts.

However, with the advent of globalization processes in the contemporary age there has been an increase in the political and economic power of non-state actors. These states, held total control of their political and economic aspects during the modern age, and, in the present day, observe such transfer control to global corporations, through the passage of economic liberalism to neoliberalism. In other words, global corporations obtained therefore a sovereign autonomy away from national regulations.

In addition, one of the examples that we can observe of global corporation is the IOC, because it reflects the whole process and has a connotation that it exists not only to ensure the holding of Olympic Games, but to ensure its commercialization as a consumer product, making it a spectacle. For that, obtaining a global hegemonic power and its legitimation, the IOC starts to interfere and to participate in political events external to it, trying to create efforts to minimize or to resolve international conflicts related to its associate members.

One of these efforts is the constitution of IOA because such a delegation is given without any official national representation and allows athletes of nationalities, who have suffered punishments arising from political processes, to participate in the greatest sporting sociocultural event worldwide. Moreover, the creation of that new delegation reflects a strengthening of relationships as the IOC dialogues with the international community, especially with the UN.

Therefore, it is with the transformation of an international institution to a global corporation that the IOC has acquired not only a global power but also a legitimacy to interfere in processes and political conflicts that surround the world, mostly those that refer to its associated members. That legitimacy goes through the IOA establishment, which evidences above all the social and political power that the IOC has at the present time.

It is worth thinking of critical political decisions in relation to the attitude of the IOC toward political conflicts and processes. Because it is clear that in the history of sport in the twentieth century, there were conditions for the anticipation of the establishment of the IOA, including the anticipation of the idea of the Olympic Truce, considering that the IOA was and is a great solution/alternative to the resolution of internal and external problems associated with the IOC.

Notes

1. Jean-Loup Chappelet and Brenda Kübler-Mabbott, *The International Olympic Committee and the Olympic System: The Governance of World Sport* (New York: Routledge, 2008).
2. NOC, 'International Olympic Committee', Olympic.org, http://www.olympic.org/national-olympic-committees (accessed 23 April 2016).
3. Ibid.
4. Chappelet and Kübler-Mabbott, *The International Olympic Committee and the Olympic System*, 49.
5. Melo de Carvalho and José Manuel Constantino, *O que é o olimpismo: pequeno manual de iniciação* [What is Olympism: A Small Manual of Initiation] (Lisboa, Portugal: Livros Horizonte, 1986).
6. Chappelet and Kübler-Mabbott, *The International Olympic Committee and the Olympic System*.
7. Ibid.
8. Ibid., 50.
9. NOC, 'International Olympic Committee'.
10. Elga Castro Ramos, 'Puerto Rico is Not the Only One: Politics and Disparity Between the United Nations and the IOC Membership' (Paper presented at the Sixth International Symposium for Olympic Research, Ontario, Canada, October 2002, 256), http://library.la84.org/SportsLibrary/ISOR/ISOR2002zg.pdf (accessed 22 March 2016).
11. Chappelet and Kübler-Mabbott, *The International Olympic Committee and the Olympic System*.
12. Sportreference.com, 'Competitors Under the Olympic Flag, Summer Games', http://www.sports-reference.com/olympics/about/nationalities.html (accessed 30 April 2016).
13. 'East Timorese Athletes in Sydney', *Olympic Review* 26 (2000), 50.

14. Heather L. Reid and Christos Evangeliou, 'The Political Heritage of the Olympic Games Relevance, Risks, and Possible Rewards', in Robert Knight Barney, Janice Evelyn Forsyth, and Michael K. Heine (eds.), *Rethinking Matters Olympic: Investigations into the Socio-Cultural Study of the Modern Olympic Movement* (International Centre for Olympic Research, University of Western Ontario, 2010), 404–11. In Ancient Greece, the so-called Olympic Truce or *ekecheiria*, which protected pilgrims travelling to the Games, and the competition area itself from military aggression, was generally (although not universally) respected. Because the varied city states who participated in the Games were often at war with one another, the Olympic festival provided a safe place for them to negotiate with enemies, form alliances with friends, and perhaps even pray to the gods for victory in full view of their rivals.
15. Ramos, 'Puerto Rico is Not the Only One'.
16. Fékrou Kidane, 'The IOC and the United Nations', *Olympic Review* 26 (1995), 1–2.
17. Alpha Ibrahim Diallo, 'The IOC and United Nations System', *Olympic Review* 26 (1995), 2.
18. Naufumi Masumoto, 'The Birth of the Modern Olympic Truce: The Chronological Approach', in R.K. Barney, M.K. Heine, K.B. Wamsley, and G.H. MacDonald (eds.), *Pathways: Critiques and Discourse in Olympic Research* (Beijing: International Centre for Olympic Research, University of Western Ontario, 2008), 498.
19. Sufyan El Droubi, 'Notas sobre as resoluções obrigatórias do Conselho de Segurança da ONU e sua introdução no direito brasileiro' [Notes on Binding UN Security Council Resolutions and its Introduction into Brazilian Law], *Revista Imes Direito* 12 (2006), 47.
20. 'Decision of the 99th Session', *Olympic Review* 299 (1992), 3.
21. Patrícia Galvão Teles, *Autodeterminação em Timor Leste: Dos acordos de Nova Iorque à consulta popular de 30 de agosto de 1999* [Self-determination in East Timor: From the New York Agreements to the Popular Consultation of 30 August 1999] (New York: Documentação e Direito Comparado, 1999), 76.
22. Lucas Kerr de Oliveira and Igor Castellano Silva, 'South Sudan: New Country, Huge Challenges', *Revista Meridiano* 12 (2011), 10.
23. Philip Barker, 'Testing Time for London', *Journal of Olympic History* 19 (2011), 2.
24. Pedro Guerreiro, 'Antilhas Holandesas deixam de existir no mapa' [Netherlands Antilles Cease to Exist on the Map], *Revista Sol*, 11 (2010), 2.
25. Barker, 'Testing Time for London'.
26. José Jobson Arruda, *A grande revolução inglesa, 1640–1780: Revolução inglesa e Revolução industrial na construção da sociedade moderna* [The Great English Revolution, 1640–1780: English Revolution and Industrial Revolution in the Construction of Modern Society] (São Paulo: Hucitec, 1996); and Luiz Alberto Pilatti, 'Reflexões sobre o esporte moderno: Perspectiva Histórica' [Reflections on Modern Sport: Historical Perspective] (Paper presented at I Prêmio INDESP de literatura desportiva for the Instituto Nacional de Desenvolvimento do Desporto, Brasília, Brazil, 1999).
27. Luiz Carlos Bresser-Pereira, 'Império e nação na sociedade global e o Brasil' [Empire and Nation in the Global Society and Brazil], 2010 Annual Report (June 2011), 1–17.
28. Norbert Elias and Eric Dunning, *A busca da excitação* [The Pursuit of Excitement] (Lisboa: Editora Memória e Sociedade, 1992).
29. Eric Hobsbawm and Terence Ranger, *A Invenção das tradições* [The Invention of Traditions] (São Paulo: Paz e Terra S.A, 1997).
30. Valter Bracht, *Sociologia crítica do esporte: uma introdução* [Critical Sociology of Sport: An Introduction] (Ijuí: Editora Unijuí, 2005).
31. Elias and Dunning, *A busca da excitação* [The Pursuit of Excitement].
32. Bracht, *Sociologia crítica do esporte* [Critical Sociology of Sport: An Introduction].
33. Ibid.
34. Elias and Dunning, *A busca da excitação* [The Pursuit of Excitement].
35. Eric Hobsbawm, *Nações e nacionalismo desde 1780: programa, mito e realidade* [Nations and Nationalism Since 1780: Program, Myth and Reality] (Rio de Janeiro: Paz e Terra, 1990); Elias and Dunning, *A busca da excitação* [The Pursuit of Excitement]; and Richard Giulianotti, *Sociologia do futebol: Dimensões históricas e socioculturais do esporte de multidões* [Sociology

of Football: HISTORICAL and Sociocultural Dimensions of the Sport of Crowds] (São Paulo: Editora Novalexandria, 2002).
36. Dietrich Quanz, 'Civic Pacifism and Sports-Based Internationalism: Framework for the Founding of the International Olympic Committee', *Olympika* 2 (1993), 1–23.
37. Dietrich Quanz, 'Formatting Power of the IOC Founding the Birth of a New Peace Movement', *Journal of Olympic History* 3 (1995), 6–16; and Bulletin du Comité International des Jeux Olympiques, *Revue Olympique* (1894).
38. Reid and Evangeliou, 'The Political Heritage of the Olympic Games Relevance, Risks, and Possible Rewards'. See the comment at note 14.
39. Dietrich Quanz, 'Civic Pacifism and Sports-Based Internationalism', 9–10.
40. Chappelet and Kübler-Mabbott, *The International Olympic Committee and the Olympic System*.
41. Ibid., 20.
42. Ramos, 'Puerto Rico is Not the Only One', 255.
43. Olympism in Action. 'International Olympic Committee', Olympic.org, http://www.olympic.org/olympism-in-action.
44. 'Pierre de Coubertin, Philosophic Foundation of Modern Olympism', *Le Sport Suisse*, vol. 31 (1935), in Norbert Muller (ed.), *Olympism: Selected Writings. Pierre de Coubertin 1863–1937* (Lausanne: IOC, 2000), 580–3.
45. Ibid., 581.
46. Bulletin du Comité International Olympique, *Olympic Review* 38 (1953), 9–10. In the same Olympic document, it observed the philosophical and technical bias of the slogan. *Citius*: not only faster in the race but also in the sense of understanding of speed, the intelligence liveliness; *Altius*: higher, not only with respect to a desired aim, but also for the moral improvement of the individual; *Fortius*: not only bolder in fighting within the sportive environment, but also in the vital struggle.
47. 'Pierre de Coubertin, Philosophic Foundation of Modern Olympism', 583.
48. Hywel Iowerth, Carwyn Jones, and Alun Hardman, 'Nationalism and Olympism: Towards a Normative Theory of International Sporting Representation', *Olympika* 19 (2010), 81–110.
49. Dietrich Quanz, 'Formatting Power of the IOC Founding', 12.
50. Ramos, 'Puerto Rico is Not the Only One'.
51. Katia Rubio, *Esporte, educação e valores olímpicos* [Sports, Education and Olympic Values] (São Paulo: Ed. Casa do Psicólogo, 2009).
52. The Olympic Flag, 'Lettre d'informations Newsletter', *Olympic Review* 2 (1967), 15.
53. Bresser-Pereira, Império e nação na sociedade global [Empire and Nation in the Global Society and Brazil], 7.
54. Reginaldo Moraes, 'Reformas neoliberais e políticas públicas: Hegemonia ideológica e redefinição das relações Estado-Sociedade' ['Neoliberal Reforms and Public Policies: Ideological Hegemony and Redefinition of State-Society Relations'], *Educação e Sociedade* 23 (2002), 13.
55. Octavio Ianni, *Teorias da Globalização* [Theories of Globalization] (Rio de Janeiro: Civilização Brasileira, 2001), 101.
56. Michèle Verdier, 'The IOC and the Press', *Olympic Review* 25 (1996), 65–6.
57. Chappelet and Kübler-Mabbott, *The International Olympic Committee and the Olympic System*, 35.
58. Ibid., 36.
59. Ibid.
60. Boaventura de Sousa Santos, *A globalização e as ciências sociais* [The Globalization and the Social Sciences] (São Paulo: Cortez, 2002).
61. Ianni, *Teorias da Globalização* [Theories of Globalization], 13.
62. Ibid.

Disclosure Statement

No potential conflict of interest was reported by the authors.

ORCID

Tiago Del Tedesco Guioti ⓘD http://orcid.org/0000-0002-4225-643X

The Legacy of the Games of the New Emerging Forces and Indonesia's Relationship with the International Olympic Committee

Friederike Trotier [iD]

ABSTRACT
The Games of the New Emerging Forces (GANEFO) often serve as an example of the entanglement of sport, Cold War politics and the Non-Aligned Movement in the 1960s. Indonesia as the initiator plays a salient role in the research on this challenge for the International Olympic Committee (IOC). The legacy of GANEFO and Indonesia's further relationship with the IOC, however, has not yet drawn proper academic attention. This paper analyzes Indonesia's interactions with the IOC until the present time, with a focus on the country's involvement in sporting events under the patronage of the IOC (such as the Asian and Southeast Asian Games). In addition, two case studies demonstrate the variable relationship between the two actors. First, Indonesia only narrowly escaped sanctions over a dispute on the use of the Olympic logo in 2015. Yet, the country is named as host of the 2018 Asian Games, hence showing high ambitions to re-enter the international sports arena. These incidents illustrate the significance of conformity of local agencies towards the IOC with regard to political positions and power structures. The study opens the field to local – Asian – perspectives on interactions with the IOC.

Introduction

Indonesia – although the largest South-East Asian country – does not have a reputation as a sporting nation and has therefore received little attention during international sporting events such as the Olympic Games. Yet, one episode makes Indonesia prominent in the history of the Olympic Movement. The country created a counter platform for sporting events, challenging the International Olympic Committee (IOC). The so-called Games of the New Emerging Forces (GANEFO) often serve as an example of the entanglement of sport, Cold War politics and the Non-Aligned Movement in the 1960s. The research on this conflict between the 'Old Established Forces' and the 'New Emerging Forces' – using President Sukarno's words – has shed light on Indonesia's role.[1] However, the legacy of this politically motivated sporting event for the host country, as well as for Indonesia's further relationship with the Olympic Movement have so far drawn little attention.

Starting with a summary of GANEFO, its challenge of the IOC and the role of Indonesia, this paper analyzes Indonesia's further relationship with the IOC until the present with the focus on the country's involvement in sporting events under the patronage of the IOC, concentrating on the Asian Games and the Southeast Asian Games. The focus lies on the first Southeast Asian Games with Indonesian participation in 1979. The changes within the structure of Indonesian sports bodies reflect the specific domestic policies, as well as the modality of interaction with other Indonesian and international sports organizations. In addition, two cases demonstrate the variable relationship between Indonesia and the IOC, including the Olympic Council of Asia (OCA). On the one hand, Indonesia only narrowly escaped sanctions over a dispute regarding the use of the Olympic logo in 2015. On the other hand, the country was named host of the forthcoming Eighteenth Asian Games in 2018 and thus showing high ambitions to re-enter the international sport stage. These incidents illustrate the significance of conformity of local agencies towards the IOC with regard to political positions and power structures. Yet, depending on the circumstances, the member state can exert pressure on the international committee as well. Focusing on Indonesia, the study attempts to open the field to local – Asian – perspectives on interactions with the Olympic Movement.

GANEFO and the IOC

WE PEOPLES OF THE NEW EMERGING FORCES

conscious that sports mean to serve as an instrument to build Man and Nations, to create international understanding and goodwill, **desirous** to build this world anew, free from colonialism and imperialism in all their forms and manifestations,

aspiring to develop a community of nations imbued with the spirit of the Asian-African Conference held in Bandung 1955 which ensures respect for each other's national identity and national souvereignty [sic], strengthens friendship, fosters cooperation towards lasting peace among nations, and towards Brotherhood of Man,

have agreed to develop a new international sports movement, to secure the achievement of these ideals,

AND FOR THESE ENDS

resolve, through our representatives assembled in conference in the capital city of Djakarta, Indonesia, from 27th till 29th April 1963, to adopt the following Charter, and to proclaim an international sports movement:

THE GAMES OF THE NEW EMERGING FORCES

To be known as the

GANEFO[2]

In the era of the Cold War, the newly independent or decolonizing countries attempted to find their place in the world and to establish a force outside of the East–West confrontation. This situation brought forth the formation of the Non-Aligned Movement to offer a platform for these new international players. Following the concept of the 'Third World' – in contrast to the Western and Eastern Bloc, respectively, the 'First and Second World' – their policy was also coined *Third Worldist* policy. One of the main actors of this Third Worldist policy was the Indonesian President Sukarno, who had proclaimed Indonesian independence in 1945 and led the country until his removal from office in 1967. He was highly ambitious about his own role and the role of his country in the Non-Aligned Movement, creating his own political vision to gain a leading position. Sukarno saw two opponent groups struggling with each other: the Old Established Forces (OLDEFOs) and the New Emerging Forces (NEFOs). The Old Established Forces were the (former) colonial powers, including not only countries, but also institutions situated within the context of 'imperialism, colonialism, and capitalism'. In contrast, the New Emerging Forces constituted those countries and institutions and so on that had suffered from the oppression of the opponent group. His definition of forces created a new dimension beyond the nation state in order to address a larger part of the world, as, for example, parts of Africa were still in the process of decolonization. Furthermore, any kind of organization could thus be called a NEFO even if its geographical location was outside of the Third World.[3]

One strategy to fill his political vision of the competing forces with life was to create a platform for the NEFOs to meet and interact, yet not in a formal political context, but rather on the personal level, especially among young people. Hence, Sukarno founded the GANEFO and the event clearly bore his signature. In his perception, the newly established sporting event would strengthen his concept, as well as his own position. In 1963, the foundation of the GANEFO[4] thus had a strong link to the political agenda of the Indonesian president and his worldview. Yet, there were also some other factors which influenced the creation of GANEFO: first, there was the confrontation between Indonesia and the IOC; second, the interest of the Republic of China in creating sport games outside of the IOC; and third, the political awakening of the decolonizing countries mainly in Asia and Africa.

The conflict between Indonesia and the IOC goes back to the politicization of the Fourth Asian Games, which took place in Jakarta in 1962. When Indonesia was awarded the Asian Games in 1958, several initiatives started to secure a successful hosting of the event. On the one hand, the idea of success included following the motto of the Asian Games 'Ever onward' by reaching greater cooperation and solidarity among the Asian nations, as well as by outscoring the Western countries and their organizations (like the IOC). On the other hand, the focus lay on the development of Indonesia into a leading country for the Non-Aligned Movement. To reach the targets, the *Dewan Asian Games Indonesia* (DAGI) was formed for the preparation of the Games as along with the *Komite Gerakan Olahraga* (KOGOR), which was to secure sporting success of Indonesian athletes. From the beginning, the political targets of the Sukarno administration corresponded only partly with the concepts of the Asian Games Federation (AGF). Although one major objective was to strengthen Asian unity, the intended scope of the Indonesian organizers went beyond the core region of Asia to include African countries, for instance.[5] This rather unique perception was in line with Indonesia's foreign policy to establish the Asian Games as an event of the Non-Aligned Movement and thus support Sukarno's ideology and nation-building policy. In addition, the Fourth Asian Games became a political message of anti-Western sentiments and thus a new threat for the IOC, which was later enforced by the GANEFO.

As Lutan (2007) and Hübner (2012) have further analyzed, the Indonesian usage of the Asian Games for political messages and the deliberate mixing of sports and politics initiated a longer dispute between Indonesia and the IOC.[6] Indonesia refused to issue visas to the participants and officials from Taiwan and Israel as attribution to the amicable foreign relations with the Republic of China and the Arabic countries. This was a confrontational action against the IOC for two reasons. First, the IOC claimed to be an institution outside of political affairs warning its members of mixing sports and politics. The Indonesian leadership, in contrast, was very frank with the political statements and even proclaimed a necessity to mix sports with politics in order to reach political goals and to end the hypocrisy of the IOC. Second, the IOC could not entirely avoid positioning itself in political issues. Prior to the Fourth Asian Games, the Asian Games Federation (AGF) had attempted to keep a low profile with regard to the 'two Chinas' issue (Communist versus Nationalist China). Nevertheless, Taiwan was invited to participate at the 1954 and 1958 Asian Games as it was a member state of the AGF and Communist China was not.[7] Thus, the IOC was not able to entirely avoid a political positioning, yet the members were obliged to follow the decisions of the IOC. Indonesia refused to obey and consequently broke with the rules of the AGF concerning the attitude towards China and Taiwan.

The Indonesian perspective on the conflict was that the IOC and the AGF acted as Old Established Forces showing 'imperialistic' and 'neo-colonial' characteristics. Furthermore, the Indonesian leadership claimed that the Asian Games did not truly reflect the 'Bandung spirit', relating to the 1955 Asian-African Conference in Bandung, an event with a very high symbolic value. This meeting of the Non-Aligned Movement is perceived as the 'first and clearest manifestation of Third Worldist politics in action'[8]. The notion of solidarity became the most salient sentiment of the conference and was reflected in the metaphor of the 'Bandung spirit'. Sukarno constantly referred to this spirit during the process of establishing and organizing GANEFO. It united two important elements: on the one hand, it stood for the symbolic moment of decolonization and, on the other hand, for the beginning of a new era of international politics with Asian and African countries forming new and powerful actors.[9] The Sukarno administration saw the necessity to follow its own political ideas and to create GANEFO in reaction to the neglect of the IOC and the AGF to follow the 'Bandung spirit' and to include Third Worldist policy in their agendas. Hence, GANEFO evolved as a result of Indonesia's unsuccessful attempt to reshape the Asian Games as a tool for the Non-Aligned Movement and as a tool to propagate the solidarity of the new forces in Asia, Africa, and Latin America.[10]

The politicization of sport in Indonesia had a strong effect on the sport organizations in the country. Already in 1946, one year after the declaration of independence, the Indonesian Sports Association (*Persatuan Olahraga Republik Indonesia*, PORI) was founded with its base in Yogyakarta, a nationalist stronghold. PORI organized the newly established National Games (*Peran Olahraga Nasional* [PON]), which constituted a crucial tool for nation building in the young and not yet internationally recognized country.[11] The first PON took place in Surakarta in 1948 and aimed to create and demonstrate national unity. A further goal of the Indonesian government was to gain international recognition, and the participation at international sporting events such as the Olympic Games or the newly established Asian Games was perceived as a promising step to reach this target. After becoming a member of the United Nations in 1950, Indonesia participated in the First Asian Games in 1951 and prepared for the Olympic Games in 1952. In the year of the Olympic Games in Helsinki, the IOC welcomed Indonesia with the Indonesian Olympic Committee (at first *Komite Olympiade Republik Indonesia*, KORI, later changing to *Komite Olympiade Indonesia*, KOI) as a new member. In the 1950s, elite sport and competitions on both national and international levels became more widespread in Indonesia.[12]

In 1962, prior to the Asian Games, the Ministry of Sport (*Departemen Olahraga* [DEPORA]) was founded and headed by Minister Maladi, who later played a vital role in the conflict with the IOC, pushing sport as a tool for nation building. When Indonesia had to leave the IOC, the Indonesian Olympic Committee was disbanded. The following creation of GANEFO enforced the mixing of the spheres of politics and sport; and the newly created Sports Council of the Republic of Indonesia (*Dewan Olahraga Republik Indonesia* [DORI]) embodied this entanglement, as it was an arm of the government. The head of the Sports Council, for instance, was the Indonesian president. After its foundation in 1964, all prior existing sports organizations were integrated into the *Dewan Olahraga*. Its tasks had a wide range covering national and international activities, for instance, to organize and oversee all sporting activities in the country and on the international level, to construct and maintain facilities, to develop sporting industries and to conduct and support research on sports and sports medicine. In addition, the Ministry of Sport had to administer the preparations of the First GANEFO in Jakarta. Hence, the *Dewan Olahraga* monopolized great power in the sport sector and beyond with access to funds and forces and the backing of the government.[13]

The perspective of the IOC and the AGF in the conflict with Indonesia concentrated on the Indonesian violation of the Olympic ideals and the immanent rule to keep sport and politics separated. The discrimination against two member states called for a reaction. Although the opinions on the nature of punishment were diverse – ranging from renaming the Fourth Asian Games to excluding Indonesia from the IOC – the members agreed on the necessity to rebuke Indonesia for its 'misbehaviour'. The Asian Games took place unhampered, yet the punishment occurred one year later with Indonesia's exclusion from the Olympic Movement.[14] The IOC stated that it would refuse reinstating Indonesia as long as the government did not declare its will to respect the Olympic rules.[15] The fact that Indonesia decided to leave the Movement before the official expulsion only demonstrates the will of the Indonesian government to play an active rather than a passive role. Indonesia resigned officially from the IOC in February 1963, but continued its confrontation with the IOC as a perceived 'tool of imperialism' by creating GANEFO as a competing platform for international sporting competitions.[16]

In combining the call for quitting the IOC and establishing the GANEFO, Sukarno demonstrated determination, in his course to fight the IOC's 'constant discrimination especially against Asian-African and Latin American nations,'[17] thus seeing Indonesia as a main victim of the Committee's 'imperialistic' and 'colonialist' attitude. In a further step, he conjured up Indonesia's strength and future greatness as an independent country that does not depend on the Olympic platform. Hence, the assurance of Indonesia not being 'a nation of frogs and toads'[18] had more significance than the exclusion from the 1964 Olympic Games in Tokyo. Consequently, the newly founded GANEFO Federation with Sukarno as 'Founder and Honorary President'[19] and the headquarters in Jakarta embodied the initiative of Indonesia and other emerging countries, but also a signal to the IOC about its falseness and failures.

Besides Indonesia, the other main initiator in the realization of GANEFO was the Republic of China, which demonstrated a similar confrontational attitude towards the IOC. The Chinese showed an immense interest in the project of GANEFO since they were not part of the IOC, but rather already in opposition with the entire Western and Communist World. The new sporting event embodied a promising opportunity for China to fight the IOC, as well as the United States, as their proclaimed enemies.[20] China's full support of GANEFO included political, organizational and financial concerns. China provided immense financial support and thus enabled the implementation of the First GANEFO and the participation of athletes and officials from many poor countries.[21] Therefore, similar to the Indonesian situation, GANEFO provided an outstanding opportunity for Communist China to take the lead among the countries of the Third World. With diplomatic communication and sporting success, China gained centre stage during the sporting event in Jakarta and improved its international image considerably.[22]

The implementation of the First Games of the New Emerging Games in Jakarta provided the Sukarno administration with the opportunity to realize the targets of the previous Asian Games. Thus, the event left behind the regional scope of the Asian Games and became a global project with a strong link to the Non-Aligned Movement. Furthermore, Jakarta could claim to be the first Asian host of a truly international sporting event, outscoring Japan as the host of the 1964 Olympic Games.[23] In addition, the event fostered a feeling of solidarity among the participants as well as a feeling of national pride in Indonesia. The host was able to convey a positive image of its culture, such as the value of *gotong royong* which literally means to share a burden and to be mutually cooperative. As a core value in Javanese community life,[24] it fitted well into the idea of solidarity among the NEFOs. Another Indonesian principle claimed by the GANEFO Federation was *musjawarah*, a system of consultation, mutual dialogue and decision-making based on consensus.[25] This principle further strengthened Indonesia's key role for the GANEFO.

Although scholars still discuss the actual threat of GANEFO, these Games nevertheless challenged the monopoly of the IOC. The Olympic Committee or its regional franchises, offered newly decolonized countries membership of the respective organization, but sometimes lacked the sincerity to pay attention to the needs and wishes of the new members. When GANEFO challenged the IOC, the organization did not try to increase its appeal, but rather threatened to exclude those countries labelled as NEFOs from the 1964 Olympic Games if they followed Indonesia and GANEFO.

Indonesia, with a strong grievance and an ambitious leader, aimed to break the hegemony of the IOC and to challenge the distinctively Western structure of the Olympic Movement. On the one hand, the official statements issued by the GANEFO Federation demonstrated a modest and non-confrontational attitude towards other sports organizations – including the Olympic Movement – with the intention to be attractive for a large range of countries and organizations.

> Ganefo is the manifestation of the demand of our new world itself. As such it is the manifestation of progress and improvement … It is logical then that the Ganefo can co-exist with all international sports organizations except those hostile to the ideals of Ganefo. The Ganefo movement, working on the basis of fraternal equality and mutual cooperation, practices tolerance in all its undertakings. Tolerance accompanied with a sense of respect for the customs, traditions and national policies of respective members.[26]

On the other hand, Sukarno torpedoed this strategy when attacking the IOC as being a hypocrite. He accused the IOC of acting politically and of denying this fact, supporting his point of view with examples from the treatment of Communist China, Egypt and North Korea. Sukarno emphasized:

> Now let's frankly say, *sports have something to do with politics*. Indonesia proposes now to mix sports with politics, and let us now establish the Games of the New Emerging Forces, the GANEFO … against the Old Established Order.[27]

Consequently, the GANEFO Federation had to struggle permanently to find a balance between open confrontation and aggression and a moderate course to avoid a deterrent effect for the Asian, African and Latin American countries. Furthermore, in spite of the confrontation, Indonesia still felt the appeal of the Olympic Games and wanted to be part of the 1964 Games in Tokyo. Yet, from the Indonesian perspective, the imperialist nature of the IOC forced the newly decolonized countries to form their own event with an agenda that was truly in accord to the Olympic spirit.

Indonesia from the First GANEFO to the Southeast Asian Games (SEA Games)

GANEFO depicted a tool of Sukarno's foreign policy in the 1960s. Yet, in spite of the large-scale struggle against imperialism, colonialism and capitalism, the policy of GANEFO also had a regional focus on South-East Asia. On the one hand, Sukarno exploited the First GANEFO in Jakarta for his anti-Malaysia propaganda, combining the slogan of the Games with his *konfrontasi* policy:[28] 'Sukseskan GANEFO Ganjang Malaysia' [Success to GANEFO Crush Malaysia].[29] Furthermore, the official motto of the Games, 'Onward! No Retreat!', served as the slogan of the confrontation with Malaysia even after the Games were over.[30] On the other hand, Indonesia used GANEFO to stress diplomatic relations with other countries in the region. As participants from Laos, Thailand, Burma and Cambodia took part in the Games, these countries were on rather positive or neutral terms with Indonesia. The closest cooperation existed between Indonesia and Cambodia. Although a detailed study on Cambodia's role in the GANEFO movement has yet to be undertaken, there are several indications to assume that the country had a strong interest in the Third Worldist Movement and in supporting GANEFO. When Cambodia cancelled the regional event of the Southeast Asian Peninsular Games in 1963, the declared reason was not the continuous disputes with Thailand but rather a statement of solidarity with Indonesia against the IOC.[31] Furthermore, Cambodia agreed on hosting the First Asian GANEFO in 1966.[32] It is likely that Indonesia and Cambodia worked closely together to successfully implement the Asian GANEFO in Phnom Penh and that is why they were the driving forces of the first regional GANEFO.

Indonesia's confrontation policy against the IOC ended with the country's political turnover, General Suharto's seizure of power, and one of the darkest chapters of Indonesian history with the killings of hundreds of alleged communists. Suharto, as the new president, followed a political agenda contrary to Sukarno's. GANEFO, as a manifestation of Sukarno's rapprochement to communist China, contrasted Suharto's anti-communist policy and was therefore excluded from the national memory in the anti-communist New Order regime. One example of the complete political turn from Sukarno to Suharto was Indonesia's position in the AGF with regard to the 'Two Chinas' question. In 1962, Indonesia had prevented Taiwan from participating at the Asian Games and was therefore severely punished. About 10 years later, in 1973, Indonesia voted for Taiwan to remain a member of the Federation, but the majority voted for the inclusion of the Republic of China.[33] Another example was the project of establishing the National Museum (*Museum Sejarah Monumen Nasional*, Museum Monas) with dioramas representing Indonesian history and identity. In Sukarno's planning, one diorama was dedicated to the First GANEFO featuring himself and Maladi as well as the slogans of the Games 'Onward! No Retreat!' and 'Build the World anew'. With a continuation of the Guided Democracy, GANEFO would not just have entered the Museum Monas, but also national history. The snapshot of the Games had the intention of demonstrating Indonesia's return to greatness and the nation's role in world history. Yet, General Suharto's power seizure prevented Sukarno's concept of the museum from realization. Instead, Suharto's new museum committee revised the concept and changed and omitted certain dioramas. Among others, the scene of the GANEFO was excluded and thus prevented from entering national memory. Other events, which supported the New Order vision of the past and provided legitimacy to the regime, replaced GANEFO and Sukarno's struggle for national unity and greatness, as well as national advancement towards socialism.[34]

Hence, only after the fall of Suharto, the rehabilitation of Sukarno beyond his role as the father of independence entailed a new perspective of the Fourth Asian Games, as well as GANEFO. Both sporting events receive an increased appreciation, especially in the current preparation period of the 18th Asian Games. The legacy of GANEFO is therefore linked to the perception of Sukarno, who is officially proclaimed a 'national hero' and enjoys an increased popularity since the democratization process in Indonesia. References to GANEFO, therefore, occur in the context of acknowledging Sukarno and his striving for national unity.[35]

The change of government, starting in 1965, entailed a realignment of the Indonesian sport organizations. As early as December 1965, DORI (Sports Council of the Republic of Indonesia) was officially 'freed' from political influence and renamed Indonesian Sports Council (*Komite Olahraga Nasional Indonesia*, KONI). In 1967, President Suharto confirmed KONI as a non-governmental and autonomous body with the mission to help the government in the sports sector, but to remain outside of politics. The presidential decree thus established that KONI should not be controlled by any power elite, but rather be returned to Indonesian society. The new body simplified the structure of the sports sector in Indonesia. The responsibilities of the Sports Council concentrated on Indonesian elite sport and the representation at the IOC and AGF including the planning of preparations of the Indonesian athletes for international sporting events.[36] The head of the 'new' KONI was Sultan Hamengku Buwono IX, the Sultan of Yogyakarta and the second Indonesian vice-president (1973–1978). He functioned as the Indonesian member of the IOC between 1967 and 1972. The Sultan's involvement in sporting organizations occurred at a time when the position as vice-president left him only ceremonial power. He continued his activities in the sports sector after resigning from the office as vice-president.[37]

Suharto's foreign policy aimed to end Indonesia's isolation from the Western countries and to re-integrate the country into international organizations such as the IOC. The reconsolidation with the IOC included Indonesia's participation at the Fifth Asian Games in Bangkok in 1966, at the 1967 Universiade in Tokyo and, most importantly, at the 1968 Olympic Games in Mexico. In October 1968, Indonesia was officially reinstated into the IOC with Sultan Hamengku Buwono IX as Indonesia's representative. Furthermore, the new guidelines for sports in Indonesia concentrated on the benefit for body and soul for sportspersons and on the aspect of competitiveness for international events. In accordance with *pancasila*, Indonesia's state ideology, the sports institutions and activities were continuously depoliticized.[38]

Suharto's domestic policy focused on the economic development of the country with *pembangunan* (development) as the central parameter of success. Therefore, the new formation of the sports sector followed a so-called 'scientific approach' with the target being effective, objective and reliable in order to support Indonesia's development.[39] The foreign policy emphasized the importance of the Asia-Pacific region, especially the ASEAN countries. Indonesia as the biggest country in the ASEAN region had a strong interest in a leading position among its neighbouring countries. In this strategy, one promising soft power tool had been neglected in the early years of the *Orde Baru* (New Order) government, namely sport and the hosting of sporting events. The country was not part of the major multi-sport event in the region, which had regularly taken place since 1959. In 1958, during the Third Asian Games in Tokyo, representatives of Thailand, Burma, Cambodia, Laos, Malaya and South Vietnam founded the Southeast Asian Peninsular Games Federation. The Southeast Asian Peninsular (SEAP) Games followed the concept and idea of the Asian and Olympic Games and were thus situated under the supervision of the IOC. Besides devoting itself to the Olympic ideals of friendship and sportsmanship, the main target of the SEAP Games was regional solidarity. The means to reach this goal was to link sport as a popular activity with diplomacy and cultural programmes.[40] Under Thailand's leadership, the Games developed into a regular event, taking place every two years in a changing host country. The decision to hold the Games in the years between the two major sporting events, the Olympic and the Asian Games, reflected the intention to provide a platform to prepare for the big and prestigious events and to raise the competiveness of the South-East Asian athletes. The similar sporting level was perceived as a promising condition to improve the skills of the athletes, who were often behind in international competitions.[41] Political changes within the region led to adaptations within the SEAP Games Federation, for example concerning the Confederation of Malaysia, Singapore and Vietnam.

Between 1958 and 1977, Indonesia had no link with the sporting event in the neighbouring countries. Not only had the regional focus on mainland South-East Asia kept Indonesia from the SEAP Games; it also excluded Sukarno's politics in the 1950s and 1960s. His flirt with communism stood in contrast to the anti-communist agenda of the Federation.[42] A change of paradigm occurred in 1975 when, finally, the SEAP Games Federation decided to expand its regional scope by including the countries of insular South-East Asia, Indonesia, Brunei, and the Philippines. The official admission of the three countries into the Federation

Figure 1. Flag of the Southeast Asian Peninsular Games. Source: https://rankly.com/cache/236919c1104589cf6ba17555363aa599_w500_h500.jpg

occurred in 1979. Consequently, the name of the games had to be adapted to the new situation. The pragmatic solution earmarked the omission of the word 'Peninsular', and the new name Southeast Asian Games, which is currently still in use, was coined. The main force behind the new orientation of the SEAP Games was Malaysia. After perceiving difficulties to nominate a host for the 1979 Games, Malaysia suggested to expand the SEA Games and to invite Indonesia, the Philippines, and Brunei.[43] In spite of the extension, the Federation emphasized the continuity of this regional sporting event and decided to keep the numeration of the Games with the 1959 SEAP Games in Bangkok as the first. The 1979 SEA Games in Jakarta thus went down in history as the 10th Southeast Asian Games.[44] The logo kept its design and only additional rings were added to symbolize the new members (Figure 1). The new Charter issued in 1978 stressed the conformity to the Olympic ideals, for instance, with the stated aim to 'spread the Olympic principles throughout South East Asia thereby creating goodwill in the region'.[45]

In contrast to Malaysia, the main force from within the SEAP Games Federation to support the expansion of the Games, Thailand's attitude towards the newcomers was not so welcoming. In the early 1970s, Thailand was still able to prevent the expansion. Since Thailand held a dominant position in the Federation as the initiator of the regional event, it did not have an interest in integrating other regional heavyweights such as Indonesia. The SEAP Games were a Thai brainchild and thus connected to the ideas and intentions of this country. Furthermore, Thailand hosted the Games three times between 1959 and 1975 and was very successful in sporting terms during these early years. Consequently, the expansion to insular South-East Asia was against Thai policy in the region of peninsular South-East Asia.[46] In addition, Indonesia had posed a threat to the SEAP Games during the 1960s and had thus already acted willingly against Thailand as the head of this regional event. The 1963 GANEFO, and even more so, the 1966 Asian GANEFO embodied rival events challenging the Peninsular Games with a contrasting ideology. Indonesia's leading role in GANEFO was an argument against the country's integration in the SEAP Games Federation. Nevertheless, the difficulty to find suitable hosts among the participants for the biennial event finally led to the renewal of the SEAP Games.

Indonesia showed a high interest in joining the SEA Games. The country aimed to emphasize an image of capability, as well as cooperation, with the other ASEAN countries. One of the stated targets of the 1979 SEA Games was to 'cultivate and develop the holding of the South East Asia Games as a means in realizing utmost cooperation and solidarity of the South East Asian nations, through these venues of sports'.[47] One example of good neighbourly relations was the showcased gratefulness towards Malaysia. The complete turnabout from 'Ganyang Malaysia' to thanking Malaysia for providing an example worthy of imitation reflects the entirely different political standpoints of the Sukarno and the Suharto era. The country did not attempt to make a grand entrance as the host of the SEA Games, but followed a script of humbleness and cooperation with the other countries. A manifestation of the cooperation and mutual understanding with an Indonesian flavour was the concept of *gotong royong*. Thus, the SEA Games unintentionally followed the orientation of the GANEFO, which had also upheld the value of mutual help and solidarity. In the context of the SEA Games, *gotong royong* found translation into 'the spirit of national Cooperation',[48] and thus became a link between Indonesian, respectively Javanese, culture, and the international event. Following this concept, the suggested image of Indonesia was one of a good neighbour who is eager to play an even more active part of the community than before. Although

Indonesia was not a new member of ASEAN, the hosting of the SEA Games provided the possibility to increase its soft power among the South-East Asian countries. The SEA Games, under the umbrella of OCA,[49] helped Indonesia to demonstrate its willingness to cooperate and to forget the period of confrontation with the IOC and the AGF.

One of the important figures in the preparation of the 10th SEA Games was the already mentioned Sultan of Yogyakarta Hemengku Bowono IX. He was the president of the Organizing Committee and thus jointly responsible for the implementation of the Games. In Indonesia, he is not only well known and respected as a political leader and national hero, but also as a *tokoh olahraga*, a key figure of Indonesian sport.[50] In the context of hosting the Tenth SEA Games, the Indonesian sports bodies KONI and KOI were combined but had different functions in order to improve the efficiency. The Indonesian Olympic Committee (KOI) was the international branch and the Sports Council (KONI) was the national branch. Both bodies had the same president; a system, which led to a great concentration of power on the highest management level.

From 1979 on, Indonesia remained one of the core countries in the SEA Games Federation, hosting the Games in 1987, 1997 and 2011. Every time Indonesia hosted the SEA Games, the target was to strengthen the country's position as an economic and political stronghold in the region. Especially the latest Games in 2011 aimed to emphasize Indonesia's re-emergence after the turmoil of the democratization and decentralization processes following the fall of President Suharto. The main theme of the Games was the kingdom of Srivijaya, with the slogan 'Srivijaya: The Golden Peninsula'. Srivijaya was one of the last Hindu-Buddhist kingdoms of maritime South-East Asia and exerted influence in the region between 680 and 1400 AD. The centre of the kingdom was in South Sumatra, thus fitting well as the co-host of the Games Palembang, the capital of South Sumatra. The theme evoked positive associations since the kingdom and the concept of the golden peninsula suggested values like peace and tolerance. Srivijaya, for instance, is praised as a peaceful kingdom of trade where people of diverse ethnic backgrounds and even religious affiliations could interact without any barriers.[51] Naturally, the Indonesian leaders were keen to link this image of a prosperous and peaceful polity with the young Indonesian democracy. The theme of the SEA Games was thus supposed to convey a picture of the host country as diverse but united, as tolerant towards all ethnic and religious groups, as powerful and influential but not dominating and suppressing and as a strong economy. As the SEA Games coincided with Indonesia's ASEAN chairmanship, the leaders of the country saw 2011 as the year of the manifestation of Indonesia's re-emergence and positioning as the region's leader. The sporting success of the Indonesian athletes underlined the country's ambition.[52]

Current Trends of Conflict and Cooperation

Conflict: The Dispute Over the Olympic Rings

After decades of conformity to the Olympic Movement, Indonesia returned to a more confrontational attitude towards the IOC in recent years. Although the issues were of minor importance compared to the escalations in the 1960s, Indonesia was still warned and even threatened with punishment. The starting point for the first confrontation in 2008/2009 was an internal conflict between the Ministry of Youth and Sports Affairs and the KONI. When the Ministry of Youth and Sports Affairs launched a 'Top-Tier Athletes Program' in

2008, this was perceived as an unwelcome government intervention and an intrusion into the territory of the Sports Council. The IOC intervened because it saw a violation against the Olympic Charter, which promotes no government interventions. The unauthorized launching of the programme by the Indonesian Ministry of Youth and Sports Affairs was thus judged as severe enough to call for action. The IOC, as well as the OCA, issued a warning that KONI's international membership might be suspended and Indonesia banned from international competitions.[53]

Although this first incident did not have far-reaching consequences, as Indonesia was able to avoid a suspension, some years later another clash between the IOC and the Indonesian sport committees made the headlines even beyond those of the Indonesian press. The confrontation in 2015 had its background in another internal conflict between the two main sports bodies in Indonesia: the Indonesian Sports Council (*Komite Olahraga Nasional (Indonesia)*, KON or KONI) and the Indonesian Olympic Committee (*Komite Olimpiade Indonesia*, KOI). In general, the separation of tasks is clear: the main task of the Sports Council is to organize sports development projects within the country, including the organization of the National Games, whilst the Indonesian Olympic Committee is responsible for the international relations with the IOC and other world governing bodies. Thus, the letter is nominally responsible for the preparation for international events such as the Olympic, Asian and Southeast Asian Games. Nevertheless, the source of conflict was the question of responsibility of preparing the Indonesian sports teams for these international multisport events. The dispute was in part a legacy of the new formation of the committees in 2005. Although the organizations KONI and KOI had already long existed, in 2005, a new law reorganized the Indonesian landscape of sports committees trying to put an end to the unclear and changing responsibilities of the preceding decades. Hence, the separation of tasks between KON and KOI as mentioned above was established. Yet, already in 2007, further changes occurred and the acronym KON returned to KONI, followed by further arrangements, which again shrouded the distribution of responsibilities.[54]

In accordance with the general separation of responsibilities, the IOC interacted with KOI as the representative of the country. This included certain rights and obligations shared by all member committees of the IOC. One aspect is that only national Olympic committees, which the IOC has officially accepted, are allowed to use the iconic Olympic logo featuring the five different coloured interlaced rings. Any other organization or individual adopting this logo without permission violates the property rights of the IOC. In 2014, KONI integrated the Olympic rings into its own logo, claiming to have the right to do so as the Indonesian representative at the Olympic Committee. This claim led to a conflict not only with the Indonesians, but even with the IOC. The quarrel even threatened Indonesia's right to host the 2018 Asian Games.[55]

The logo itself, with the red flame in the centre and the yellow wings linked with three red interlocking rings, has a long history as the official logo of the Indonesian Sports Council. Yet, only recently did KONI see itself as entitled to add the Olympic rings at the head of the logo. The Indonesian Olympic Committee gave the Olympic rings a very prominent position in the centre of the logo just below the Indonesian flag, thus emphasizing its own claim on the Olympic Movement (Figure 2). The struggle between KONI and KOI led to the stalemate that both bodies attempted to monopolize the copyright of the five rings and thus the status as the official member of the IOC. The Olympic rings thus became the symbol of the rightful National Olympic Committee (NOC) of Indonesia. KONI's argument was that

Figure 2. Logo of the Indonesian Sports Council with the Olympic rings. Source: http://static.republika.co.id/uploads/images/inpicture_slide/logo-koni-pusat-_150206164629-530.png

Figure 3. Logo of the Indonesian Olympic Committee. Source: http://sp.beritasatu.com/media/images/original/20,151,001,163,537,886.jpg

it has the longer history (since 1978) as the official NOC; KOI's perspective, in contrast, underlined the current separation of tasks giving the realm of international activities to KOI (Figure 3). The position as the official Indonesian NOC promised a higher degree of power and influence not only for the institution, but also for the powerholders within the committees. The subliminal power struggle between KONI and KOI had accompanied the diverse changes of laws and arrangements concerning the two bodies since 2005. The moment of escalation in 2015 can be linked to the awarding of the 18th Asian Games to Indonesia – a unique opportunity for the Indonesian sports bodies to gain attention, power and large funds. Both committees thus perceived the event as a chance to improve their positions especially in direct comparison with the 'opponent' committee.

Following the concept of Aspinall (2013), the Asian Games embody a huge *proyek* (project) combining neoliberal economic policies with clientelism.[56] Aspinall shows that 'project hunting' penetrates every sphere of the Indonesian social and political life, ranging from political parties to nongovernmental organizations to religious groups. Sporting events are a prime example of a *proyek* as they promise a relatively large slice of patronage resources. A major event such as the Asian Games generates a considerable budget for diverse kinds of investments, yet it also offers niches for money to disappear into clientist networks and private channels. Hence, leaders of KONI and KOI compete over the *proyek* Asian Games as well as the small projects related to the international event, its preparation and implementation.

The tension due to the conflict increased in early 2015 when the IOC issued its warning regarding the unauthorized use of the Olympic rings. The IOC called upon the Indonesian government to solve the problem and defend the interest of the Olympic Committee, reinforcing the demand by threatening to withdraw the award of the upcoming Asian Games. It was a strong message of discontent when Thomas Bach, as the head of the IOC, and Sheikh Ahmad Al Fahad Al Sabah, as the president of the OCA, addressed a letter to the Indonesian President Joko Widodo for a call for action. As a consequence, the government was under pressure to end the conflict between KONI and KOI and to satisfy the IOC. The most promising method to make the Sports Council compliant was to cut the funding. Presumably, this threat depicted the main reason for the Sports Council to finally comply with the demand and to change the logo. The following messages issued by the Indonesian government and representatives of the Indonesian Sports Council eagerly stressed the wish of cooperation and the common striving for a successful preparation and implementation of the Asian Games.[57]

When the IOC threatened Indonesia with heavy penalties, the South-East Asian country had to fear losing the hosting award of the 18th Asian Games. This event is a milestone in Indonesia's history of hosting sporting events and, therefore, the threat was very serious. Consequently, the Indonesian government had to react and to demonstrate its conformity with the demands of the IOC. Although the dispute began as an internal power struggle between the Indonesian sports bodies, the involvement of the IOC changed it into an international affair. The non-conformity and arbitrary action of the Indonesian Sports Council endangered cooperation with the IOC and thus with the OCA as well. The IOC, as the patron institution of the Asian Games, had the upper hand in the conflict with Indonesia, demonstrating its power by exerting pressure on the Indonesian government. The supra-national character and the lack of competing institutions make the IOC a very potent body that is able to threaten and penalize not only NOCs, but even national governments.

Indonesia, which had once resisted the IOC and had borne the consequences, had a weak stand in this dispute. The country depended on the IOC and OCA to implement the 2018 Asian Games. In the year 2015, however, there was no political clash of ideologies comparable to the 1960s. Indonesia's fundamental attitude towards the IOC was not confrontational but rather conforming.

Cooperation: The XVIII Asian Games

In the last decade, Indonesia has shown an increased interest in hosting sporting events. After the consolidation of the young democracy, political leaders rediscovered sporting events as a promising tool for domestic and foreign policy. By hosting the 2008 inaugural Asian Beach Games, the 2011 Southeast Asian Games, the 2013 Islamic Solidarity Games and the 2014 ASEAN University Games, Indonesia entered the 'event circuit' following other emerging economies. The peak of the efforts is the prospect of hosting the 18th Asian Games in 2018. In comparison with 'normal' bidding processes for international sporting events, the path leading to Indonesia's awarding of the Games was rather intricate. Consequently, there were also more interactions between Indonesia and the OCA in the process.

The bidding process began in March 2010 when potential candidates handed in their proposals. In 2012, only two candidates remained; namely Hanoi, Vietnam, and Surabaya, Indonesia. Hanoi won the bid and was awarded the 2019 Asian Games. Vietnam's success was accompanied by the decision to change the rhythm of the Games from the even to the uneven years between the Summer and Winter Olympics. Surprisingly, Vietnam withdrew in April 2014 and a new host had to be found. The only serious candidate was Indonesia; in contrast to the original bid, however, the potential host city was not Surabaya but Jakarta with one or several co-hosts as supporters. During the 2014 Asian Games in Incheon, Indonesian representatives signed the contract to become the new host of the 18th Asian Games.

The pressure on the OCA to find a new host put it into a rather weak position in negotiations, whereas Indonesia's position was strong in contrast due to the lack of competitors. Consequently, Indonesia was able to negotiate the return to the four years interval and to implement the Asian Games in 2018. Indonesia could thus enforce national interests over the OCA's planning. The reason to prefer 2018 was to avoid a collision with the presidential elections in Indonesia in 2019. Furthermore, due to the unusual situation and the limited time, the process of the 'second bid' did not follow the normal rules of the OCA. Indonesia, as the host country, was already confirmed before having a final decision on the host city or cities. Hence, the competition between the cities, which usually occurs prior to the official bidding process, now came last. The result is a novelty in the history of the Asian Games, as for the first time, there will be two official host cities for the Games, namely Jakarta and Palembang, the provincial capital of South Sumatra. Again, the Indonesian – in this case Palembang's – interest overruled the concept of the OCA.

After both cities were officially acknowledged and incorporated into the logo, the negotiations over the distribution of the specific events began (Figure 4). Representatives of the OCA, Jakarta and Palembang had to decide about the venue of the opening and closing ceremonies, as well as the venues of the 38 sports and disciplines. The OCA preferred to have as many events as possible in the Indonesian capital, reducing the logistic challenges entailed in the concept of two host cities on different islands. In the Council's point of view,

Figure 4. Logo of the XVIII Asian Games. Source: http://static.republika.co.id/uploads/images/inpicture_slide/logo-baru-asian-games-2018-_160728140344-630.jpg

Palembang's infrastructure and facilities do not meet the international requirements or will not be ready in time. Following the news coverage on these debates reveals contrasting positions and tough negotiations. One controversial issue is the host for the opening and closing ceremonies; events with very high prestige and external impact. Palembang is very eager to host at least one of these ceremonies and Jakarta agrees to share the task and to organize only the opening ceremony. The OCA, in opposition, demands to have both ceremonies in Jakarta. Officially, the agreement to have two co-hosts for the Asian Games is based on the condition to follow the Council's guideline. Yet both Indonesian parties strongly supported Palembang's endeavours. Even Jakarta's Governor Basuki Tjahaja Purnama gives preference to the South Sumatran capital. Consequently, the OCA is under pressure and might submit to the Indonesian concept.

Nevertheless, not only does the OCA feel the pressure. Indonesia has very limited time for the preparation facing many obstacles with regard to the infrastructure and also for the preparation of the athletes. On the one hand, the building project of the athletes' village in Jakarta, the infrastructure projects such as the monorail and the upgrade of some venues need resources and good planning strategies. On the other hand, in sporting terms, Indonesia has not performed well during the last Asian and Southeast Asian Games. The target to have a strong performance similar to the one in 1962 when Indonesia hosted the Asian Games, coming in second in the medal tally is very ambitious and needs a new orientation as well as an organization of the entire sporting sector in Indonesia.

Conclusion

GANEFO put Indonesia on centre stage in a conflict with the IOC. The South-East Asian country aimed to position itself as the leader of the decolonizing world, challenging the Old Established Order, including the IOC. The charismatic leader President Sukarno used the Games to enforce his ambition in the Third Worldist policy and to challenge the monopolist in the international sporting sector. The IOC, in reaction, put pressure on the Third World countries by threatening them with exclusion, thus enhancing the confrontation. Hence, the alternative sporting event imposed a serious threat to the IOC, yet the struggle for supremacy was short lived. Even in the core country of GANEFO, the event did not generate a long-lasting legacy. The political turnover and President Suharto's extreme anti-communist policy erased the sporting event from the Indonesian memory. The new government tried to heal the rift with the IOC by approaching the Western, capitalist countries, reorganizing the sports institutions in the country and joining the regional Southeast Asian Games under the umbrella of the IOC. Playing an important role in the anti-communist orientated SEA Games emphasized the conformity to the concepts of the international sports bodies IOC and AGF, respectively OCA.

After a long time of conformity, Indonesia found itself in a dispute with the IOC. Whilst the conflict over the use of the Olympic rings was originally an internal struggle about power structures and a fight for a large profit of the '*proyek* Asian Games', the involvement of the IOC changed it into an international affair with two unequal opponents. The IOC had the power to exert pressure on the Indonesian government to enforce its demand. During the negotiations and preparations for the 18th Asian Games, in contrast, Indonesia held a rather strong position towards the OCA. Yet, the limited time for the preparation put the host cities, as well as the Council, under pressure. The 2018 Asian Games, therefore, depict a great opportunity for Indonesia to demonstrate its ability as a host and its conformity with the Olympic principles on the one hand; yet, on the other hand, the event is also a big challenge and failures could lead to further tensions with the IOC or the OCA.

Notes

1. For detailed research on GANEFO see: Ewa T. Pauker, 'Ganefo I: Sports and Politics in Djakarta', *Asian Survey* 5, no. 4 (1965), 171–85; C.A. Connolly, 'The Politics of the Games of the New Emerging Forces (GANEFO)', *The International Journal of the History of Sport* 29, no. 9 (2012), 1311–24; Rusli Lutan and Fan Hong, 'The Politicization of Sport: GANEFO – A Case Study', in Fan Hong (ed.), *Sport, Nationalism and Orientalism: The Asian Games* (Abingdon: Routledge, 2007), 22–36; Terry Vaios Gitersos, 'The Sporting Scramble for Africa: GANEFO, the IOC and the 1965 African Games', *Sport in Society* 14, no. 5 (2011), 645–59.
2. Permanent Secretariat of the GANEFO Federation, *GANEFO (Games of the New Emerging Forces): Its Principles, Purposes and Organization* (Jakarta: GANEFO Federation, 1965), 31. The quotation appears with original emphasis and formatting.
3. Gitersos, 'The Sporting Scramble for Africa', 646, 648.
4. Komite Nasional GANEFO, *Djakarta, 1963: Tugas Dan Kedudukannja. Siaran No. 1* (Jakarta: Komite Nasional GANEFO, 1963), 4.
5. Tan Liang Tie and Ang Hong To, *Asian Games Ke-IV, Djakarta, 24 August–4 September 1962: Suatu Bahan Pegangan Untuk Penonton, Untok Penggemar Olahraga* (Jakarta: P.T. Kinta, 1962), 7.
6. Rusli Lutan, 'Indonesia and the Asian Games: Sport, Nationalism and the "New Order"', in Fan Hong (ed.), *Sport, Nationalism and Orientalism: The Asian Games* (Abingdon: Routledge, 2007), 11–21; Stefan Hübner, 'The Fourth Asian Games (Jakarta 1962) in a Transnational Perspective: Japanese and Indian Reactions to Indonesia's Political Instrumentalisation of the Games', *The International Journal of the History of Sport* 29, no. 9 (2012), 1295–310.
7. The People's Republic of China had withdrawn from the IOC in 1958 and isolated itself from the capitalist as well as the communist world over political issues such as the 'two Chinas' question. See Fan Hong and Yiong Xiaozheng, 'Communist China: Sport, Politics and Diplomacy', in J.A. Mangan and Fan Hong (eds), *Sport in Asian Society: Past and Present* (London/Portland: Frank Cass, 2003), 326–8.
8. Gitersos, 'Sporting Scramble for Africa', 647.

9. Naoko Shimazu, 'Diplomacy as Theatre: Staging the Bandung Conference of 1955', *Modern Asian Studies* 48, no. 1 (2013), 227f.
10. Stefan Hübner, *Pan-Asian Sports and the Emergence of Modern Asia, 1913–1974* (Singapore: NUS Press, 2016), 186.
11. For a detailed description of the National Games in the 1950s and their national significance see Colin Brown, 'Sport, Modernity and Nation Building: The Indonesian National Games of 1951 and 1953', *Bijdragen tot de Taal-, Land- En Volkenkunde (BKI)* 164, no. 4 (2008), 431–49.
12. Iain Adams, '"Pancasila": Sport and the Building of Indonesia: Ambitions and Obstacles', in J.A. Mangan and Fan Hong (eds.), *Sport in Asian Society: Past and Present* (London / Portland: Frank Cass, 2003), 297–9.
13. Adams, '"Pancasila": Sport and the Building of Indonesia', 309; Direktorat Jenderal Olah Raga, *Sejarah Olahraga Indonesia* (Jakarta: Departemen Pendidikan Nasional 2003), 57–8.
14. Lutan and Hong, 'The Politicization of Sport', 23; Hübner, 'The Fourth Asian Games', 1305f.
15. Direktorat Jenderal Olah Raga, *Sejarah*, 80.
16. Lutan and Hong, 'The Politicization of Sport', 25.
17. Sukarno in his speech at the opening of the Conference of National Front Committees on 13 February 1963, cited in George Modelski, *The New Emerging Forces: Documents on the Ideology of Indonesian Foreign Policy* (Canberra: Australian National University, 1963), 90.
18. Ibid., 88.
19. Ibid., 94. Quotation with original formatting.
20. Connolly, 'The Politics of the Games of the New Emerging Forces', 1313.
21. Hong and Xiaozheng, 'Communist China: Sport, Politics and Diplomacy', 329f.
22. Pauker, 'Ganefo I', 180; Russell Field, 'Re-Entering the Sporting World: China's Sponsorship of the 1963 Games of the New Emerging Forces (GANEFO)', *The International Journal of the History of Sport* 31, no. 15 (2014), 1852–67.
23. Hübner, *Pan-Asian Sports*, 193.
24. On *gotong royong* see for example Dwita Hadi Rahmi, Bambang Hari Wibisono and Bakti Setiawan, 'Rukun and Gotong Royong: Managing Public Places in an Indonesian Kampung', in Pu Miao (ed.), *Public Places in Asia Pacific Cities: Current Issues and Strategies* (Dordrecht: Springer Netherlands, 2001), 119–34.
25. Modelski, *The New Emerging Forces*, 94.
26. Permanent Secretariat of the GANEFO Federation, *GANEFO*, 20.
27. Pauker, 'Ganefo I', 174.
28. The *konfrontasi* (confrontation) policy attacked the formation of the Malaysian Federation. Sukarno branded Malaysia as a mere puppet state of the British imperialists. For more information of the confrontation policy see for example Matthew Jones, *Conflict and Confrontation in South East Asia, 1961–1965: Britain, the United States, and the Creation of Malaysia* (Cambridge/New York: Cambridge University Press, 2001); Greg Poulgrain, *The Genesis of Konfrontasi: Malaysia, Brunei, Indonesia, 1945–1965* (London: Hurst, 1998).
29. Pauker, 'Ganefo I', 179. The word 'ganjang' is in the original spelling. Today, the spelling is ganyang.
30. Ibid.
31. Simon Creak, 'Representing True Laos in Post-Colonial Southeast Asia: Regional Dynamics in the Globalization of Sport', in Katrin Bromber, Birgit Krawietz and Joseph Maguire (eds), *Sport Across Asia: Politics, Cultures, and Identities* (New York: Routledge, 2013), 110.
32. Connolly, 'The Politics of the Games of the New Emerging Forces', 1320.
33. Ali-Mohammad Amirtash, 'Iran and the Asian Games: The Largest Sports Event in the Middle East', in Fan Hong (ed.), *Sport, Nationalism and Orientalism. The Asian Games* (Abingdon/New York: Routledge, 2007), 54.
34. Katharine McGregor, 'Representing the Indonesian Past: The National Monument History Museum from Guided Democracy to the New Order', *Indonesia* 75 (2003), 115–22.
35. See for example Ahmad Faizin Karimi, 'Hari Pahlawan, GANEFO dan Nasionalisme Kita', n.d. https://ahmadfk.wordpress.com/2009/11/08/hari-pahlawan-ganefo-dan-nasionalisme-kita/ (accessed 10 May 2016).

36. Direktorat Jenderal Olah Raga, *Sejarah*, 94–5; KONI, Sejarah KONI http://koni.or.id/index.php/id/about-us?showall=1&limitstart= (accessed 10 May 2016); Adams, '"Pancasila": Sport and the Building of Indonesia', 310.
37. John Monfries, *A Prince in a Republic: The Life of Sultan Hamengku Buwono IX of Yogyakarta* (Singapore: Institute of Southeast Asian Studies, 2015), 287–9.
38. Direktorat Jenderal Olah Raga, *Sejarah*, 98–100, 111–2.
39. Ibid., 107.
40. Simon Creak, 'Sport as Politics and History: The 25th SEA Games in Laos', *Anthropology Today* 27, no. 1 (2011), 14.
41. Creak, 'Representing True Laos in Post-Colonial Southeast Asia', 102; Sombat Karnjanakit and Supitr Samahito, 'Thailand and the Asian Games: Coping with Crisis', in Fan Hong (ed.), *Sport, Nationalism and Orientalism: The Asian Games* (Abingdon: Routledge, 2007), 38.
42. Creak 'Representing True Laos in Post-Colonial Southeast Asia', 104.
43. Dharmawan Tjondronegoro, *10th SEA Games, Jakarta 1979, September 21–30: Souvenir Programme - Buku Petunjuk* (Jakarta: Organizing Committee of the Tenth South East Asia (SEA) Games, 1979), 47f.
44. Dharmawan Tjondronegoro, *Official Guide Book 10th SEA Games, Jakarta 1979, September 21–30* (Jakarta: Organizing Committee of the Tenth South East Asia (SEA) Games, 1979), 35.
45. SEA Games Federation, South East Asian Games Federation Charter and Rules http://voc.org.vn/Portals/0/2013-SEAG%20Charter.pdf (accessed 10 March 2016).
46. Creak, 'Representing True Laos in Post-Colonial Southeast Asia', 101–4.
47. Tjondronegoro, *10th SEA Games, Jakarta 1979, September 21–30: Souvenir Programme*, 49.
48. Tjondronegoro, *10th SEA Games, Jakarta 1979, September 21–30: Souvenir Programme*, 52.
49. The Asian Games Federation was reorganized and changed its name to OCA in 1982.
50. For more information on Sultan Hemengku Bowono IX as a sport figure see Andibachtiar Yusuf and Ekky Imansyah, 'Sri Sultan Hamengku Buwono IX: Sebagai Tokoh Olahraga', *Prestasi Hidup Anda d'Maestro* 1, no. 5 (2004), 16–7.
51. Dougald J.W. O'Reilly, *Early Civilizations of Southeast Asia* (Lanham: AltaMira Press, 2007), 59f; Simon Creak, 'From Bangkok to Palembang: The Southeast Asian Games and a Cultural Approach to Studying Regionalism', www.cseas.kyoto-u.ac.jp/edit/wp…/NL6515-17.pdf (accessed 5 March 2013).
52. Simon Creak, 'National Restoration, Regional Prestige: The Southeast Asian Games in Myanmar, 2013', *Journal of Asian Studies* 73, no. 4 (2014), 860.
53. Niken Prathivi, 'Indonesia faces suspension from IOC, OCA', *Jakarta Post*, 4 September 2009, http://www.thejakartapost.com/news/2009/09/04/indonesia-faces-suspension-ioc-oca.html (accessed 15 April 2016).
54. KOI, Sejarah KOI, http://www.nocindonesia.or.id/about-us/history.html (accessed 10 May 2016).
55. Wina Setyawatie, 'Konflik KONI-KOI Meruncing', *Pikiran Rakyat*, 10 February 2015, http://www.pikiran-rakyat.com/olah-raga/2015/02/10/315,725/konflik-koni-koi-meruncing (accessed 20 March 2016).
56. Edward Aspinall, 'A Nation in Fragments: Patronage and Neoliberalism in Contemporary Indonesia', *Critical Asian Studies* 45, no.1 (2013), 27–54.
57. 'Indonesia Could Lose the 2018 Asian Games Because of Olympic Logo Copyright Violation', *Coconuts Jakarta*, 12 February 2015, http://jakarta.coconuts.co/2015/02/12/indonesia-could-lose-2018-asian-games-because-olympic-logo-copyright-violation (accessed 28 April 2016).

Disclosure Statement

No potential conflict of interest was reported by the author.

ORCID

Friederike Trotier ⓘ http://orcid.org/0000-0001-5991-0242

'The Sole Anti-Democratic Federation in the Entire Olympic Movement': Early International Association of Athletics Federations Development Initiatives Between Commercialization and Democratization, 1974–1987

Jörg Krieger

ABSTRACT
Studies on the development of Olympic Solidarity as a tool of the International Olympic Committee (IOC) to enable National Olympic Committees of developing countries access to resources and influence in the Olympic Movement exist. However, historical scholarship has relatively neglected the development of aid programs by International Federations to explain how they made use of resources to gain influence in international sport politics. Based on extensive multi-national and multi-lingual archival research in the archives of the International Association of Athletics Federation (IAAF) and the German Sport University Cologne, this article explores the establishment and development of the IAAF's Technical Aid Program, which had been installed in 1974. Referencing a large amount of previously unknown protocols and written correspondence, the paper critically discusses the IAAF's development activities in light of two parallel occurring processes that shaped the federation's character in the 1970s and 1980s decisively: its increasing commercialization and its path towards democratization in its voting system. It is argued that the IAAF development programs served as a tool to enforce commercial and sport political interests whilst the nature of support remained without clear guidance until the mid-1980s.

Introduction

The development activities of international organizations in general and sporting bodies in particular have been subject to considerable criticism in recent years. However, there are only a few studies dealing with the establishment of international sport development efforts, such as excellent research on the foundation of the Committee for International Olympic Aid (CIOA) and Olympic Solidarity.[1] In this context, little is known about the development efforts of the core sport federation within the Olympic Movement, the International Association of Athletics Federations (IAAF),[2] despite it engaging in development activities since the 1970s. Connor and McEwen have studied the IAAF's current strategies, arguing that the IAAF is engaging in 'classic Western development rhetoric' through its Regional Development

Centers (RDCs).[3] While they briefly touch upon the origins of the RDCs, Connor and McEwen do not elaborate in detail on the initiation of the IAAF's development activities. Consequently, this paper attempts to create an understanding of the genesis of the IAAF's sport development initiative, which cannot be evaluated without critically discussing two parallel occurring processes that shaped the federation's character in the 1970s and 1980s decisively. First, its increasing commercialization, second, its path towards democratization in its voting system. Thereby, this paper focuses on the development *of* sport which aims to increase participation and improve performance in a specific sport, in this case in athletics.[4] It is argued that the IAAF development programs served as a tool to enforce commercial and (sport) political interests whilst the nature of support remained without clear guidance until the mid-1980s.

From the analysis, three main phases (1974–1976, 1977–1983, 1984–1987) evolved. The starting year for this research is 1974 as it marked the beginning of the IAAF's development initiatives. The investigation ends in 1987 because this year proved to be a major turning point for the IAAF's development aid and power struggles. The presented results are based on an historical analysis of IAAF Council and Congress meeting minutes, written correspondence by IAAF Council members and files of the IAAF Development Commission, compiled from the IAAF Archives (Monaco) and the Carl und Liselott Diem-Archive of the German Sport University Cologne (Germany).

Initial Attempts to Address the Needs of Emerging IAAF Member Federations

The need for development aid in sport became an issue to international sport organizations as a result of the growing membership applications and in light of decolonialization after the Second World War. A notable example for this is the International Olympic Committee (IOC). Claiming for universality;[5] it accepted 48 new National Olympic Committees (NOCs) from Asia and Africa from the 1950s to the 1970s.[6] The emergence of the NOCs led to the foundation of the CIOA in 1961.[7] Henry and Al Tauqi argue that the IOC aimed to provide an ideal way for the development of elite athletes and a Western sporting culture as the CIOA would only provide equipment and coaches, with Western countries benefiting from the exchange.[8] As the IOC's leaders, IOC President Avery Brundage (USA) and IOC Vice-President David Burghley (United Kingdom), also IAAF President, became concerned about what they thought to be 'political' involvement, the CIOA's activities were sidelined from 1963 onwards. Only after the threat of the Games of the Newly Emerging Forces (GANEFO), did the IOC increase its efforts on the African continent again. It eventually supported the 1965 African Games in order to avoid a withdrawal of Africa from the Olympic Movement.[9] The GANEFO crisis clarified that the IOC had to bring African countries closer to the core of its movement, although the leading figures only intended for participation, not decision-making. This was most clearly reflected in the establishment of Olympic Solidarity in 1972, considered a compromise to ensure the compliance of NOCs whilst also keeping them at arm's length. The IOC at first refused to provide financial support but only provided training.[10] Thus, the IOC's path to the establishment of its development activities was clearly linked to the conflict between Western sporting powers and developing countries.[11]

As the biggest international sports federation within the Olympic Movement, the IAAF faced similar challenges in the 1960s and 1970s, and monitored the IOC's development activities closely. In 1964, the IAAF had already discussed a potential development aid program for the first time.[12] However, extensive debates about the possibility to support the development of athletics globally only took place in September 1973 in Edinburgh, following the establishment of Olympic Solidarity.[13] During an IAAF Council meeting, IAAF General Secretary John Holt (United Kingdom) and IAAF Honorary Treasurer Frederick W. Holder (United Kingdom) emphasized that the federation was in a much better financial situation following the receipt of its share of the television income from the 1972 Munich Olympic Games.[14] John Holt proposed to use the additional revenues to support the increasing number of member federations from developing countries in their development of athletics through advancing technical and practical experience of local coaches, strengthening 'the sport and practice of Athletics ... in all regions'.[15] Clearly, the development strategy was a response to the rapid increase in the IAAF membership. By 1974, the number of official IAAF member federations had for the first time risen to over 150 members with Bermuda, Botswana, Burundi, Montserrat, Rwanda and St Vincent becoming members that year. Thus, decolonialization and globalization also increasingly began to influence the structure of the IAAF – if only a decade after the IOC. The delay in addressing the issue was linked to the lack of financial resources available to the federation. Therefore, it is logical that the initiation of the IAAF development activities was linked to its slowly growing budget. Moreover, it is unsurprising that the IAAF intended to follow the IOC's strategy to provide only coaching assistance. With a long-established, conservative leadership under David Burghley in place, the IAAF Council wanted to restrict the flow of direct money to keep control over the usage of possible development activities. Such a careful approach had its roots also in the federation's growing problems with regional athletic events at the beginning of the 1970s, similar to the IOC.[16] Continental athletic events sought recognition from the IAAF whilst on many occasions not being in compliance with IAAF regulations.[17] At the same time, athletics confederations were founded on all continents that aimed to increase the influence of smaller member federations.[18] Hence, the IAAF Council saw the necessity to gain more influence on a global scale and considered the installation of development initiatives as a starting point to do so. It created the IAAF Technical Aid Program in 1974 and officially approved a development concept by John Holt and the Hungarian IAAF Council member Jozsef Sir, who had already pushed for the involvement of the IAAF in aid activities in the 1960s.[19] The concept foresaw the initiation of coaching and instructional courses in developing countries in order to improve the technical and practical experiences of coaches. The decision marks the official beginning of IAAF development activities.

The recorded communication between Western IAAF Council members and their colleagues from developing regions revealed concerns about the nature of the proposed training activities for athletics coaches from the very beginning. They agreed that the final approval for the usage of the funds had to be made by 'Area Group Representatives' from the respective regions. However, it is important to note that the single African representative on the IAAF Council, Hassan Agabani from Sudan,[20] argued that the organizational difficulties in most African member federations would make it complicated to organize coaching courses. Instead, he saw the need for more infrastructural and administrative support before coaching courses should be offered. Jozsef Sir and John Holt dismissed the warning, however, and referred to the success of other national and international bodies that had started to run sport development programs.[21] It appeared more important to them that the IAAF could wield its authority as 'the world governing body for athletics' and coordinate all international development activities in its sport.[22] The nature of the support remained unchallenged. Hence, the IAAF intended to follow a typical development strategy applying a Western training philosophy in developing countries. The initiative to install a Technical Aid Program anticipated a hierarchical top-down approach to show an intention to support smaller member federations whilst keeping control over what kind of support was provided. The IAAF saw itself as an expert organization that felt aware about the needed development.[23]

The reflection upon Hassan Agabani's doubts mirrored that of the perceived suppression of smaller member federations within the IAAF that became contested from the 1970s onwards. During this time, the IAAF still employed a voting system that allowed some national member federations more power than others. It categorized its national federations into five different groups according to athletic infrastructure. Such a classification resulted in higher membership fees for the larger federations but also in a different number of votes at the IAAF Congress.[24] Consequently, the majority of the member federations only had the minority of the voting power. The increasing number of IAAF members from developing countries had continuously complained about this principle and proposed changes at the 1972 and 1974 IAAF Congresses. Their representatives stated that the voting scheme was anti-democratic and discriminatory.[25] The leading IAAF figures rejected such charges vigorously. IAAF president David Burghley argued that the IAAF was not a political body,[26] whilst IAAF Council member Adriaan Paulen (The Netherlands) was quoted in the official protocol: 'when using words like fair play, discrimination, and democracy, it would be even less justified if under the proposed system the USSR had the same votes as Gibraltar or Liechtenstein'.[27] Affected by the group voting system in place, the IAAF Congresses voted against any change in 1972 and 1974. However, discussions in the IAAF Council reveal that the Western leadership of the federation did begin to reconsider the growing influence of developing countries after all in the following years, if not on the Congress level. In the last years of his presidency, David Burghley proposed constitutional changes in the IAAF Council. In particular, he saw the need to address the 'expansion of our International Federation and its activities in the top echelon'.[28] Hence, he extended the IAAF Council membership to 21 members: President, four Vice-Presidents (at least one from outside Europe), Honorary Treasurer, seven individuals and six Area Group Representatives (Africa, Asia, Europe, North/Central America, Oceania, South America).[29] The inclusion of the Area Group Representatives in the IAAF Council and the expansion of the body were considered key in the reassurance of the concerns of inequality and a concession towards the decentralization of the federation. This was directly stated by the new IAAF president Adriaan Paulen, elected in 1976, who wanted to avoid a 'violent political struggle'.[30] However, by unremittingly rejecting changes to the voting system in the IAAF Congress, which was the main decision-making body of the federation, representatives of the leading nations ensured that they could keep control over all significant processes. Clearly, a power play of interests emerged. Whereas difficulties as a result of globalization were recognized and discussed, neither did the Technical Aid Program nor the changes in the IAAF Council appear to deal with the problems efficiently and appropriately according to the representatives from developing countries. Further evidence for this contention was given by the fact that a motion proposed by Arabic countries to include Arabic simultaneous translation at Congress meetings was dismissed officially at the 1976 IAAF Congress.[31]

Besides the emerging contestations for power in the IAAF, finance became a key issue in connection with the development initiatives. The Technical Aid Program remained minimal until the end of 1976. In 1974, the federation had spent a mere £1711 on minor coaching activities in Africa.[32] For 1975 and 1976, the budget was raised to £15,000 as the first IAAF coaching course took place in Zambia in April 1975.[33] Thus, the initial Technical Aid Program remained a commendable strategy on paper while barely having an effect in terms of practical implementation. In light of this situation, a new strategy emerged within the IAAF Council. Western IAAF Council members blamed the lack of resources and pushed for the generation of more income for the federation through hosting international athletic events. Therewith, so they argued, the IAAF would make itself less dependent on the television money of the Olympic Games allocated through the IOC.[34] Significantly, main speakers in the IAAF Council such as Adriaan Paulen and Primo Nebiolo (Italy) constantly argued that more money was needed to support the Technical Aid Program. The Area Group Representatives supported this stance as they saw a benefit for their continents. In 1977, the IAAF installed the IAAF World Cup with continental teams, organized for the first time in Düsseldorf (West-Germany) and intended to explore a possibility for generating revenue through an international athletics event.[35] During an IAAF Council meeting in March 1977, Adriaan Paulen communicated that the purpose of the event was mainly to increase the financial possibilities of the IAAF's development activities: 'Now all must realize how important it was that the World Cup in September should be a financial success, to ensure the carrying out and expansion of the Development Program'.[36] The statement shows that the technical development initiatives served as a tool to justify the commercialization of the IAAF and athletic sport.

Against the background of the power imbalance but also the prospective new financial possibilities, IAAF Council members openly voiced discontent with the poor implementation of the Technical Aid Program at the end of 1976.[37] Specific criticism came from the elected Council members from developing countries and the Area Group Representatives, such as Hassan Agabani, Amadeo Francis (Puerto Rico) and Charles Mukora (Kenya). They made very pragmatic suggestions on improving specific features of the program such as an extension of the coaching activities, the provision of technical equipment, more consideration of regional differences and direct financial support.[38] In light of the prospect of more income, the IAAF Council also considered it necessary to make more funds available and undertook efforts to contract a sponsor to finance the aid program.[39] The intended expansion of the activities but also the prospect of increasing income led to an adaption of the organizational structure of the development initiatives by founding a permanent IAAF Development Committee in 1976.[40] It consisted of Jozsef Sir, John Holt, Primo Nebiolo and Frederick Holder.[41] No IAAF Council member from a developing country was elected but the six Area Group Representatives acted as advisors.[42]

In summary for the first investigated phase, the development aid of the IAAF was from the very beginning embedded into the federation's broader expansion. Initially, it was a project by John Holt and Jozsef Sir, who saw the potential to support the sport of athletics worldwide through increasing television income from the Olympic Games. Despite these commendable efforts, no effective support program to address the needs of its poorer member federations appears to have been implemented. Instead, the development initiatives quickly turned out to become a means to an end for leading figures in the IAAF Council. This can be related to two reasons. First, it presented them with a tool to satisfy the increasingly demanding needs of a growing number of member federations, especially from Africa, Asia and Oceania. As the program only foresaw courses for coaches in the different areas, it can be considered a compromise to ensure the compliance of developing countries whilst it allowed the IAAF an expansion of its dominance over the world of athletics during rapid globalization of the sport. Second, the rhetoric of Western IAAF Council members shows that the development activities were beginning to be used to justify the IAAF's efforts to host international athletics events under its umbrella. Individuals such as Adriaan Paulen and Primo Nebiolo, who evidently wanted to propel the IAAF in a commercial direction, used the generation of revenue for development as a key argument for the establishment of the IAAF World Cup.

Coordinating and Expanding the Development Efforts: Struggles for the Shares of an Increased Income

The second phase of the IAAF's development activities lasted from the foundation of the IAAF Development Committee in November 1976 until the end of 1983. The IAAF Development Committee was off to a slow start although Jozsef Sir presented a new four-year development plan with more coaching activities for the African and South Asian member federations in March 1977.[43] Clearly, he was willing to continue with his strategy and to expand the educational courses. However, as only a few initiatives took place in the first months and the plans continued to lack the involvement of the Area Group Representatives, varying opinions on the work of the Development Committee remained. Generally, the smaller member federations perceived the activities as too slow and without specific support for most areas.[44] Moreover, contention on the geographical distribution of the assistance began to increase.[45] Such debates heralded the emerging conflict for more development activities in light of a potentially increased income. Hence, one has to consider the commercialization processes within the IAAF and the growth of its development program jointly in this second phase.

The increasing generation of revenue through the staging of their own international athletic events had a direct effect on the aid activities. In 1977, the Development Committee still worked with an annual budget of £15,000 and surplus from previous years. This original financial plan was raised with an additional $15,000 that Primo Nebiolo had negotiated with Olympic Solidarity.[46] However, the development work really became boosted by the fact that the net surplus from the 1977 IAAF World Cup exceeded DM 1 million.[47] The revenue resulted in an increase in the overall budget for development activities but also in the creation of a 1977 World Cup Development Fund, for which member federations could apply independently (see Table 1). The new fund was coordinated by the Development Commission and money distributed in agreement with the respective Area Group Representative. However, there were no clear guidelines on the distribution of the money and no proof for its usage through the continental delegates.

In parallel, the IAAF Council continued its strategy to defend commercializing efforts with its development aid activities. In 1978, the IAAF contracted *Dubai International*, acting for the emirate of Dubai, to sponsor the staging of the 'Golden Mile' race until 1980.[48] According to the contract, *Dubai International* paid $400,000 over a three-year period for the sole purpose of the IAAF's development initiatives.[49] The few critical voices such as by IAAF Council member Max Danz (West Germany), who pointed out the dangers of increased commercialization in the federation, remained unheard.[50] On the contrary, the need for more money because of the development activities was cited as a priority.

Table 1. Expenditures of the IAAF for development activities (1977–1984).

Year	Expenditures from general development fund (in $/£)	Expenditures from 1977 world cup development fund (in £)	Total (in $/£)
1976	£2,713	–	£2,713
1977	£25,999	–	£25,999
1978	£47,610	£15,512	£63,122
1979	£44,838	£75,616	£120,454
1980	£48,192	£14,113	£62,305
1981	£49,793	£22,318	£72,111
1982	$100,000	–	$100,000
1983	$80,000	–	$80,000
1984	$150,000	–	$150,000

Moreover, nobody seemed to question the intentions of the consortium either. Rather, the IAAF Council followed the advice of marketing consultant Patrick Nally, who led the talks on behalf of the emirate. He was to become a key figure in the continuing commercial efforts of the IAAF and also had a strong interest in opening the markets of developing countries for corporates.[51] Additional proof for the link between commerce and development is that of a comment by IAAF President Adriaan Paulen: 'As a result of the financial contribution that we are to receive from Dubai International, we will now be able to achieve athletics objectives in terms of coaching and technical development not previously possible'.[52] Thus, the case of *Dubai International*'s sponsorship verifies the infiltration of commercial interests into the IAAF on the back of the development activities. This is also true for the installation of IAAF World Championships that the IAAF Congress ratified in 1978.[53] In contrast to the 'Golden' events and the IAAF World Cup, World Championships revenue was not specifically designated for development activities, but the establishment of the event was mainly a reaction of the federation to the ongoing difficulties in negotiations on the share of the Olympic television money.[54]

The prospect of more access to financial resources for developing countries heated up the discussion in the IAAF Council on the distribution of the money in subsequent years. It was again Amadeo Francis who demanded an increase in the overall development budget following the 1977 World Cup, considering the low budget 'ridiculous'.[55] Moreover, he and the African IAAF Council members Hassan Agabani, Charles Mukora and Lamine Diack (Senegal) asked for more support in terms of administration and leadership education.[56] However, the other IAAF Council members continued to disagree with their demands and only granted a special grant of $15,000 from the World Cup Development Fund to the running of the secretariat of the African Athletics Confederation, based in Dakar (Senegal), due to the administrative problems.[57] Besides this specific aid, it was the opinion to restrict the support mainly to coaching activities. At the same time, other Area Group Representatives also wanted to have a larger share, with Oceania demanding one sixth of the World Cup income be separated equally between the areas instead of an overall fund.[58] They brought the argument forward that such a weak association as Oceania was always being criticized for poor performance but could not develop without the provision of sufficient financial aid. The proposal was, however, outvoted. Such debates show that despite the slowly growing resources for development, the concerned member federations did not express gratitude but rather dissatisfaction with the IAAF leadership about the quantity and quality of the support. Adriaan Paulen, John Holt and Primo Nebiolo shrugged off the demands by referring to the still insecure financial situation of the federation due to increasingly

Table 2. Number of IAAF staged development courses (1978-1986), including courses in cooperation with Olympic Solidarity.

Year	Number of courses (coaching, judges, administration, walking)
1986	60
1985	57
1984	45
1983	39
1982	37
1981	37
1980	15
1979	19
1978	7

complicated TV negotiations with the IOC and the other IFs.[59] Such growing tensions provide evidence for the intensifying power game between more powerful federations/individuals and member federations with less-developed athletic infrastructure as a result of the growing financial possibilities. Western leaders were prepared to increase technical support but the aid continued to be imposed rather than negotiated.

Hence, even though the Development Commission under leadership of Jozsef Sir extended its activities from 1978 onwards, the main focus remained on coaching courses (see Table 2).[60] During this period, the IAAF also increased its cooperation with Olympic Solidarity due to numerous talks between Primo Nebiolo and the IOC. As a result, Olympic Solidarity began to initiate and finance courses that were in practice realized by the IAAF.[61] Because the nature of the development activities did not change considerably, African, Asian and Latin American IAAF Council members reiterated their criticism on this approach persistently in meetings. The African federation even went to the lengths of considering independent continental sponsorships to support athletic development and approached *Nike* about the possibility.[62] In contrast to this, Jozsef Sir saw the courses as the main possibility to grant technical support and continuously reiterated that it was the federation's policy to focus on education rather than material assistance and direct financial support.[63] For example, the Development Commission did not consider the demands by federations such as India and Guatemala with underdeveloped athletic infrastructure for more financial support and the provision of technical equipment.[64] This was also the case for growing inquiries about the effect of the initiated courses. Already in 1978, IAAF Congress members had asked for an evaluation of the staged courses but the Development Commission did not implement such measures at the time.[65] Thus, only changes in quantity but not in the quality of the courses appeared to have taken place at the end of the 1970s.

The African continent proved to be a specifically problematic region in terms of developing the athletic infrastructure. The African member federations never ceased to highlight the lack of administrative arrangements and asked for support from the Development Commission. Lamine Diack, who increasingly became more influential as he was elected to IAAF Vice-President, and wrote in the report about the African area to the 1980 IAAF Congress: 'everyone in our sport recognizes the immense potentialities of our Continent, but these will never be realized unless we really improve the level of our administrative and technical operation'.[66] What sounds like self-criticism and awareness of the root of the problem, was in reality also caused by Lamine Diack himself. As the IAAF Council protocols from the beginning of the 1980s detail, he had continuously failed to draw up a budget and provide evidence for the usage of the $15,000 that the African Athletics Confederation had received for administrative support.[67] In Lamine Diack's unexcused absence, other IAAF Council members accused him of non-transparency and blamed his lack of leadership abilities for the problems within the African continent. Such allegations became even worse towards the end of 1982, when IAAF Council member August Kirsch (West Germany) reported about 'total chaos' in Africa.[68] Primo Nebiolo was quoted as saying that Africa should do more to help itself rather than constantly demanding more financial resources that were unlikely to be adequately used.[69] Similar statements by other Western IAAF Council members showed that such behaviour reinforced the prejudice that the African continent could not yet be trusted with big amounts of financial support. Rather, aware that financial aid might foster corruption, it led the IAAF Council to introduce a regular and detailed system for the submission of reports from the different areas in 1983. It required the Area Group Representatives to outline the application of provided funds.[70] Furthermore, it strengthened the IAAF's control mechanism over the development activities even though the arrangements in place were still some way off today's good governance standards. These guidelines aim to prevent corruption on the back of development activities.[71]

With more general income for the IAAF, the member federations from developing countries intensified their efforts to overcome the imbalance in the voting system. Significantly, the representative of the USSR in the IAAF Council, Leonid Khomenkov, initiated the next serious attempt at reform. The USSR knew of a block of smaller, politically linked member federations which backed it. Moreover, as in the case of the CIOA,[72] it wanted to increase its influence in developing countries in order to pile pressure on sporting bodies during the boycott era of the Olympic Movement but also for broader political reasons.[73] It constantly promoted its international policies of equality and anti-colonialism in order to gain influence in developing regions. Soviet sport authorities had provided sporting aid in the form of coaches, the construction of sport facilities and sport administrators to developing countries. Between the end of the 1950s and 1978, more than 600 Soviet coaches had worked in Africa, Asia and Latin America.[74] Within this context, Leonid Khomenkov submitted a written request to the IAAF Council in 1978, in which he advocated for an equal voting system in the IAAF Congress with 'one vote for one country'. He quoted the IAAF statutes, which read that the IAAF strived to 'ensure that no racial, religious, political or other kind of discrimination be allowed in athletics'.[75] According to him, the voting system provided a stark contrast to this principle and called for an 'irreversible democratization' of the IAAF.[76] The IAAF members from developing nations supported the USSR proposal in Congress debates.[77] The initial response of the IAAF Council was to install a Working Group to investigate the issue in detail. The body admitted that the scheme in place was indeed not democratic but another system would be impossible to implement:

> There is a strong case for giving a more powerful voice to National Federations with long experience and proved [sic] success in athletics in their own countries, than is given to a newly-fledged Federation in a country where the sport is barely established ... The present system of weighting the votes from 1–8 is in fact a compromise which favours the smaller and weaker Members.[78]

Their argumentation to justify the existing system was based on the assumption that the traditional athletic nations could make more informed decisions. This strategy had the objective to maintain the existing power balance. By referring to the development activities of the IAAF, the Working Group continued by arguing that as a result of the aid given, member federations had the possibility to obtain an upgraded status and subsequently

Table 3. Budget for IAAF development activities (1985–1987).

Year	Budget shared between the six areas (in $)	Budget for permanent centres (in $)	Total (in $)
1985	$300,000	$100,000	$400,000
1986	$315,000	$210,000	$525,000
1987	$330,750	$330,750	$661,500

secure more votes. On the recommendation of the Working Group, the 1978 IAAF Congress rejected the USSR's proposal, even though more than 70% of the federations were in favour of it.[79]

Curiously, amid continuous complaints, the Working Group focused in the following years on regrouping rather than the introduction of an equal voting system. In 1980, it recommended to the IAAF Congress to reduce the number of groups from five to four. This suggestion was not an active step towards equality but rather a result of 'considerable overlapping standards between the A, B and C Groups'.[80] Arguments, such as that brought forward by Lamine Diack that 90% of the member federations supported one vote per federation, remained blighted.[81] Due to the 1980 Olympic boycott,[82] the decision was postponed to the 1981 IAAF Special Congress in Rome, where the reduction was approved).[83]

In summary of the second phase of the IAAF's development program from 1977 until 1983, there is evidence of an intensification of the main processes detected in the first period. First, leading IAAF figures stepped up their efforts to create income for the federation. Their attempts were closely linked to the development program because they continuously stated the need to invest in athletic sport in weaker member federations as a main reason for the IAAF's commercial interests. Hence, the development program also remained a tool for power expansion with little incorporation of developing countries. Second, despite expanded activities and a growing development budget, there was overt frustration about the provided aid. The development program still lacked an evaluation of the implemented courses and the member federations from developing countries did not see any concrete improvements or results. It appears that the supported regions were not integrated in the design of the aid programs, leading to the initiatives being perceived as unrewarding. Third, severe administrative problems from the African continent were brought into focus in consequence of the boosted financial funds. Such behaviour underpinned the preconception by Western leaders that the African continent was not to be trusted with high amounts of financial benefits. This was in contrast to the attempts by African representatives that considered direct financial support more important than the money spent through the development courses.[84] Fourth, the development efforts of the IAAF did not belie its member federations from perceiving the power balance in the IAAF Congress inequitable. With politically-motivated support from the USSR, they continued to speak out against the felt discrimination implemented through the voting system but found little sympathy amongst the leading athletic federations and individuals at the time.

Extended Development Initiatives Become a Presidential Affair

The third phase of the IAAF's development efforts, beginning in 1984, is closely linked to the federation's fourth president, Primo Nebiolo. As outlined, he had been an influential figure in the IAAF in general and its development activities in particular, already prior to his election as IAAF President in 1981.[85] Once appointed, Primo Nebiolo accelerated the process of commercialization in the federation through the acquisition of additional sponsorships,[86] retention of high revenues through the income of television rights for the inaugural IAAF World Championships in 1983 and the installation of further IAAF events.[87] It allowed him to make the federation less dependent on the sales of the broadcasting rights of the Olympic Games through the IOC.[88]

Under Primo Nebiolo's leadership, the World Championships turned out to be a great financial success for the federation. The IAAF divided its total income of $5.5 million amongst the participating countries to cover accommodation and travel expenses (65%, $3.6 million), the six areas (10%, $0.5 million in total, $90,000 for each of the six areas) and the IAAF (25%, $1.4 million).[89] The development initiatives also benefited considerably from the income: the IAAF Council raised the budget for the Development Committee from $150,000 to $300,000 for the year 1984.[90] The IAAF Council members from the developing countries much appreciated this decision and there was also praise from Leonid Khomenkov, who emphasized that such support for the development of athletics could not have been imagined 30 years ago and now 'opportunities existed to increase such help'.[91] At the same time, the IAAF did also expect more support from Olympic Solidarity through anticipated additional income for the IOC from the television rights sales of the 1984 Los Angeles Olympic Games.[92]

On the back of much more available revenues, Primo Nebiolo got officially involved in the development work from 1984 onwards. This was benefitted by the official retirement of Jozsef Sir from the IAAF Council in August 1984. Primo Nebiolo's involvement saw a change in his approach, as in the first years of his presidency he had focused on the preparations for the World Championships.[93] By 1984, however, he was put under increasing pressure regarding the voting system by the member federations with permanent support from the USSR. In fact, on the recommendation of the IAAF Council, the Congress voted for a further reduction of the group system, down to only three different groups, whilst 'the one vote for one country' system did not achieve a two thirds majority.[94] Of 172 member federations in total, 35 members were grouped in Group AA (eight votes), 50 members in Group A (six votes) and the remaining 87 members in Group B (four votes).[95] Hence, the traditional athletic nations maintained control, for now, but their power started to crumble progressively.[96] Against this background, Primo Nebiolo appointed himself as chairman of the IAAF Development Commission in August 1984 and it appears that he took over this role to gather support amongst the majority of the small member federations as he anticipated that the unequal voting was eventually to be overturned in upcoming IAAF Congresses.[97] He needed the backing of small federations to hedge his presidential position and in turn promised more funds for development activities. He did not disappoint in implementing a different approach as he oversaw extensive changes in the organizational structure of the IAAF's development program, which became possible through the increased financial possibilities, in 1984.[98] The new structure also answered evolving criticism on the existing development activities from Western IAAF representatives, who argued that all initiatives had been run 'without a plan'.[99] Primo Nebiolo changed the internal structure of the Commission and installed Jozsef Sir as Director and Jim Alford (Great Britain), who had closely worked with Jozsef Sir in previous years, as Program Coordinator.[100] Moreover, he named Lamine Diack as deputy chairman to include regional knowledge into the leadership. With these changes, he gained the immediate support of the Area Group Representatives.[101]

In contrast to his previous statements, it is noticeable that Primo Nebiolo stated grand aspirations for the development work under his leadership:

> [Primo Nebiolo] said it was important to have an ambitious program; in the past, we had been too modest and had not utilised all our resources and the expertise available through our Member Federations and other agencies.

> The President said he wanted to be involved personally, and he thought this work was most important. He felt his presence on the Working Group as President of the IAAF and with all his personal contacts, would be beneficial.[102]

Clearly, his attitude towards an expansion of the development activities greatly changed and his apparent rethink was closely linked to the available resources and the apparent need to secure his power. The IAAF Council members August Kirsch and Amadeo Francis criticized Primo Nebiolo for this strategic move, arguing that the federation's development activities would suffer from his lack of time.[103] August Kirsch also condemned the IAAF President for appointing Jozsef Sir as Director because he considered it significant to advance the aid activities through new input.[104] Notwithstanding the critique, Primo Nebiolo confided in Jozsef Sir and they together submitted a three-year plan for the development activities from 1985 until 1987 (Table 3).

Despite the increased budget, however, the nature of the initiatives was still coaching courses and the demanded input from the developing countries remained limited.[105] Continuing demands for support in administration and infrastructure, in particular from Africa,[106] were also unaddressed, even though Olympic Solidarity and the IAAF agreed that this was a major area of concern.[107] In essence, the development work remained a top-down approach regardless of the available budget. The most significant change concerned the introduction of Permanent Centres (today IAAF Regional Development Centres) to support the development of athletics in specific areas. This idea reached back to the first IAAF technical aid plan from 1974, which had already envisaged regional hubs.[108] The IAAF officially opened the first Centre in Patiala (India), in 1986.[109] The structure of the Centre mirrored the overall development scheme of the IAAF as it had a main emphasis on coaching courses lasting four months, courses for judges, a few offers for administrators and training facilities for athletes.[110] However, struggles for power also influenced the intended expansion of the Permanent Centres to all areas. In particular, the process to select two locations (Arabic-speaking and English-speaking) in Africa proved to be a challenge. Twelve African countries applied to host a Permanent Centre and eventually Nairobi (Kenya) and Cairo (Egypt) were chosen, although there were unclear specific selection guidelines with IAAF Council members supporting the bids from their own countries.[111] Moreover, the applications displayed a primary intention for increasing national prestige as well as developmental aims. This is clearly stated in the Kenyan bid.[112] Kenya had intended to apply for the 1996 Olympic Games and it was the objective of national sports leaders to strengthen its international standing through an official IAAF sporting complex.[113]

Problems also continued regarding the nature of the support and little guidance as to how to improve administration. It emerged in 1987 that there was still no follow-up and evaluation from the staged activities, meaning that it remained unclear whether the participants actually used their knowledge to advance athletics in their home communities.[114] As a result from pressure in the IAAF Council,[115] Primo Nebiolo agreed to the installation of a permanent Development Officer in Björn Wangemann (West

Germany) and handover of the chairmanship of the Development Commission to August Kirsch in January 1987.[116] Simultaneously, the IAAF set up a permanent Development Department in the IAAF Bureau.[117] Primo Nebiolo insisted, however, that he would deliver the Council's and Development Commission's report to the IAAF Congress in 1987. Therein, he emphasized the need to support all member federations equally, highlighting that 'the sport is administered in a way which benefits all members of the athletics family'.[118] It is no coincidence that the IAAF President gave emphasis to the community feeling in his organization as the perception of the weaker member federation towards equality in the IAAF differed considerably from Primo Nebiolo's statements. Their stance is best reflected in an open letter by Ethiopian journalist and sport administrator Fekrou Kidane, who addressed the IAAF President directly in 1987:

> The IAAF is, in fact, the sole anti-democratic federation in the entire Olympic movement … I am well aware, as no doubt are you, that if all the member countries of your federation are present at the Rome Congress, that the amendment will possibly be adopted. In that case, the Third World will owe neither you, nor its opponents anything. If on the other hand, you should manage, on the occasion of your federation's 75th anniversary, to convince your democratic anti-democratic friends, for whom democracy is rather as a one-way system, it is time that was a change of policy, then I would say 1987 is really the year of athletics … Athletics is a simple sport which does not need complications. It is a peaceful struggle conducted between individuals, whose performances are kept track of by computerized equipment which does not take account of voting rights. Until such time as this problem is resolved; a problem which concerns the dignity of your partners in the Third World, you will always be accused of presiding over a federation, where demagogy and cynicism reign. And I fear that you would be held responsible for the possible ensuing consequences.[119]

With pressure from African members heavily increasing within the IAAF Council, too, Primo Nebiolo eventually recommended to the 1987 IAAF Congress that the 'one vote one country' proposal should be adopted.[120] In his speech, he now emphasized 'the importance that everyone should be allowed to express their views equally'.[121] Therewith he concluded a gradual U-turn in the IAAF's stance towards voting equality in the federation.[122] Paradoxically, the gathered support from developing countries secured Primo Nebiolo's leadership in the coming years as he remained IAAF President until his death in 1999. Lamine Diack, the first non-White and non-European IAAF President, succeeded him.

To sum up the IAAF's development effort from 1984 until 1987, the aid activities remained contested by various stakeholders even though a significant step into the professionalization of the support initiatives was made. With the income from the inaugural World Championships having led to a significant increase in funds for development, it became possible to extend the scope of activities. However, the nature of the top-down approach continued to be the same and involvement for the developing countries was still limited. Consequently, it was difficult to advance changes to the system as voiced continuously by August Kirsch throughout the entire presidency of Primo Nebiolo. In contrast to previous periods, however, the IAAF President paid considerably more attention to the development processes. He chaired the IAAF Development Commission from 1984 until 1987, even though he was not heavily involved in the actual processes. It appears that he also used his role in order to advance his influence in member federations worldwide and thus, maintain a dominant role in light of the dooming change of power relations mirrored specifically in the voting system of the federation.

Conclusion

The review of the establishment and early history of the IAAF's development aid activities identifies that IAAF presidents, Council members and member federations all used the development program as a playing field of power. The processes of cooperation and conflict between key stakeholders of the athletic world explored in this paper reveal that the IAAF's development activities were interlinked with the parallel occurring commercialization and the battle for democratization within the federation. This is coherent with findings that highlight the link between the increased commercialization and a shift of power that is an outcome of the globalization in sport.[123]

The IAAF development activities focused mainly on coaching activities that tied the small member federations to the dominating powers in the IAAF. Even when more resources became available to the federation from the end of the 1970s onwards, little adaptation to the cultural context of developing countries took place. Instead, the IAAF supported a top-down approach.[124] This paper also provides evidence for the fact that the developing countries lacked the economic, administrative and (sporting) infrastructural preconditions to benefit from the provided aid in an adequate manner. Representatives of those countries continuously stated concerns but did not appear to have the assertiveness to achieve changes. At the same time, considerable weaknesses in their own administration hindered their position. The IAAF expanded its activities considerably at the beginning of the 1980s, however, the nature of the development aid remained largely unaddressed. There was only little evaluation concerning the effects of the activities and it was only in 1987 that the IAAF Development Commission discussed what 'development' actually meant to the IAAF.[125]

It is noteworthy that other authors consider the IAAF as a transnational corporation because the federation 'does not fit the model of an "aid" organization'.[126] For them, the IAAF aims to create maximum profit and return on its own activities and consequently they question the reasoning for the federation's development aid. This paper has provided evidence that the rise of the IAAF to a commodified sport organization is inextricably linked to its development efforts. Particularly from 1977 onwards, Western key figures in the IAAF Council adopted a twofold rhetoric regarding development and commercialization. On the one hand, they used the apparent need to improve the sport of athletics globally in order to justify their rapidly expanding efforts to generate resources for the federation. Therewith, they condemned concerns about the evident commercialization that eventually led to the installation of lucrative international athletic events and multi-million dollar sponsorships deals under the presidency of Primo Nebiolo. However, there appeared little worry about the widening gap between developing nations and leading athletic powers due to the rapid professionalization of the sport of athletics. In fact, it allowed the West to extend its control over economic, technological, political and knowledge resources in global sport.[127] On the other hand, the analyzed material shows that the same individuals used the increasing funds for development in an attempt to satisfy the members from developing countries against the background of growing pressure to gain equal electoral rights. This aim for equality within the IAAF Council and the IAAF Congress was contested heavily by the dominating athletic nations and their representatives for more than a decade. They were content to approve athletic development because there was a benefit for the IAAF through global participation, public relations and the opening of new markets for (predominantly Western) sponsors and broadcasters at stake. In contrast, until the mid-1980s a potential change to the IAAF

Congress' group voting system was considered a threat to the Western-led, authoritative power structure in place. This also did not change through the presidency of Primo Nebiolo but he understood that eventually an equal voting right system would become inevitable. Once the pressure became too high, he appears to have supported development efforts more vigorously to secure backing from smaller member federations and eventually recommended a change to the voting system, leading to the end of the IAAF's reputation as the 'sole anti-democratic federation in the entire Olympic Movement'. Thus, non-Western federations were able to gain more influence, a tendency also evident at the example of the *Fédération Internationale de Football Association* (FIFA) around the same period.[128]

Notes

1. Ian Henry and Mansour Al-Tauqi, 'The Development of Olympic Solidarity: West and Non-West (Core and Periphery) Relations in the Olympic World', *The International Journal of the History of Sport* 25, no. 3 (2008), 355–69; and Dikaia Chatziefstathiou et al., 'Cultural Imperialism and the Diffusion of Olympic Sport in Africa: A Comparison of Pre- and Post-second World War Contexts', in Nigel B. Crowther, Robert K. Barney and Michael K. Heine (eds), *Cultural Imperialism in Action: Critiques in the Global Olympic Trust. Eight International Symposium for Olympic Research* (London: The University of Western Ontario, 2006), 278–92.
2. The IAAF was founded under the name of International Amateur Athletic Federation on 12 July 1912 in Stockholm. Its founding member countries were Australia, Austria, Belgium, Canada, Chile, Denmark, Egypt, Finland, France, Germany, Greece, Hungary, Norway, Russia, Sweden, United Kingdom and the United States of America. The first President was Sigfrid Edström (Sweden), elected at the 2nd IAAF Congress in 1913. He remained in office until 1946, when he was elected President of the IOC. Ansgar Molzberger, *Die Olympischen Spiele 1912 in Stockholm: Zwischen Patriotismus und Internationalität* [The 1912 Olympic Games in Stockholm: Between Patriotism and Internationalism] (St Augustin: Academia, 2012), 91.
3. James Connor and Melissa McEwen, 'International Development or White Man's Burden? The IAAF's Regional Development Centres and Regional Sporting Assistance', *Sport in Society* 14, no. 6 (2011), 805.
4. Roger Levermore and Aaron Beacom, 'Sport and Development: Mapping the Field', in Roger Levermore and Aaron Beacom (eds), *Sport and International Development* (Basingstoke: Palgrave MacMillan, 2009), 8.
5. John M. Hoberman, *The Olympic Crisis: Sport, Politics and the Moral Order* (New Rochelle, NY: Caratzas, 1986), 29.
6. Henry and Al-Tauqi, 'The Development of Olympic Solidarity', 359. The applications of new NOCs to the IOC were a result of the European decolonialization after the Second World War that saw the most extreme increase in states. Between 1945 and 1978, the United Nations' membership rose from around 50 states to more than 150 states. Andrew Heywood, *Global Politics* (Basingstoke: Palgrave Macmillan, 2014), 37.
7. Chatziefstathiou et al., 'Cultural Imperialism', 284.
8. Henry and Al-Tauqi, 'The Development of Olympic Solidarity', 363ff.
9. Terry V. Gitseros, 'The Sporting Scramble for Africa: GANEFO, the IOC and the 1965 African Games', *Sport in Society* 14, no. 5 (2011), 363.
10. Henry and Al-Tauqi, 'The Development of Olympic Solidarity', 363.
11. There are numerous varying terms for regions described in this paper as developing countries. Other used phrases are 'low and middle income countries', 'Third World', or 'Global South'. In order to avoid misunderstanding and allow for a clear understanding, the term developing countries is used throughout, however. Nico Schulenkorf and Daryl Adair, 'Sport-for-Development: The Emergence and Growth of a New Genre', in Nico Schulenkorf and Daryl Adair (eds), *Global Sport-For-Development: Critical Perspectives* (Basingstoke: Palgrave Macmillan, 2014), 6.

12. August Kirsch, 'Entwicklungsarbeit aus der Sicht der IAAF [Development Work from the Perspective of the IAAF]', 19 August 1987 (Carl and Liselott Diem-Archive, Cologne).
13. IAAF, Minutes of the Meeting of the IAAF Council, Edinburgh, 7–9 September 1973 (Carl and Liselott Diem-Archive, Cologne).
14. The IAAF had ended the year 1973 with a general fund of £192,315. IAAF, 'Financial Report by Frederick W. Holder to the IAAF Council', 15 August 1974 (Carl and Liselott Diem-Archive, Cologne).
15. IAAF, 'Report by Jozsef Sir and John Holt', 1974 (Carl and Liselott Diem-Archive, Cologne), 5.
16. The end of the 1960s and the beginning of the 1970s saw the emergence of continental athletic events on the developing continents. The first Central American and Caribbean Athletics Championships were organized in Mexico in 1967 and the first Asian Athletics Championships took place in the Philippines in 1973. The first African Athletics Championships were staged considerably later, in 1979, in Senegal.
17. A prominent example, discussed in Edinburgh extensively, was the participation of athletes from the People's Republic of China (PRC) in regional athletics events in Africa, although the IAAF did not recognize the PRC at the time.
18. After officially allowing the formation of continental associations in 1968, the IAAF recognized European Athletics Association in 1969. The Oceania Amateur Athletics Association was founded in 1973. This was followed by the establishment of the African Athletics and the North American, Central American and Caribbean Athletic Association in 1973 and the foundation of the Asian Amateur Athletics Association in 1974. The South American Athletics Confederation had already existed since 1918.
19. IAAF, 'Protokoll', 28–29 August 1974 (Carl and Liselott Diem-Archive, Cologne).
20. IAAF, Minutes of the Meeting of the IAAF Council, 7–9 September 1973, 13.
21. IAAF, 'Report by Joseph Sir and John Holt', 1974 (Carl and Liselott Diem-Archive, Cologne), 1f.
22. Ibid., 2.
23. This approach is also referred to as 'technical' projects in the sport for development sector, in which the agency assumes to have an advantage over the user groups through expert knowledge. There is little communication between the two groups and contents are barely negotiated but rather imposed. Richard Giulianotti and Gary Armstrong, 'The Sport for Development and Peace Sector', in Nico Schulenkorf and Daryl Adair (eds), *Global Sport-For-Development. Critical Perspectives* (Basingstoke: Palgrave Macmillan, 2014), 27.
24. Group AA: eight votes, Group A: six votes, Group B: four votes, Group C: two votes, Group D: one vote. IAAF, Minutes of the 28th Congress, Munich, 30 August and 10–11 September 1972 (Carl and Liselott Diem-Archive, Cologne).
25. IAAF, Minutes of the 28th Congress, August and 10–11 September 1972, 42ff.
26. IAAF, Minutes of the 29th Congress, Rome, 29–31 August 1974 (IAAF Archive, Monaco), 19.
27. IAAF, Minutes of the 28th Congress, August and 10–11 September 1972, 43.
28. IAAF, Minutes of the 29th Congress, 29–31 August 1974, 38.
29. IAAF, Minutes of the 30th Congress, Montreal, 20–22 July 1976 (IAAF Archive, Monaco), 44.
30. IAAF, 'Changes in IAAF Constitution', September 1975 (Carl and Liselott Diem-Archive, Cologne).
31. The discussion on the inclusion of Arabic as a sixth official language had already taken place at the 1974 IAAF Congress in Rome at which it was decided that the Arabic speaking member federations had to bear the costs for the translation if this was technically possible. Hence, the Saudi Arabian Athletic Federation financed the costs for the Arabic translation at the 1976 IAAF Congress in Montreal (IAAF, Minutes of the 30th Congress, 20–22 July 1976, 49).
32. IAAF, Minutes of the Meeting of the IAAF Council, Nairobi, 18–20 April 1975 (IAAF Archive, Monaco), 2.
33. August Kirsch, 'Entwicklungsarbeit'.
34. In fact, the discussions on the distribution scheme of the IOC's broadcasting revenues had intensified in the mid-1970s with the IAAF pressured by smaller international sport federations to give up its large share of the Olympic television money. Robert K. Barney, Stephen R. Wenn

and Scott G. Martyn, *Selling the Five Rings: The International Olympic Committee and the Rise of Olympic Commercialism* (Salt Lake City: University of Utah Press, 2002), 98.
35. Jörg Krieger, 'Born on the Wings of Commerce: The World Championships of the International Association of Athletics Federations', *The International Journal of the History of Sport*, 33, no. 4 (2016), 418–33.
36. IAAF, Minutes of the Meeting of the IAAF Council, Düsseldorf, 18–20 March 1977 (Carl and Liselott Diem-Archive, Cologne).
37. IAAF, Minutes of the Meeting of the IAAF Council, Amsterdam, 13–14 November 1976 (IAAF Archive, Monaco).
38. Ibid.
39. Ibid.
40. Ibid.
41. This decision was in line with the general efforts to increase the administrative structure of the federation as it also created a permanent bureau in London (IAAF, Minutes of the 30th Congress, 1976, 43).
42. IAAF, Minutes of the Meeting of the IAAF Council, 13–14 November 1976, 28.
43. IAAF, Minutes of the Meeting of the IAAF Council, 18–20 March 1977.
44. Ibid.
45. For example, Amadeo Francis wanted to see more action in the American nations in need, arguing that not all aid activities should focus on the African continent. Ibid.
46. IAAF, Minutes of the Meeting of the IAAF Council, Düsseldorf, 5–6 September 1977 (IAAF Archive, Monaco), Appendix A.
47. IAAF, Minutes of the 31st IAAF Congress, San Juan, 5–6 October 1978 (IAAF Archive, Monaco), 9.
48. IAAF, 'Press Release Dubai International and IAAF agree to hold Golden Mile', 12 September 1978 (Carl and Liselott Diem-Archive, Cologne). Steve Ovett (Great Britain) won the 1978 'Golden Mile' race ahead of Francis Gonzalez (France) and Graham Williamson (Great Britain). Ovett had also won the 1500 m race at the inaugural IAAF World Cup in 1977. Besides the one-mile run, it was decided that the IAAF would promote other 'Golden' events. Hence, in 1979, it organized 'Golden Sprints' (Zurich, Switzerland), 'Golden 10,000 m' (Brussels, Belgium) and 'Golden Javelin' (Budapest, Hungary) besides the 'Golden Mile' (Oslo, Norway). In 1980, only the 'Golden Mile' (London, Great Britain) and a 'Golden Vault' (Nice, France) event took place.
49. Ibid.
50. IAAF, Minutes of the Meeting of the IAAF Council, San Juan, 3–4 October 1978 (Carl and Liselott Diem-Archive, Cologne), 13.
51. Krieger, 'Born on the Wings of Commerce', 427. Especially multi-national sport companies such as Nike, Adidas and Puma had an interest in the opening and expansion of markets for their sporting goods. At the same time, those companies finance a wide range of sport-in-development activities on the African continent. Gerard Akindes and Matthew Kirwin, 'Sport as International Aid: Assisting Development or Promoting Under-Development in Sub-Saharan Africa?' in Roger Levermore and Aaron Beacom (eds), *Sport and International Development* (Basingstoke: Palgrave MacMillan, 2009), 224.
52. IAAF, 'Press Release Dubai International and IAAF agree to hold Golden Mile', 12 September 1978.
53. IAAF, Minutes of the 31st IAAF Congress, 5–6 October 1978.
54. Krieger, 'Born on the Wings of Commerce', 425.
55. IAAF, Minutes of the Meeting of the IAAF Council, Seoul, 14–16 April 1978 (IAAF Archive, Monaco), 12.
56. Ibid., 15. Also see: IAAF, Minutes of the 31st Congress, 5–6 October 1978, 22.
57. IAAF, Minutes of the Meeting of the IAAF Council, Dakar, 26–27 April 1979 (IAAF Archive, Monaco), 25.
58. IAAF, Minutes of the Meeting of the IAAF Council, Paris, 10–11 March 1980 (IAAF Archive, Monaco), 15.

59. IAAF, Minutes of the Meeting of the IAAF Council, 14–16 April 1978, 12ff.
60. IAAF, Minutes of the 31st IAAF Congress, 5–6 October 1978, Appendix E.
61. IAAF, 'Honorary Treasurer's Report to Congress AAF Accounts for the Years 1980 and 1981', 1982 (Carl and Liselott Diem-Archive, Cologne).
62. IAAF, Minutes of the Meeting of the IAAF Council, Helsinki, 5–6 August 1983 (Carl and Liselott Diem-Archive, Cologne), 9.
63. IAAF, 'Major Decisions of the XXXIIIrd IAAF Congress', 7 September 1982 (Carl and Liselott Diem-Archive, Cologne), 4.
64. IAAF, Minutes of the 32nd Congress, Moscow, 21–22 July 1980 (IAAF Archive, Monaco), 15.
65. IAAF, Minutes of the 31st IAAF Congress, 5–6 October 1978.
66. Ibid., 72.
67. IAAF, Minutes of the Meeting of the IAAF Council, Kingston, 18–20 April 1982 (IAAF Archive, Monaco), 8.
68. At this point, it is considered to move the main office of the African Athletics Association (AAA) away from Senegal to another country. August Kirsch, 'Gesamtwertung des IAAF Council in Helsinki' 14 December 1982 (Carl and Liselott Diem-Archive, Cologne).
69. IAAF, Minutes of the Meeting of the IAAF Council, Helsinki, 10–12 December 1982 (IAAF Archive, Monaco), 16.
70. IAAF, 'Letter to all IAAF Council Members', 1 February 1983 (Carl and Liselott Diem-Archive, Cologne).
71. Heywood, *Global Politics*, 379. Andrew Heywood argues that aid – in a political context – is usually provided through the hands of a few individuals with little established mechanisms of accountability in place in developing countries. Such conditions foster corruption and oppression as it allows leaders to benefit personally from provided financial aid and to widen their power.
72. Chatziefstathiou et al., 'Cultural Imperialism'.
73. Cesar R. Torres and Mark Dyreson, 'The Cold War Games', in Kevin B. Wamsley and Kevin Young (eds), *Global Olympics: Historical and Sociological Studies of the Modern Games* (Amsterdam: Elsevier, 2005), 55–82.
74. James Riordan, *Soviet Sport: Background to the Olympics* (Oxford: Basil Blackwell, 1980), 157.
75. USSR Light Athletics Federation, 'IAAF Membership Groups', 5 September 1977 (Carl and Liselott Diem-Archive, Cologne), 1.
76. Ibid.
77. IAAF, Minutes of the 31st Congress, 5–6 October 1978, 38ff.
78. USSR Light Athletics Federation, 'IAAF Membership', 2.
79. IAAF, Minutes of the 31st Congress, 5–6 October 1978, 39.
80. IAAF, Minutes of the Meeting of the IAAF Council, 10–11 March 1980, 7.
81. Ibid., 8.
82. IAAF, Minutes of the 32nd Congress, 21–22 July 1980, 7ff.
83. IAAF, 'Information about Grouping Changes', 14 September 1981 (Carl and Liselott Diem-Archive, Cologne).
84. IAAF, Minutes of the Meeting of the IAAF Council, 5–6 August 1983, 8.
85. Primo Nebiolo was the only candidate that stood for election as the previous IAAF President Adriaan Paulen withdrew his candidacy in order to avoid a crucial vote. It appears that he was aware that Primo Nebiolo had secured the majority of the votes already prior to the Congress, especially from the smaller member federations. IAAF, Minutes of the Special IAAF Congress, 1–2 September 1981 (IAAF Archive, Monaco), 29.
86. For example, ahead of the 1983 IAAF World Championships, the IAAF contracted Canon, Coca-Cola, Iveco and TDK to sponsor the event and the federation. IAAF, 'Major Decisions of the IAAF Council Rome, Italy – April 21st to 23rd, 1983', 1983 (Carl and Liselott Diem-Archive, Cologne).
87. Krieger, 'Born on the Wings of Commerce', 427ff.
88. Primo Nebiolo, in his new role as president of the General Assembly of International Sports Federations (GAIF), had conceded that the income through the sales of the broadcasting

rights for the Olympic Games should be shared equally amongst the recognized international sport federations. Aware that the World Championships would yield more revenues than the Olympic Games, this strategical move allowed him to manifest his leading role within GAIF. GAISF, Minutes of the Meeting of the Association of Summer Olympic Federations, 31 May 1983 (Carl and Liselott Diem-Archive, Cologne), 6f.

89. IAAF, 'World Championship Finance', 16 December 1983 (Carl and Liselott Diem-Archive, Cologne).
90. Ibid.
91. IAAF, Minutes of the Meeting of the IAAF Council, Manila, 16–18 December 1983 (Carl and Liselott Diem-Archive, Cologne).
92. Barney, Wenn and Martyn, *Selling the Five Rings*.
93. IAAF, Minutes of the Meeting of the IAAF Council, Los Angeles, 12 August 1984 (Carl and Liselott Diem-Archive, Cologne).
94. IAAF, Minutes of the Meeting of the IAAF Council, Rome, 16–19 March 1984 (Carl and Liselott Diem-Archive, Cologne), 26ff.
95. IAAF, Minutes of the Meeting of the IAAF Council, Rome, 29–31 March 1985 (Carl and Liselott Diem-Archive, Cologne), Appendix 8.
96. The decision on a potential change of the voting system was purposely put on the Congress agenda after the elections to prevent the new system already being applicable in 1984. IAAF, Minutes of the Meeting of the IAAF Council, 16–19 March 1984.
97. In its own publications, the IAAF states that Primo Nebiolo became Chairman of the IAAF Development Commission when he was elected to IAAF President in 1981. However, the consulted archival material reveals that Primo Nebiolo took over this role only in 1984, following the first IAAF World Championships in Helsinki in 1983. See, for example, Björn Wangemann and Bill Glad, *IAAF Development Cooperation: A Situation Analysis and a Strategy for the World-Wide Development of Athletics* (London: IAAF, 1991), 6.
98. August Kirsch, 'Entwicklungsarbeit'.
99. 'Aktennotiz', 17 August 1984 (Carl and Liselott Diem-Archive, Cologne), 3.
100. This was the first meeting held under the chairmanship of Primo Nebiolo. IAAF, 'IAAF Development Program Report to Council of the main points arising from the Development Commission Meeting', 26 March 1985 (Carl and Liselott Diem-Archive, Cologne).
101. IAAF, Minutes of the Meeting of the IAAF Council, 12 August 1984, 5 and 'Aktennotiz', 17 August 1984 (Carl and Liselott Diem-Archive, Cologne), 3.
102. IAAF, Minutes of the Meeting of the IAAF Council, Canberra, 23–25 November 1984 (Carl and Liselott Diem-Archive, Cologne), 13.
103. August Kirsch, 'Letter to Primo Nebiolo', 3 September 1984 (Carl and Liselott Diem-Archive, Cologne).
104. Ibid.
105. IAAF, Minutes of the Meeting of the IAAF Council, 12 August 1984, 5.
106. IAAF, Minutes of the Meeting of the IAAF Council, 29–31 March 1985, 21.
107. IAAF, 'Meeting between Olympic Solidarity and the Development Commission of the IAAF', 23 February 1984 (Carl and Liselott Diem-Archive, Cologne).
108. IAAF, 'Report by Jozsef Sir', 4.
109. Extensive coaching courses took place in Patiala from 1985 onwards.
110. IAAF, 'IAAF Development Program', 28 March 1985 (Carl and Liselott Diem-Archive, Cologne), 4.
111. IAAF, Minutes of the Meeting of the IAAF Council, Athens, 15 July 1986 (Carl and Liselott Diem-Archive, Cologne), 10.
112. IAAF, 'Report of Dr. Jozsef Sir on his Visit to IAAF Asian Permanent Coaching Centre at Patalia', 1985 (Carl and Liselott Diem-Archive, Cologne), 1.
113. IAAF, 'Meeting of the Development Commission Sub Group to Discuss Nominations for IAAF Development Centre(s) in Africa', 21 February 1986 (Carl and Liselott Diem-Archive, Cologne), 4.

114. IAAF, 'Report of Dr. Jozsef Sir on his Visit to IAAF Asian Permanent Coaching Centre at Patalia'.
115. Björn E. Wangemann, 'Letter to August Kirsch', 21 September 1987 (Carl and Liselott Diem-Archive, Cologne).
116. IAAF, 'Report of the Development Commission to the XXXVI IAAF Congress', 26 August 1987 (Carl and Liselott Diem-Archive, Cologne), 4.
117. Wangemann and Glad, *IAAF Development*, 14.
118. IAAF, 'IAAF Council Report to the 36th Congress of the IAAF – Rome, 1987', 1987 (Carl and Liselott Diem-Archive, Cologne).
119. Ibid.
120. IAAF, Minutes of the Meeting of the IAAF Council, Rome, 24–25 August 1987 (Carl and Liselott Diem-Archive, Cologne), 23.
121. Ibid., 23.
122. Even on today's website of the IAAF, it is listed amongst Primo Nebiolo's main achievements: 'A pivotal moment in the political history of the IAAF came in 1987 when Nebiolo insisted on changes to the voting structure of Congress, which had been biased towards the "traditional powers", to one-member one-vote', IAAF, Past Presidents of the IAAF (IAAF, 2016), http://www.iaaf.org/news/news/past-presidents-of-the-iaaf.
123. Torsten Wojciechowski, 'Sportentwicklung im internationalen Vergleich', in Eckart Balz and Detlef Kuhlmann (eds), *Sportentwicklung. Grundlagen und Facetten* (Aachen: Meyer & Meyer, 2009), 234.
124. John Brohman, 'Economism and Critical Silences in Development Studies: A Theoretical Critique of Neoliberalism', *Third World Quarterly* 16, no. 2 (1995), 297–318.
125. IAAF, Minutes of the Meeting of the IAAF Development Commission, Rio de Janeiro, 7 January 1987 (Carl and Liselott Diem-Archive, Cologne), 6.
126. Connor and McEwen, 'International Development or White Man's Burden?' 810.
127. Joseph A. Maguire, 'Power and Global Sport: Zones of Prestige, Emulation and Resistance', *Sport in Society* 14, nos 7–8 (2011), 1013.
128. Wojciechowski, 'Sportentwicklung', 232.

Disclosure Statement

No potential conflict of interest was reported by the author.

Sport in Singapore (1945–1948): From Rehabilitation to Olympic Status

Nick Aplin ⓘ

ABSTRACT
After the Japanese Occupation ended in September 1945, Singapore experienced a brief period of British Military Administration. During the next three years of rehabilitation under civil administration, sport in Singapore became an instrument of identity creation. Administrators and stakeholders strove to establish an international profile. There was a desire to forge a Pan-Malayan sporting body and then the priority was to join the Olympic Movement. Tensions arose between interdependent organizations and the individuals representing interest groups. Civil administrators were predominantly British. The Chinese, who retained strong affiliations to nationalist China, represented the vast majority of the population. These two communities had their own ideas on how best to promote sport. A complicating factor was the growing threat of communism and the transition in political power in China. Two plans evolved that created a unique setting for representative sport in Singapore. Membership of the International Olympic Committee was the first step for athletes aspiring to represent the new Singapore Colony team itself. For the Chinese there was an alternative path. They became motivated to attend the China Games in Shanghai, with the hope that it would lead to selection for the China team at the Olympic Games in London.

Introduction

> The colony of Singapore is a new creation, where the experiences of war and of enemy occupation have radically altered both the way of life of its inhabitants, and their mental attitude towards it.[1]

As identified by Patrick McKerron in the Annual Report, the rapid social, economic and political transitions that occurred in Singapore during the period immediately after Second World War, also marked the beginning of the British version of the democratization of sport on a small but densely populated equatorial island.[2] Issues of severely limited housing, rampant disease and poor living conditions, changing national and international identity, and political volatility underpinned the dramatic upheaval of both society and sport that occurred after the Japanese Occupation. This paper seeks to examine three of the most significant recurring themes in the evolution of sport between 1945 and 1948 in colonial Singapore.

First, the desire to increase general access to sporting experiences for a multi-cultural population is identified. Restoring decaying facilities and coordinating the actions of a diversity of sporting figurations during a period of British Military Administration (BMA) represented the initial concerns. Then balancing the social, economic and political needs of society became the main priorities once the civil administration took over in 1946. Sport was an important tool in re-establishing equilibrium. In a multi-cultural setting it represented a common interest, and it was certainly a significant distraction from the general deprivation that existed, particularly for the younger generation and a small section of the numerically dominant Overseas Chinese (*hua qiao*) population. Within this context of multiple interests and concerns, the prospect of self-government heightened awareness of a new process of nation building, a process involving power relations and interdependencies reflected both in the committee rooms and on the playing field.

Second, the willingness to create an enduring mark on the international sporting scene as part of a geo-politically sensitive and culturally diverse location is revealed. Joining the Olympic Movement was an early ambition borne from the relief experienced at the end of global and regional conflict. This short-lived euphoria brought with it the need to re-examine existing and often antiquated ideas about the organization and promotion of sport. To paraphrase Baker, Singapore sport was 'a creation of its past and an anticipation of its future', implying a tussle would occur between continuity and change.[3]

Third, the re-emergence of a strong cultural connection with China takes on a brief, yet significant, role in establishing sport as an enduring feature of Singapore's international relations. Close sporting ties with China, which was rapidly entering a phase of communist revolution, generated strong motivations amongst the local-born Chinese to confirm and enhance their sporting identity. Many of the local Chinese preferred to speak English rather than Chinese and yet still reserved a strong sense of affiliation with the motherland that would motivate the creation of new sports federations. There would follow the opportunity to compete on the international stage. To represent China at the Olympic Games became a serious challenge. The Overseas Chinese community is represented as a group of autonomous figurations, linked by culture, yet divided in terms of dialect, class and ideology.[4] The Chinese happily accommodated ideas of dual-nationality when appropriate situations arose. Leading figures in the Chinese sporting community contributed financial backing for the China team attending the London Olympics in 1948 and for training and preparation of the individuals selected to represent Singapore after the Chinese Communist Revolution in 1949.[5]

To what extent sport managed to fulfil its ambitions depended on a system that relied on coordinated individual and group endeavour. Initially rejecting the legacy of the Japanese, various figurations and interdependencies re-emerged in an attempt to revive a moribund laissez-faire colonial approach to sport. This appeared to be an emotionally acceptable path. Freedom had been achieved, so it was time to enjoy the fruits of victory. But new challenges provoked new types of responses.

Pulling together various interest groups from 1945 to 1948 created a platform for later sporting successes. From an Eliasian perspective the various figurations and significant individuals, who created the interdependencies that had re-emerged, found difficulty in working together cohesively. The interdependencies that were required to forge a unified set of ambitions met with problems of mutual misunderstanding and resistance.

Framework for Analysis

The process-sociology approach of Elias provides an appropriate perspective for examining the inter-relationships that emerged in sport in Singapore after the war. Elias's approach encompasses a broad range of social forces, developments and trends with diverse power balances and tensions existing within the various figurations.[6] Emerging from Japanese Occupation, the desire to rehabilitate the pre-war sporting model or to create a new more democratic and internationally aware system immediately reveals significant areas of individual and group interactions.

It has been highlighted that there are three phases in a 'process-oriented methodology' that also constitutes a theory-driven empirical study:

- Reconstructing the rules and social structure of the figuration.
- Reconstructing the individual's placement within, perception of and ability to change the figuration.
- Reconstructing the socio-genesis of the figuration.[7]

The first methodological objective of this study is to reconstruct the social structure of the figurations involving the BMA and other communal parties interested in sport. Assuming that a figuration consists of interdependent individuals held together by norms, preferences, values and rules,[8] there was an immediate problem in that an unusual power balance had been created after the surrender of the Japanese. The BMA possessed the ultimate authority over the Chinese community, but had limited tangible resources to facilitate rehabilitation. The Chinese were well capable of pursuing private and nationalistic interests with substantial financial backing. In one way the established administrative group were simultaneously outsiders when it came to shaping the future of competitive sport. Somewhat cynically it was noted some years later that influential Chinese generally steered clear of civil administrative challenges, preferring the British to shoulder the responsibilities.[9]

> What was more surprising still, or should have been, was the entire absence among Asian leaders of any manifest yearning towards that independence, or taking the responsibility of running the Government. Apart from extremists, the Singapore Chinese community seemed perfectly content to leave Government in all its branches in European hands while they engaged whole-heartedly in commercial pursuits under the Union Jack in a stable British Colony.[10]

A small group of BMA officers was designated to advise how best to coordinate local elements of Chinese Affairs.[11] These officers had worked within the Malayan Civil Service before the War, either on the peninsula or in Singapore. Some were also members of Force 136, which had worked with Chinese communist resistance fighters on the peninsula during the War. The officers were considered to be in the best position to help restore lines of communication and reintegrate former guerrilla fighters. The group, described as 'meagre' in the official report on BMA, was also instructed to contact members of local associations and impose operating procedures. These established administrators had been involved with the running of Chinese sport in Singapore before 1942. Largely autonomous, the Chinese sporting clubs requested a return to the status quo and might not have fully understood, nor accepted, the military-style directions being issued. Passive, yet deliberate resistance to imperial hegemony had always been an issue under colonial rule.[12] The pre-war laissez-faire approach needed to become more assertive, and so a relatively passive form of conflict can be seen as a consequence.

Primary documents which reveal sport-related figurations involving the BMA after the war are few and far between. The official report mentions only the requisitioning of 51 clubs and associations in the Singapore Division for temporary military use.[13] Some correspondence does exist, which highlights British caution and lack of resources and Chinese enthusiasm to recreate their own exclusive amateur sports federation.[14] During the two-year period that followed BMA, the Chinese community most closely associated with sport, steadily assumed a stronger financial position for their activities. This enabled them to extend their interest both inside and outside Singapore. Wealthy supporters, such as Aw Kow, the eldest son of Aw Boon Haw, the philanthropist and newspaper magnate, had been evacuated from Singapore before the Japanese invasion. On his return, Aw Kow, became Chairman and patron of both the Malayan Chinese Amateur Athletic Federation and the Singapore Chinese Amateur Sports Federation in early 1947.[15] The second phase is to emplace the individuals within their respective figurations in order to establish their position within and consequently their freedom or lack of freedom to act.[16] Autobiographical documents go some way to providing insights into the contributions of well-placed individuals within the BMA, who influenced the process of change. The danger is to accept the British experience (the one which is accessible) to the exclusion of the broader Asian population. Hence, the need to examine the Chinese experience (the one which is less easy to identify) presents itself.

The third logical phase is then to 'reconstruct the socio-genesis of the figuration'.[17] This involves identifying a specific timeframe during which figurations become relevant. In the case of Singapore after the war, it is appropriate to start with the surrender of the Japanese and the inauguration of BMA. However, it should be recognized that many figurations would have been created before the war and perceptions of those interdependencies, as they were being re-created post-1945, will have been fresh in the minds of many of the survivors and re-builders.

Under colonial rule, which was characterized by hegemony and segregation, the club system was usually operated on the basis of race. Asians were generally denied access to European Clubhouses, but were invited to play on the club pitches, such as the *padang* adjacent to the Singapore Cricket Club (SCC). Different racial groups were able to mingle successfully on the playing field, if not at the bar afterwards. Oswald Gilmour,[18] a senior Municipal Engineer suggested in 1941 that many European club competitions were actually being expanded to include local Asian clubs.

> It is on these playgrounds of land and water ... that we find the best comradeship between the many races of this city.[19]

Not all clubs were single-race based. There were multi-racial clubs that proved the exception, for example the Race Course Golf Club was formed in 1926. It was later relocated and became known as the Island Club. Established in 1932 the Club boasted a golfing membership of 170, including 40 Europeans, 20 Eurasians, 40 Japanese, 50 Chinese and 20 Malays and Indians.[20] Attempting to refute claims of discrimination, Hugh Bryson, the Acting Colonial Secretary in 1946 and later the first President of the Singapore Olympic and Sports Council (SOSC) insisted that clubs 'admitted without distinction' senior Malay officers who were in the Civil Service.

> ... once a man of different race had been accepted as a member, there was quite distinctly no sign of any discrimination.[21]

However, it has been suggested that the pursuit of sport tended to reinforce the divisions that existed between the British and the Chinese.[22] Most British residents were indifferent to Chinese activities, as long as their own privileges were not threatened. The Chinese would emulate British practices when it was expedient, but would turn a blind eye to happenings in Singapore and focus on the emerging interest in sport in China.

> If the British were concerned with encouraging the Chinese to adopt sporting systems that supported the control of imperial possessions, then the Chinese used sport to maintain important links with China.[23]

Before the War, a loose form of symbiotic relationship had evolved between the British and the Chinese as far as sport was concerned. Sharing entertainment and sporting rivalry figured in the equation, but sharing a national identity did not. Playing together on the same field was symbolic of mutual respect. In reality, physical access to European club facilities and activities by Asians after the war remained a stumbling block.

Rehabilitation

The immediate processes of establishing an administration capable of initiating rehabilitation and restoration can be identified. Figurations can be closely associated with the subsequent requirements of the BMA to requisition appropriate physical resources, for example buildings and open spaces. Once these elements were de-requisitioned, it was possible to revive an essentially colonial club system of sport. New figurations were also created with the formation of new associations and councils that better reflected the changing nature of sport in Singapore itself and beyond.

The process of rehabilitation was initiated, at least at a conceptual level, soon after the Japanese occupation had begun in 1942. In London, the stark realization that the British Empire was doomed, encouraged thoughts of loosening the ties with many colonies and yet retaining some global influence. The new Malayan Planning Unit (MPU) began a process to introduce self-government once hostilities were over. The assumption was that the British would regain control of Singapore eventually. The best people to undertake and lead the process of rehabilitation were perceived to be those with a close personal affinity to the colony: those who had been engaged in aspects of administration before the War. This included those who had been interned during the Occupation or who had escaped and who were going to be able to return to an island that had been their home. These individuals were often those who termed themselves 'Malayans' or 'Malayans in exile'.[24]

Before the Japanese Occupation, the residents of the Straits Settlements (Singapore, Malacca, and Penang) and peninsular Malaya shared many legacies, among them their sporting preferences. Sportsmen talked of themselves as Malayan sportsmen, even though they came from towns as far apart as Ipoh and Singapore. The sporting traditions that existed were based on generations of inter-state competitions in predominantly British sports.[25]

British Military Administration (1945–1946)

Little research has been undertaken to identify the interdependencies and associated processes that were required to revive the culture of sport in the years immediately after the War. Hone, who was Chief Civil Affairs Officer (CCAO) responsible for the official report into BMA, included no specific mention of sport.[26] Similarly, Yeo and Lau made no reference to the link between BMA and the revival of sport, preferring to focus on political developments that involved the potential for communist insurgency.[27] Turnbull likewise declined to consider the role of sport during this period.[28]

The main objectives of BMA during the first six weeks after the Japanese surrender were:

(1) The disarming and concentration of 70,000-strong Japanese Forces.
(2) The repatriation of Allied prisoners-of-war and internees.
(3) The relief and rehabilitation of the civil population.
(4) Preparation for the restoration of civil administration at the earliest possible moment.[29]

Oswald Gilmour was among the first to reflect on the physical degradation to the environment that was the legacy of Japanese occupation.[30]

> There was little opportunity of playing games, even for those who had the leisure. Most of the tennis courts and playing fields had been dug up, or diverted to other use. The Padang furnished one football pitch and nothing else. Jalan Besar Stadium ground was playable, but Anson Road was piled high with Jap litter.[31]

McKerron and the British Military Administration

Brigadier Patrick A.B. McKerron returned with the British Forces in September 1945.[32] As Deputy Chief Civil Affairs Officer, during a tortuous 208-day period of BMA that followed, he was constrained by the knowledge that communism was challenging the proposed rule of democracy in the colonies, and that Singapore itself was moving irrevocably, and with a significant possibility of violence, towards a state of uncertain self-government.

The BMA lasted until April 1946, during which time it had to, *inter alia*, restore law and order, organize food, shelter and medical supplies, repair the buildings and provide for better electricity and water supplies and the disposal of refuse, for the whole population.[33] The beginning of the reconstruction of the colony was an important part of their portfolio, and the revival of banking and the restoration of the economy were high on the agenda. The immediate priorities of BMA concerned restoring basic services, essential economic potential and restoring social stability within an atmosphere of ideological conflict. The period of BMA was characterized socially by deep mistrust, corruption and crime, so that McKerron's main objectives were to establish civil equilibrium before embarking on secondary issues.

It is not surprising that the rejuvenation of sport would play a part in the restoration of civil order as it could provide a positive form of distraction and a sense of a return to normality. The first beneficiaries were former allied prisoners of war (POWs) and internees who received hospitality from the Young Men's Christian Association (YMCA).[34] However, the main beneficiaries were the new military groups that were arriving, rather than the civilian population. For example, the SCC was a prominent meeting place for the armed forces, which utilized the facilities within days of re-occupation.[35] The YMCA, which had been granted the right to occupy the SCC premises, played an important, if neglected, role in restoring the sporting environment.

Requisitioning

The privileges afforded to the Military touched a raw nerve with civilians of all races during BMA. At the forefront of the problem was the process of requisition. There was a serious housing shortage and with the inflow of military personnel this shortage became more acute. The military seized the opportunity to satisfy extensive claims for recreational amenities, clubhouses and open spaces. As the BMA established itself, it became necessary to requisition a variety of properties to accommodate the rapid influx of soldiers, engineers, administrators and civil servants. This practice was a necessity, but the slow return of those properties proved to be frustrating experience for those whose collective voices could actually be heard. For example, the European civilian members of the Singapore Swimming Club (SSC) were determined to resist a lengthy period of requisitioning.[36] Recreational facilities were an important resource for all the main communities. A club setting acted as a safety valve to counter frustration. However, many establishments were inaccessible or unusable.

What might appear to be surprising was that manpower was also allocated, during the first weeks of BMA, to the specific task of coordinating a sporting revival with the various Asian communities. Sport represented an important means of restoring harmony between the returning British and the Overseas Chinese majority. The Chinese had established a widespread network of clubs and associations before the war. The Straits Chinese Football Association league had been flourishing as early as 1911 and during the immediate pre-Second World War years league interest had been boosted by the visits of touring teams from Hong Kong. In late 1945, there were local teams such as Chinese Athletic who were particularly keen to revive league play.

Hugh Pagden, an Adviser on Chinese Affairs, was given a military commission and with it the task of initiating and coordinating aspects of recreation for the wider community.[37] His brief was to communicate with representatives of the sporting fraternity and to restore appropriate facilities and playing fields to usable condition. Pagden had been a senior civil affairs official with the Agricultural Department in Kuala Lumpur before the outbreak of war. Then as a Force 136 officer, he had fought beside the Malayan People's Anti-Japanese Army (MPAJA) behind enemy lines in the Malay Peninsula.[38]

Pagden's main, although short-lived, responsibility represents one of the few documented sporting exchanges from the BMA period that survives. Archival material reveals that communication between the British and Chinese communities was always vulnerable to misunderstanding. Pagden was directed to inform Chinese officials to 'motivate all sporting activities'. He received communications from the representatives of Chinese Athletic, asking for greater access to the Services-dominated Jalan Besar Stadium and a greater hand in the local organization of matches. The tone of the communications involving Pagden and the Chinese reflected a mutual uncertainty. From a BMA memorandum (dated: 26 October 1945) Pagden expresses his concerns:

> I am afraid they have entirely missed the point of my remarks to them that we were anxious to get outdoor recreation going and would put sports grounds in order and help obtain premises and equipment.[39]

One month later (dated 18 November 1945) Pagden is informing a successor about what to expect. He pinpoints an important issue:

> You will find that there is a wide gap between the English-speaking and non-English speaking Chinese Sports Clubs.[40]

Singapore: A Crown Colony

On 1 April 1946, Singapore ceased to be a Straits Settlements and McKerron was sworn in as the Officer Administering the Government.[41] The period of BMA was over. Civil administration took over as Singapore became a Crown Colony. Attaining this new status, which was to draw a line of demarcation between predominantly 'Chinese' Singapore and predominantly 'Malay' Malaya, was economically motivated. With its significant strategic location and its more vibrant economy, Singapore was to be nurtured more closely than the Malayan Union by the British.

On the sporting front, the line of division was less apparent between the Colony and the Union. Inter-state games and competitions were portrayed as reinforcing existing ties and relations. Nevertheless, the division was to raise thorny issues of affiliation and identity when the time came to become involved in international sporting competitions.

De-Requisitioning and Revival

BMA had officially ended but this was a 'fade-out' process rather than a 'lights out' process. The process of de-requisitioning premises and facilities organized by the new civil administration was underway, albeit in a hesitant and sometimes discriminatory fashion. Private sporting clubs had been prime targets for occupation by the returning British armed forces Officers. British Other Ranks (BORs) frequented the Navy, Army, Air Force Institutes (NAAFIs) that had been created.

At the beginning of July 1946, the SSC was finally derequisitioned and returned to its members.[42] The SCC was also released in July. The Tanglin Club, an even more elite institution – associated with officers – was only returned to civilian members in August 1946.[43] In order to cater for officers who were to remain in Singapore, a rationing system was introduced whereby any officer was only permitted membership of one civilian club.[44]

Members of the Chinese Swimming Club (CSC) complained about the release process affecting their premises. The honorary secretary accused the de-requisitioning committee of discrimination.[45] His concern was the delay of de-requisitioning in comparison with other clubs and the continuing use of its ground floor by the NAAFI canteen operators.[46] There was discontent and the British clubs appeared to them to be at the top of the release list. Quick press rebuttals were issued pointing out the Singapore Chinese Recreation Club (SCRC) had not been requisitioned at all, and that other sports clubs were in a similar state of suspension.[47] One day later the premises were fully released and the indignant requisitioning committee declared the Chinese Swimming Club was, in fact, the first to be fully returned to its members. Other clubs were still occupied.[48]

Public facilities were slower to return to use than the private clubs, an indication of a predictable power imbalance. Privilege outweighed public priority. The Mount Emily Swimming Pool, for example, was handed back to the Municipal Commissioners in August 1946, but then it was announced that the pool might not be re-opened for public use for some years to come. It was felt that the water supply position was unresolved and releasing large quantities of water for the purpose of swimming was a non-starter.[49]

The target date which was set for the release of all requisitioned properties was 1 October 1946. One year after the occupation, there were increasing calls for access to recreational spaces.[50] The attention of the Municipal Commissioners was directed to the essential opening of parks, playing grounds, pitches and swimming pools. For sports spectators and players the release of the Jalan Besar Stadium was a step in the right direction. However, the Services retained use of the ground on Mondays, Wednesdays and Fridays, while civilian sides under the control of the Singapore Amateur Football Association (SAFA) had to make do with Tuesdays, Thursdays and Saturdays.[51]

The fate of the citadel of football in Singapore – the Anson Road Stadium – was more depressing. Built in 1922 as part of the Malaya Borneo Exhibition, the Stadium was converted in 1924 and became the venue for major league, cup and tour games during the 1930s. Built near the Telok Ayer Basin dock area, it became a location for gun emplacements at the beginning of the Japanese invasion and subsequently a target for bombing. At the end of the War, it was left in a totally dilapidated state and used as a dumping area. It was only derequisitioned in April 1947.[52] As a prime location for industrial and economic development, the site became a bone of contention. Should an iconic sports stadium be built or should essential businesses and associated facilities occupy the water-front?

The revival of sports clubs and associations took place in parallel with the de-requisitioning of facilities, but not all parts of the process coincided before the target date. As late as December 1947, the ground used by the Girls' Sports Club (GSC) was still inaccessible. The GSC was the only women's sports club with its own ground and had still not been derequisitioned.[53] The club, essentially a recreational hub for Eurasian girls, had close ties to the Singapore Recreation Club (SRC). The netball and hockey teams were granted use of the SRC grounds. The GSC was clearly going to be dependent on the benevolence of the sporting fraternity. They estimated the cost for restoring their facilities to be $25,000.[54] One year later no real progress had been made. With a membership of 107 young women, the club was no further advanced in its plans and had no tennis courts of its own.[55]

Associations Revived: The YMCA and the Singapore Amateur Swimming Association

As early as September 1945, the YMCA catering for Services personnel had occupied the SCC clubhouse. Activities and amenities were provided in an abbreviated form. By the end of 1946 the original YMCA grounds in the heart of the city were being restored. Army caterpillar scrapers filled in the slit trenches that had been created by the Japanese. Table tennis was again available for members at the tennis pavilion on Bras Basah Road opposite the YMCA building.

Plans were made to re-establish the YMCA. These included the creation of branch centres around the island, as well as a radical refurbishment of the main building which had been occupied by the Kempeitai for interrogation and torture during the Occupation. A restoration fund was initiated in August 1946 just as the building was about to be released. Individuals and corporate bodies were approached. There were 1005 members in April 1947.[56] An indication of the strength of the link between the Armed Services and the YMCA was demonstrated when all Services Club funds were transferred to the YMCA ($22,348.77).[57] The target of $70,000 was reached at the end of 1947, but by then costs had soared and more funding was required for the buildings, sports ground and pavilion.[58] The process of restoration was slow, being eventually completed in August 1949.[59] The YMCA's new sports pavilion and playing field in Balestier Road added to the existing facilities.

SASA, a relatively young association that had only been inaugurated in 1939, was revived at a meeting at the YMCA in May 1947.[60] Rowland Lyne, the retiring president of SASA and coincidentally the General Secretary of the YMCA itself and Goh Hood Kiat, Vice-President of the CSC, were appointed to act as the association's delegates to any new initiatives. The pre-war rotation system was still in use. The SSC provided the President of SASA and CSC provided the Vice President of SASA for a one-year period and then switched the following year.

Apparently, this was a gesture of cooperation and diplomacy between the two dominant clubs: the European SSC and the Chinese CSC.[61] The cordiality implied by the rotation system did not extend to the members of these private clubs. Clearly visible were elements of SSC discrimination from pre-war years. In the SSC, women had only been permitted to share the club amenities on a Sunday morning. However, some progress was made when their access was extended to all day Sunday.[62] Asians were not eligible for membership, nor were they invited as guests. Daytime use was the privilege of the BORs, who used the pool from 10 am to 4:30 pm.[63] Only in April 1947 was the SSC to restrict use by the Services.[64]

One year later, the SSC members rejected a motion to accept Asian guests in the clubhouse by a slender majority of four votes – 44 to 40. This was hardly a fair representation of the total membership's feelings, but it was an indication of indifference in club matters. A few members expressed their disappointment that racial harmony was not being promoted particularly as members of Asian clubs were enthusiastic about inviting European guests to their premises.[65]

The Singapore Olympic and Sports Council

The creation of associations is a reflection of a mutual desire to forge alliances. Interdependencies between different sports associations and clubs became more pronounced as the sporting culture was gradually restored in Singapore. The complexity of relationships also increased as an international profile for Singapore was envisaged. The ambition and priority for many sports officials was to create an organization, sufficiently large, to justify sending a representative team to the London Olympics in 1948.

In March 1947 invitations had been sent out to prospective participants in the Olympic Games. There was no central Olympic sporting body in Singapore, or Malaya, to receive the invitation. But there were clearly informal connections. Initially the intention had been to create a Pan-Malayan sports federation. A combined team from Singapore and Malaya was more likely to make an impact than two independent teams. The ties that bound the two regions were strong and it was confidently predicted that weightlifters, for example, could reach world standards. Becoming affiliated to the IOC was a step forward, but sending a competitor and carrying the new national flag in the Olympic arena became a burning ambition.

The first step was to inaugurate a Singapore sports federation. Then the Malayan Union representatives could follow suit. If those objectives were achieved simultaneously then a Pan-Malayan body could be established and be represented at the Games.[66] Singapore was ahead of the game, and as the Malayan Union was not ready to link up with its southern neighbours, it was a solo run. In May 1947 more than 50 representatives of the sports associations and sporting clubs in Singapore met to create the SOSC. McKerron expressed the hope that the council would later amalgamate with a similar body in Malaya.

Soon there was news from London. It was announced that both Malaya and Singapore would be welcomed to the Olympic Games, but that matters of affiliation should be expedited. Singapore now had an official body, but Malaya had yet to comply with requests from its southern neighbour. It was thought that separate invitations for Singapore and the Malayan Union could be offered when the IOC met in June. The division between Singapore and Malaya – and their respective abilities to react to the available options – was later to lead to conflict.

Affiliation to the SOSC by the separate sports associations depended on their revival, the confirmation of their official links to the respective international federations, and the presence of official delegates at the foundation meeting of the SOSC. There were nine recognized amateur sports bodies in Singapore.[67]

Two committees were established, the election of the Management Committee being the main priority. As an indication of administrative respect, the Acting Colonial Secretary, Hugh Bryson, was unanimously elected the first President of the SOSC in early July 1947.[68] Goh Hood Kiat, a senior representative of many Chinese clubs and associations and Andrew Gilmour, the Secretary for Economic Affairs were elected as Vice-Presidents. Known as G.H. Kiat, the VP of the CSC had been closely involved with sport before and during the Japanese Occupation. He had considerable organizational experience and had been involved, willingly or unwillingly in the formation of the Syonan Sports Association during the Japanese Occupation.[69]

Confirming the International Link

Edward Strickland, President of the Singapore Amateur Athletic Association (SAAA) wrote to IOC headquarters to ask for authority to form an Olympic Council in Singapore.[70] In reply, Otto Mayer the IOC Chancellor, erroneously suggested that Singapore, as a city within Malaya, could not apply independently but should wait until the Olympic Committee of Malaya was formed.[71] The ambiguity surrounding the relationship between the Malayan Union and the Crown Colony of Singapore was looming as a major bureaucratic hurdle. Representations were sent directly to Lord Burghley, the Chairman of the Olympic Organising Committee in London, to find out what options were available. No record of his reply exists. Burghley wrote to Siegfried Edstrom the President of the IOC in March 1948 because he had been requested by an unidentified individual in Singapore – possibly McKerron – to seek clarification over Singapore's status.

Burghley explained to Edstrom that Singapore was a separate Crown Colony, with its own Governor.[72] As if to make the decision to include Singapore a more palatable one, Burghley indicated that Singapore would not be sending a large contingent, indeed 'their chief interest being a high-jumper who has been producing some fine performances lately'. The fact that the SAAA was already affiliated to the IAAF added balm to Burghley's persuasive tone. Edstrom's brief reply from Stockholm provided the SOSC with just the affirmation it required – 'I agree that Singapore be recognised as an Olympic country. I have notified our office at Lausanne'.[73]

In the first of a number a small twists, Mayer had to check first with Burghley to establish the address to which to send the confirmation of accreditation for the SOSC.[74] This was relatively insignificant, but a year later, and well after the Games had been concluded, a problem arose. The status of the SOSC was questioned by parties unknown and Mayer told

Associated Press in Lausanne that the SOSC had been admitted to the Olympic family 'by mistake'. Only countries, not cities, were granted Olympic status, he said. It was apparent that the original agreement orchestrated by Burghley and Edstrom had not been communicated in full to Mayer.

The Proposed Aims of the SOSC

The espoused values underpinning the aims of the SOSC were ambiguous. Exclusive rather than inclusive, no mention was made of the general population and the values remained close to the ideals laid down in earlier colonial times. There were five main aims. The first was a simple admission that many Singapore citizens had been disregarded in the past.

(1) To promote the general interest of amateur sports in the colony, and in particular to ensure that Singapore would be provided with a stadium and adequate training facilities.

On one issue there was a consensus: the need for a modern stadium and ancillary facilities to raise the standard of sport performance. Large crowds were required in order to generate gate money to pay for the running expenses. The ground-swell of interest in creating an appropriate infrastructure for sport came to its peak in May 1947. Officials representing most branches of amateur sport were in support of a plan to build a new stadium that would accommodate 50,000 sports fans. The second aim was designed to pull the Chinese into the colonial mainstream and thus impose more extensive control over administration and even funding.

(2) To act as the co-ordinating body for amateur sports associations in Singapore.

This was a very vague statement, considering that the Overseas Chinese community had been following its own path since the mid-1930s. Indeed, they had already created the Singapore Chinese Amateur Sports Federation in December 1946.[75] The third aim was to provide Singapore sport with a more compelling and authoritative voice within the region.

(3) To represent Singapore Amateur Sports Associations in negotiations with similar bodies in other territories and in the organization of Inter-State or international competitions.

The fourth aim was to demonstrate that Singapore was, if necessary, ready to move ahead on its own in applying for IOC approval.

(4) To act as the Singapore body for the planning, selection and administration of any Singapore Olympics team, whether representing separately or as part of a joint team with the Malayan Union and for this purpose to apply for affiliation to the International Olympic Committee.

The creation of the Crown Colony did not sever sporting ties with the Malayan Union, indeed the desire to maintain connections and forms of interdependency became an important issue. The possibility of joining the Olympic Movement induced a response that a Pan-Malayan representation on the world stage would be ideal, as it would maximize the potential of the respective sets of communities.

The SOSC Board of Control for Games had initially asserted that Singapore would not participate in the Olympics. Instead, it proposed to organize a Malayan Olympic meet in 1949 utilizing the North versus South format. The fact that the Malayan Union was still without a central Olympic organization may have been the motivation for this suggestion. There must have been frenetic lobbying behind the scenes in early 1948 because at the next monthly meeting of the SOSC the atmosphere had changed. The Secretary for Economic Affairs, Andrew Gilmour, who was presiding over the meeting, confirmed the selection of Lloyd Valberg, a Eurasian high jumper. He was described as Malaya's lone representative to the World Olympics to be held in London.[76] The fifth aim was a perennial call to generate money to finance sporting endeavours. Donations and personal subscriptions had been the traditional method, with the government usually reluctant to dedicate resources that were needed for more pragmatic reasons focusing on social rehabilitation.

(5)   To raise and administer any funds for the furtherance of the above objectives.[77] On 8 August 1947, the first full SOSC Committee meeting was held at the YMCA Building. The Council decided to appeal to the public for funds in order to erect a centrally located stadium. It had become clear that there could be little if any financial support from the government for such a project.[78] Continuing calls for support invariably fell on deaf ears.[79]

Stadiums and Playing Fields

Plans were put on hold as the national issue of a national stadium was being considered by the SOSC.[80] Impatient observers and soccer fanatics had become desperate for the return of the annual league and cup programmes. People had been asking the question: when will the Anson Road Stadium be released? Together with Jalan Besar Stadium it was the only ground capable of accommodating crowds in excess of 10,000.

In April 1947 the Anson Road Stadium had been de-requisitioned, but it was to remain unused.[81] A new Stadium Plan was proposed when it was suggested that the Stadium be rebuilt and placed under the control of SAFA.[82] The Kallang Plain, an area close to the old aerodrome represented an alternative location. But there was no progress. Then the SOSC wrote to the Singapore Municipality to ascertain the availability of Farrer Park, a large open space that had originally been the colony's first turf club. Such a stadium would cost about $250,000 to erect and the Colony would benefit financially as $50,000 in entertainment and Municipal tax could be generated annually. The Municipal Commissioners rejected the proposal reasoning that the site had to be maintained as an open space for the use of the general public. An area near Mountbatten Road, east of the city was then evaluated as a potential site.[83]

The shortage of suitable playing fields continued to hamper development of sport at the school and the club level. Two of the leading boys' schools, Raffles Institution and St Joseph's Institution, were rehabilitating their fields in the heart of the town. The SCRC, embedded in China Town, was struggling to return to its former status. The Police Training Field, the Medical College and Raffles College, all needed further re-conditioning. The other communal clubs, including the Indian Association and the Ceylon Sports Club would only re-possess their fields in 1948.

Underlying the natural sense of excitement at the prospect of promoting amateur sport with the development of renovated facilities, there was a sense that the leading voices in the new council were promoting a return to traditional activities espoused by the colonialists and ignoring other possibilities. This is an example of Baker's perception of continuity rather than change.[84] There was no mention of participatory sport for the community, of providing badminton courts or basketball courts which were cheaper, and would have appealed more to the large Chinese section of the population. One reason for this was that the temporary committee that was convened to examine the proposals of the SOSC was heavily weighted in favour of Eurasian and European influence. Only one Chinese representative, G.H. Kiat, had been nominated.[85]

With the steady stream of migrants from China, India and parts of Malaya to Singapore, it could be easily anticipated that the acute problem of housing shortage and a lack of playing fields would become foremost in many minds. It was claimed that Singapore's 700,000 sport starved (Chinese) citizens had only 200 acres of playing fields – the equivalent of one acre for every 3500 people, in which to play. The ratio laid down by the National Playing Fields Association in England was one acre for every 250 people.[86]

A number of interpretations can be offered for the minimal space available. At one time there was only a small proportion of the population who were actually interested in organized games anyway. This group included the colonialists and the wealthier migrants. When the population had been much smaller the land that was accessible was utilized for domestic and industrial purposes. Additional land that had been reclaimed from the sea near the city would have provided appropriate spaces but they had been built on as well. The situation became more acute as more and more people became exposed to sport during the late 1920s and 1930s.

Now after the war, many who had been growing up during the decade before the war were drawn to organized games as the opportunities widened. This was particularly true of the Chinese who had gradually come to dominate many of the sports. Young athletes from Chinese schools were beginning to take centre-stage.

Nationality

There was one key question that had an impact on the development of sport, and it related to issues of dual nationality. Who was eligible to represent Singapore at the Games in 1948? Before the war it had always been assumed that there was insufficient sporting talent to justify the creation of an Olympic team anyway. Before the War, athletes of Chinese origin, living in Singapore, and who had wanted to compete or who had been identified as potential Olympians were eligible to represent the Republic of China.

Now decisions had to made about who might be granted British citizenship and therefore be eligible to represent Singapore at the Olympics. In 1927, Malayan born Chinese were eligible to represent China in the Far Eastern Olympiad. As British-born subjects, it was claimed, they should have either competed as subjects of Malaya or not all.[87] After the War the process of granting British passports to Chinese residents was promoted.[88] To re-establish confidence in the Empire and to stimulate trade it was felt that approving British citizenship would be a consolidating move. The implication for sport was that Singapore might benefit from a stronger Chinese presence at the Olympics. The confounding factor was that China was scouting for Singaporean talent and could rely on strong cultural ties (intensified by war-time experiences) to draw even English speaking Singapore Chinese to the team of the motherland.[89]

In December 1947, the China National Amateur Athletic Federation (CNAAF) invited the Singapore Chinese Amateur Sports Federation (SCASF) to send a contingent of athletes to the All-China Olympic Trials. The Republic of China had already participated in the 1932 and 1936 Olympics and now there were plans to send a team to London. The SCASF accepted the invitation and drew up plans for selection.[90] Selection depended on performance at the trials in May 1948. The organizations affiliated to the SCASF were responsible for the selection of athletes to attend the China Olympics. From there, Chinese officials would decide on selection for the London Games. An old tension was revived with this plan. It had been argued that Malayan Chinese athletes who were British subjects would have their eligibility questioned.[91]

International Links: The China Connection

In 1936, the Chinese national soccer team had played friendly matches at Anson Road stadium before departing for the Berlin Olympic Games. Now 11 years later a visiting South China team was scouting for talent to play in China's team that would travel to the 1948 Olympic Games.[92] The SOSC confirmed that it would only be sending Lloyd Valberg and that it would attempt to raise funds to pay for his sea passage. The process of fund raising began in earnest in January 1948. Personal donations were solicited and the proceeds from tournaments involving table tennis, badminton and football were promised. By April 1948 it had to be acknowledged that there had been limited success in appealing for funds to send Valberg.

The efforts of the SOSC were hampered because, simultaneously, funds were being sought to send Singaporean athletes – as part of the Malayan Chinese contingent – to Shanghai for the China National Games. Significantly there were other interested sportsmen who were following the path to London but by an alternative route. In March 1948 an announcement was made that a Malayan contingent (including Singapore sportsmen and women) would be selected for participation in the China National Games – due to take place two months later. A winning performance in Shanghai might bring with it selection for the China team being sent to London in July.[93]

Singapore was nominated as a Selection Centre for athletes representing China at the London Games – one of only three such centres outside China (the other two were in Taiwan and the Philippines). Officials were sent by the CNAAF in Shanghai to establish offices in order to coordinate the process. The Malayan Chinese Organising Committee met at the Goh Loo Club in Club Street in Singapore to finalize their plans for selection.[94] Financing was difficult because of deprivations caused by the war, and yet the Malayan Chinese Organising Committee was still able to send 66 of the original 103 participants selected to the China Games. For many observers the situation would be incongruous if Singaporean athletes ended up representing China and not Singapore in London. In the event, four Singaporeans donned the colours of China.[95]

In the short period remaining in the lead up to the Olympic Games the focus of attention became the Singapore's representative Lloyd Valberg. He left on 23 June in order to acclimatize and benefit from invitations to compete in pre-games competitions. Valberg's 'team' manager Jocelyn de Souza did not arrive in London until the last week of July. He had been permitted to fly to London rather than take the boat with Valberg. At the 42nd session of the IOC, which was held on 27 July 1948, six new countries including Singapore were affiliated to the IOC.[96] The Games themselves began on the 29 July.

Conclusion

The attainment of Olympic status marked by Valberg's appearance represented a significant step forward in the creation of an international sporting identity for Singapore. Even during the ensuing period known as the Emergency (1948–1960) when peninsula Malaya experienced military conflict between communist insurgents and the British army, significant elements of the sporting calendar persisted. The Malaya Cup continued with championship successes for the state football team in 1950, 1951, 1952, 1955 and 1960. The Amateur Athletic Association of Malaya Championships or Inter-State Athletics Championships were yearly highlights with Singapore winning the title against the Malayan States on eight consecutive occasions from 1949 to 1956.[97] Malaya's success as winners of the first badminton Thomas Cup in Preston, England, in 1949,[98] led to successful defences of the title in 1952,[99] and 1955,[100] when Singapore acted as the host. The emergence of regional games, e.g. the Asian Games (1951) in New Delhi and the South East Asian Peninsular Games (1959) in Bangkok demonstrated that competitive sport was playing its part in bringing people together from nations that were pursuing independence. Singapore was represented at both of these pioneering events. In 1956, Singapore sent its largest ever contingent to the Melbourne Summer Olympic Games. A total of 69 men and 2 women participated in six sports. The SOSC and its 15 affiliated associations raised $115,000 for this purpose. The Government contributed $35,000.[101]

Notes

1. P.A.B. McKerron, *The Colony of Singapore Annual Report 1947* (Singapore: Government Printing Office, 1947), 7.
2. *The Colony of Singapore Annual Report 1947* indicated that a total of 938,079 people were recorded in the census of that year: 727,863 Chinese; 114,654 Malays; 71,289 Indians; Eurasians 9012; Europeans 8718; Others 6543.
3. N. Baker, 'The Amateur Ideal in a Society of Equality: Change and Continuity in Post-Second World War British Sport 1945–48', *The International Journal of the History of Sport* 12, no. 1 (1995), 99–126.
4. K. Blackburn and K. Hack, *War Memory and the Making of Modern Malaysia and Singapore* (Singapore: NUS Press, 2012), 96.
5. N.G. Aplin, *To the Finishing Line* (Singapore: SNP, 2002).
6. R. Giulianotti, 'Civilizing Games: Norbert Elias and the Sociology of Sport', cited in R. Giulianotti (ed.), *Sport and Modern Social Theorists* (London: Palgrave Macmillan, 2004), 148.
7. N. Baur and S. Ernst, 'Towards a Process-oriented Methodology: Modern Social Science Research Methods and Norbert Elias's Figurational Sociology', *Sociological Review*, 59, s1 (2011), 117–39.
8. N. Elias, *What is Sociology?* (London: Hutchinson, 1970 [1978]).
9. A. Gilmour, *My Role in the Rehabilitation of Singapore: 1946–1953* (Singapore: Institute of Southeast Asian Studies, 1973), 38.
10. Ibid.
11. H.R. Hone, *Report on the British Military Administration of Malaya: September 1945 to March 1946* (Kuala Lumpur: Malayan Union Government Press, 1946), 37.
12. S.A. Yeoh, *Contesting Space in Colonial Singapore: Power Relations and the Urban Built Environment* (Singapore: University Press, 2003), 15.
13. Hone, *Report on the British Military Administration of Malaya*, 98.
14. National Archives of Singapore. British Military Administration, 32/1945, Microfilm Number NA 869. Sports.

15. See V. Sim (ed.), *Aw Kow: Biographies of Prominent Chinese in Singapore* (Singapore: Nan Kok, 1950), 4. Also 'Chinese Sports Federation Officials Named', *Straits Times*, 16 February 1947, 10.
16. Baur and Ernst, 'Towards a Process-Oriented Methodology', 123–6.
17. Ibid., 125.
18. Oswald Gilmour was unrelated to Andrew Gilmour. He had escaped in highly dramatic, yet tragic circumstances before Singapore fell in February 1942. He returned to England in 1942, via Sumatra and Ceylon, and was then involved with the hopeful plans to restore and reconstruct Singapore after the occupation. He was invited to join the MPU in 1943. He was responsible for evaluating the scale of restoration that would be required to rejuvenate the infrastructure of Singapore. Specifically, his job was to draw up plans for the rehabilitation of the utility services. He was also one of the first British officers to step foot on re-occupied Singapore soil on 5 September 1945.
19. O. Gilmour, cited in K. Blackburn, *The Sportsmen of Changi* (Sydney: NewSouth, 2012), 49–50.
20. *British Malaya* 7, no. 6 (October 1932), 132.
21. Bryson cited in M. Shennan, *Out in the Mid-day Sun: The British in Malaya (1880–1960)* (London: John Murray, 2000), 146.
22. N.G. Aplin and J.J. Quek, 'Celestials in Touch: Sport and the Chinese in Colonial Singapore', *The International Journal of the History of Sport* 19, nos 2–3 (2001), 67–98.
23. Ibid.
24. O. Gilmour, *With Freedom to Singapore* (London: Benn, 1950), 16.
25. A prime example was the HMS Malaya Cup for association football, which had been inaugurated in 1921. It became a symbol of friendly interstate rivalry, notably between Selangor and Singapore in the pre-war years. Also contested was the HMS Malaya Cup for rugby football.
26. Hone, *Report on the British Military Administration of Malaya*.
27. K.W. Yeo and A. Lau, 'From Colonialisation to Independence, 1945–1965', in Ernest C.T. Chew and Edwin Lee (eds), *A History of Singapore* (Singapore: Oxford University Press, 1991), 118–149.
28. C.M. Turnbull, *A History of Singapore: 1819–1988* (Singapore: Oxford University Press, 1989).
29. 'Army Rule', *Straits Times*, 24 October 1945, 2.
30. Gilmour, *With Freedom to Singapore*.
31. Ibid., 171.
32. J. Springhall, 'Mountbatten Versus the Generals: British Military Rule of Singapore, 1945–46', *Journal of Contemporary History*, 36, no. 4 (2001), 635–52.
33. McKerron, *The Colony of Singapore Annual Report 1947*, 9–12.
34. 'Y.M.C.A. Popular with Troops', *Straits Times*, 30 September 1945, 3.
35. Ibid.
36. 'S'pore Swimming Club and Requisitioning', *Straits Times*, 10 November 1945, 3.
37. National Archives of Singapore. British Military Administration, 32/1945, Microfilm Number NA 869. Sports.
38. Springhall, 'Mountbatten Versus the Generals', 638.
39. Pagden. National Archives of Singapore. British Military Administration, 32/1945, Microfilm Number NA 869. Sports.
40. Ibid.
41. McKerron played his part in restoring sport to the social calendar, choosing to identify himself with sports such as golf and yachting. He was a playing member of the Royal Singapore Golf Club and became the Commodore of the Royal Singapore Yacht Club in 1947. The course at the Golf Club had been a tapioca plantation during the Japanese occupation, but the 273 acre course was restored after nine months. The rapidity with which the course was returned to its former glory – for the few – must have raised many eyebrows as the living conditions in the overcrowded city were desperate and the amount of open space available for the general population amounted to less than 200 acres.
42. 'Singapore Lido "Freed"', *Singapore Free Press*, 2 July 1946, 8.
43. 'Tanglin Club', *Singapore Free Press*, 12 July 1946, 9.

44. 'Singapore Clubs Rationed to Officers', *Singapore Free Press*, 1 August 1946, 1.
45. 'Protest by Chinese Swimming Club', *Straits Times*, 11 July 1946, 3. 'The members would like to protest most strongly through the medium of your paper against the shabby treatment meted out against their club which is one of the premier clubs in Singapore and which has at present a membership of about 2000. Is it justice or fair-play to deprive hundreds of our members of the use of the ground floor and reserve it for a canteen used by about 30 servicemen each time it is opened? Y.S. Leong, Honorary Secretary'.
46. *Singapore Free Press*, 12 July 1946, 12.
47. Ibid.
48. 'Release of C.S.C. Today', *Straits Times*, 13 July 1946, 5.
49. 'Mt. Emily Pool Will be Closed for Years', *Straits Times*, 23 September 1946, 5.
50. 'Singapore Wants Back its Parks and Pools', *Straits Times*, 26 October 1946, 3.
51. 'Services' Control Lifted', *Straits Times*, 1 October 1946, 8.
52. 'Anson Rd. Stadium Derequisitioned', *Straits Times*, 17 April 1947, 1.
53. 'Mrs G.A. Tessensohn Named New G.S.C. President', *Singapore Free Press*, 9 December 1947, 7.
54. 'Girls Need $25,000 to Restore Sports Ground', *Straits Times*, 16 February 1947, 5.
55. 'No Funds to Rehabilitate Playground', *Singapore Free Press*, 1 December 1948, 7.
56. 'Y.M.C.A. Wants More Funds', *Straits Times*, 10 April 1947, 3.
57. *Singapore Free Press*, 20 September 1947, 5.
58. 'YMCA Fund Now Totals $70,000', *Singapore Free Press*, 27 December 1947, 5.
59. 'Opening of YMCA Sports Field', *Straits Times*, 28 August 1949, 14.
60. 'Swimming Association Elects Delegates to Council', *Singapore Free Press*, 24 May 1947, 7.
61. The membership figures for CSC were 3262 in March 1947, up from 2700 before the Japanese invasion, while the figures for the SSC were 2589 in January 1947, down from 3896 in January 1941.
62. 'Eve Defeats the SSC', *Straits Times*, 12 August 1946, 5.
63. 'SSC's Further Heavy Expenses', *Straits Times*, 27 March 1947, 5.
64. 'Restrict Use by Services', *Straits Times*, 7 April 1947, 5.
65. 'The Views of an Old SSC Member and Dr Silcock Explains the SSC Resolution', *Straits Times*, 16 July 1948, 4.
66. In Hong Kong a similar pattern of events would unfold in 1950. The Amateur Sports Federation and Olympic Committee of Hong Kong were set up in 1950, and it was formally recognized as a member of the IOC in 1951. See S.F. Lam and Julian W. Chang, *The Quest for Gold: Fifty Years of Amateur Sports in Hong Kong, 1947–1997* (Hong Kong: Hong Kong University Press, 2005), 63.
67. The Singapore Amateur Athletic Association (SAAA); The Singapore Amateur Swimming Association (SASA); The Singapore Amateur Boxing Association (SABA); The Singapore Amateur Football Association (SAFA); The Singapore Amateur Weightlifting Association (SAWA); The Singapore Hockey Association (SHA); The Singapore Badminton Association (SBA); The Singapore Basketball Association (SBBA); The Singapore Table Tennis Association (STTA).
68. 'Bryson Elected SOSC President', *Singapore Free Press*, 5 July 1947, 7.
69. M. Shinozaki, *Syonan – My Story: The Japanese Occupation of Singapore* (Singapore: Times Books International, 1982).
70. IOC Archives/Correspondence dated 22 May 1947.
71. IOC Archives/Correspondence dated 4 June 1947.
72. IOC Archives/Correspondence dated 5 March 1948. Letter from Lord David Burghley to Sigfried Edstrom.
73. IOC Archives/Correspondence – 8 March 1948. Sigfrid Edstrom to Lord David Burghley.
74. IOC Archives/Correspondence – 12 March 1948. Otto Mayer to Lord David Burghley.
75. The SCASF included the Singapore Chinese Basketball Association, the Chinese Swimming Club, the Singapore Chinese Amateur Athletic Federation and the Singapore Chinese Football Association.
76. 'Farewell to Valberg', *Straits Times*, 17 June 1948, 12.

77. 'Olympic Council is Formed Today', *Straits Times*, 27 May 1947, 12.
78. 'Plan for Singapore Sports Stadium', *Straits Times*, 9 August 1947, 7.
79. 'Poor Response to Call for Olympic Funds', *Straits Times*, 5 April 1948, 8.
80. 'Plan for Singapore Sports Centre', *Straits Times*, 3 July 1947, 12.
81. 'Anson Rd. Stadium Derequisitioned', *Straits Times*, 17 April 1947, 1.
82. 'New Stadium Plan for Anson Road', *Straits Times*, 22 July 1947, 1.
83. 'Sports Stadium Will Need 8 Acres', *Singapore Free Press*, 1 October 1947, 7.
84. Baker, 'The Amateur Ideal in a Society of Equality', 99–126.
85. 'Council Moves on Stadium Proposal "Building Should Pay for Itself"', *Straits Times*, 28 May 1947.
86. 'Playing Field Shortage Hits Sportsfans', *Malaya Tribune*, 28 October 1947.
87. 'Malayan Athletes', *Straits Times*, 24 September 1927, 10.
88. Pagden. National Archives of Singapore. British Military Administration, 32/1945, Microfilm Number NA 869. Sports, 46.
89. 'Lee Wai Tong Looking for Olympic Talent', *Straits Times*, 13 September 1947, 12.
90. 'Selections for China Olympics', *Straits Times*, 9 March 1948, 12.
91. 'Dual Nationality and Olympics', *Straits Times*, 9 April 1948, 8.
92. Ibid.
93. 'Selections for China Olympics', *Straits Times*, 9 March 1948, 12.
94. Among the members of the Singapore Chinese Amateur Sports Federation (SCASF) were Aw Kow (1914–1983), G.H. Kiat (1892–1963), and Goh Chye Hin (1905–1984), who were all delegates of the SOSC.
95. Chia Boon Leong and Chu Chee Seng were selected for the football team, Ng Liang Chiang ran in the 440 yard hurdles and Wee Tian Siak was made captain of the basketball team and was destined to carry the national flag of China at the Opening Ceremony in Wembley Stadium.
96. The other countries admitted to the IOC were Guyana, Iraq, Pakistan, Puerto Rico, and Syria.
97. *Colony of Singapore, Annual Report, 1956* (Singapore: Government Printing Office, 1956), 292.
98. *Colony of Singapore, Annual Report, 1949* (Singapore: Government Printing Office, 1949), 14.
99. *Colony of Singapore, Annual Report, 1952* (Singapore: Government Printing Office, 1952), 293. Singapore provided three players for the Malayan team.
100. *Colony of Singapore, Annual Report, 1955* (Singapore: Government Printing Office, 1955), 265. The final stages of this competition were played in May and June 1955 at the Singapore Badminton Stadium. Malaya (meaning a combined Malaya and Singapore team) retained the trophy with an 8-1 victory over Denmark in the challenge round.
101. *Colony of Singapore, Annual Report, 1956*, 291.

Disclosure Statement

No potential conflict of interest was reported by the author.

ORCID

Nick Aplin http://orcid.org/0000-0001-6219-5446

Olympics, Media and Politics: The First Olympic Ideas in Brazilian Society During the Late Nineteenth and Early Twentieth Centuries

Fabio de Faria Peres, Victor Andrade de Melo and Jorge Knijnik [ID]

ABSTRACT
The Olympic Games of the modern era are powerful global mediated events. Olympic cities receive an overwhelming examination by world media. As the 2016 Olympic host, Rio de Janeiro has been given an enormous amount of attention, both by the international media and researchers who looked at the urban spaces of Rio, the struggles over the hegemony of the city and the social meanings the Olympics bring to the host city's citizens. However, studies over the historical relationship between Rio, sport and media are rare. This paper addresses the historical uses of the term Olympic by Brazilian media during the late nineteenth and the early twentieth centuries. By looking at the main articles in the newspapers of these periods, we examine the extent to which ideologies over sports have changed the way the Olympics were represented in Brazil's national imaginary. We demonstrate how the use of expressions associated with the Olympics historically generated a closer appreciation of these events by the public. We also show how political authorities appropriated the Olympics for their own benefit. The paper concludes by asking whether or not the historical lessons from the early Olympic ideas in Brazil have been learned by the 2016 Rio Games organizers.

'The Girl from Ipanema'

When in the 1960s Frank Sinatra sang about the cool swing of 'The Girl from Ipanema' in one of the most internationally known Brazilian songs, he was not only transforming the *Bossa Nova* rhythm in a global phenomenon. More than promoting a city, its places and people, he was also broadcasting a particular notion about Brazilian inhabitants: they have sensual bodies, they dance, they do not walk and they fluctuate using samba steps. These are all elements that put the body as a key element of that social space and that culture.

Especially by bringing together one of the most famous Rio de Janeiro beaches (Ipanema) and its girls, 'The Girl from Ipanema' lyrics from Sinatra's voice were spreading an ideal that has endured over time: Brazil and particularly Rio de Janeiro are places where people cultivate their (phenomenal and irresistible, according to the song) bodies.[1]

Sinatra's example shows that, many years up to the time of being chosen as the host of the 2016 Olympics, Rio de Janeiro (hereafter just 'Rio') has historically been painted in the national and international media as a city with magnificent beaches and outstanding landscapes, where people are prone to have a healthy lifestyle by means of physical activity and sports.[2] Rio's bid to host the Olympics has ably used the mediated relationship between its beautiful, healthy people and its natural landscape – where every sport could be practised – to promote the city's candidature.[3] Similar mediated strategies have been used when Rio successfully bid to host the 2007 Pan-American Games, an event that proved to be critical in Rio's plans to organize future mega-events such as the Olympics.[4]

As one of the most potent mediated events in contemporary history,[5] the Olympics control the imagination of global audiences by establishing a strong relation between both the sociality and the spatiality of its hosting cities and countries.[6] The authors argue that this connection is central to the understanding of the mediated power of the Games as it can reveal the social and cultural importance of the Games and the myths and ideals that they can endorse and propagate.[7]

Hence, it becomes clear that the media plays a key part in marketing the Olympics ideas and messages in the global stage.[8] As the first South American city to ever host an Olympic Games, Rio has been the topic of several academic studies that have critically analyzed several facets of its Olympic candidature. Media studies have scrutinized the use of online platforms to both construct and deconstruct the images of the Olympic city.[9] The historical development and the contestations over the urban spaces of Rio, the private and public struggles over the hegemony of these spaces have also been the target of a comprehensive study that revealed the ideologies behind the changes of the urban infrastructure of the city along the decades.[10]

However, despite the central role that mediated information has had and continues to have in every major sports-event, little attention has been given in the international level to the historical association between media, sports and Olympic Games in Brazil, particularly in Rio. There are few studies that describe the ways that Brazilian media, since the early moments of modern Olympic history, has presented the Olympics to Rio's population.[11] Limited to Portuguese readers, though, these are emblematic of the gap that still exists in the international literature on the historical accounts of the role that media has played in shaping the body and sporting concepts in the country during the evolution of Rio's sports scene in the last century.

Nevertheless, since the late years of the nineteenth century, the term 'Olympic' has started to appear in the local Rio press. In 1896, at the verge of the first Olympic Games of the Modern Era to be held in Athens, the *Jornal do Brasil* (the major Brazilian newspaper of that period) published a small but celebratory note about the event on its first page. Since then, several medium-sized and also large media outlets started to use these terms with a diverse range of meanings and aims. In the same period, Brazilian athletes started to achieve some success in international competitions. Hence, national media started to broadcast sports practices as having an important role in the country's social life.

This paper addresses key moments of the early history of the mediated connections between Brazil and the Olympic Games. The paper draws upon the relationship between media, politics and sports,[12] and uses nineteenth and early twentieth-century Brazilian newspaper articles and chronicles as empirical data to show the diverse ways that media has represented sports and the Olympic idea throughout the years in Brazil. We look at how these ideals and the conceptions of Olympism have impacted Rio de Janeiro city in the first decades of the twentieth century. We also unveil the role that the media has had in the construction of a 'monopoly' of the word 'Olympics'.

We first discuss the struggles between different representations of the Olympic ideal in Rio's media even before the first modern Games took place. We unveil the mediated processes that linked these ideal to the first Games and other sports events during the first decades of the twentieth century. This discussion is documented with several extracts of newspapers from those times to point out how the Olympic ideals were used as background to transformations in the national imaginary about global sports.

Next, we describe how the media has institutionalized the use of the expression Olympics within the educated people and how this word became the 'property' of the highest social extracts of Rio's society who controlled both sports agencies and the major media outlets. As evidence of our arguments, we present extended examples of the media coverage of both the participation of the Brazilian athletes in the 1920 Antwerp Games and of the carrying out of the Latin American Olympic Games in Rio de Janeiro in 1922. In the following section, we present the political implications of the growing influence of the Olympics in 1920s Brazilian society and we finish by discussing the potential similarities between initial Olympic events in Brazil and Rio 2016.

The First Uses of the Expression 'Olympic'

In the last decade of the nineteenth century, the term 'Olympic' was constantly used by the Rio press with a range of different meanings. It is important to note that in that historical period, Rio was Brazil's Federal Capital and its press had major weight in the country's public opinion. Nevertheless, the first reference to the Olympic Games of the Modern Era was published in 1894 by the newspaper *O Paiz* ('The Nation')[13]; it was a brief note stating that the International Conference of the Athletic Games held in Paris had the intention to revitalize the Games. This short mention, though, did not generate any sort of rumours in the capital.

The array of sports brought by the Paris Conference was not new for the Rio society. On the one hand, most of those sports were already known by the city's population.[14] On the other hand, Rio's social and intellectual elite had been educated in Europe, where they had an important neoclassic training; hence, their knowledge about the Ancient Greek Games and their recurrent use of Greek history to legitimate their social and sports practices.[15]

That first newspaper article, though, placed emphasis on the status of the Paris Conference, highlighting the participation of political and artistic personalities. Furthermore, it underlined that many countries were joining the preparation of what would be the 'basis of an international regulation for the forthcoming Modern Olympic Games between the world's civilized nations'.[16] The newspaper was of the opinion that Brazil should be part of this global movement.

The newspaper article was not only a mere description of the Paris Conference; ultimately, it revealed that *O Paiz* was making an effort to be part of the modern times in consonance with the new European cultural advancements where new forms of public sociability and sensitivity were appreciated. Hence, it was not a coincidence that the article on the Olympics was published in the 'Parisian letters' section of the *O Paiz*. Other international sports events were also highlighted in that same section, such as the Paris Grand Prix (a horse racing event), a 'party' described as 'one of these notable events where any true Parisian must attend and where all significant politicians, writers, businessmen and diplomats can be seen'.[17] By publishing these sorts of notes in the same space they used to give to the arts news, the Rio press was showing their alignment with everything that was considered civilized and modern.

Therefore, all the news that arrived in Brazil about the 1896 Athens Olympic Games can be interpreted through a similar lens. Initially, the coverage of the Games was restricted to small notes published in the *Jornal do Brasil*, briefly describing the event's opening ceremony which, according to the newspaper, 'was a party that has attracted, as always, a huge amount of interest'.[18] In addition, the news informed that a royal family (from Greece? It is not clear in the text) was at the ceremony and there was a massive participation of international visitors as well. The *Jornal do Brasil*'s expectations were analogous to the *O Paiz* ones: the newspapers expected Brazil would embrace the Games, as a symbol of civilizing practices of a new era.

The more careful *Jornal do Brasil* readers, though, might have become confused by this news; a few days earlier (25 March 1896), the *Jornal do Brasil* had already published another article reporting that the Olympic Games had started on the previous day.[19] In this first note, they reported on a 'sumptuous party' that attracted 40,000 people and a few of the competition's outcomes. The mistake was probably due to the different calendar used by Greece and the other countries.[20] Despite this initial mix-up, in the days that followed until the end of the Athens Games the press coverage did not change, and brief reports were written about competition outcomes, winners and the medal tally.

In spite of the fact that the articles announced their information coming from an 'international correspondent', the fact is that *O Paiz*, the *Jornal do Brasil*, *A Gazeta de Noticias* and other Brazilian media outlets bought their material from Havas, one of the first and mainly international press news agencies in those days.

Nearly 15 days after the conclusion of the Games, the *Jornal do Brasil* and *O Apostolo* resumed publishing other news about the event. Both newspapers suggested the closure ceremony was sublime, with 60,000 people in attendance.[21] Most important, though, was that those reports were already starting to establish a relationship between sport, nationalism and internationalism. This association became key to the widespread promotion of the Olympic idea within the Brazilian press. A *Jornal do Brasil* journalist gave special attention in his chronicle to the performance of the Greek and the Olympic hymns, and finished his article by highlighting the Greek prince's final speech, which was 'an enthusiastic and vibrant patriotic discourse, which received a loudly ovation'.[22]

The most detailed reports of the Games by the Rio press were published in the *Gazeta de Petrópolis*. Under the headline 'The Restabilising of the Olympic Games in Greece',[23] the newspaper underlined the grandiosity of the event and its arguable connection with an old and glorious past; at the same time, the *Gazeta de Petrópolis* associated the Games with modern times, bringing together central aspects that would help the building up of the imaginary about the event:

> These games, the most important national festivity in Ancient Greece, which origins are lost in the pre-historic times, have finally been restored with splendour and brilliancy at the Olden Panathenaic Stadium in Athens ... During the Easter week, in front of the famous Acropolis,

with its historical and majestic ruins, powerfully electrically lighted at night, at the margins of the dried Ilissus, in front of the shiny shops at Hermes street in Athens, the train ways and the ships dropped numerous groups of sportsmen from France, England, North America, Germany, Sweden and other countries to measure their sports skills with the sons of the historical Attica.[24]

Indeed, there was a festive mode in most of the news about the Games that were conveyed by the Rio newspapers, even if those news items were not numerous. The *Gazeta de Petrópolis* reports clearly used specific written expressions articulated to the images and symbols of the event to show to its readers the grandness of the occasion: the crowning of the winners with the olive branch by the King; the constant reports equating athletes to heroes; the extensive praise to the sports arenas where the competitions took place; the acclamation of the citizens who donated funds to the Games; the positive diplomatic relationships between participant countries; and the magnificence of the party that created incredible attention in North America and Europe.

There is no doubt that the coverage of the first Olympic Games by the Rio press in 1896 was significant, most of all considering that Brazilian newspapers in that period were produced with very limited resources under amateur conditions. Nonetheless, other uses of the expression 'Olympic' were also seen in Brazilian society in general.[25]

In the political sphere, for example, the term Olympic was associated with a major achievement or a heroic act. For example, the process whereby Brazil became independent from Portugal (1822) was characterized as the 'Big Olympics'[26]; far from trivializing the expression, this denomination shows the triumph of a young nation that was looking to build its own history. Olympic Games were also used as a metaphor for politic struggles.[27]

However, the 'Olympic' expression was also employed in 1894 as a good-tempered critique to the dangers that regular Rio de Janeiro citizens faced in their everyday errands. While writing about a tram accident, a journalist wrote that walking through Rio's streets was so hard that the only way that a pedestrian could avoid these daily misfortunes was being an Olympic athlete born in Ancient Greece.[28]

The intersection between the fields of Medicine, Education and Physical Education had also become filled with references to the Olympic Games. In these fields, the use of related Olympic expressions was always associated with the advantages that physical exercise would bring to health – especially Swedish gymnastics. The meanings of having an Olympic physique were frequently connected to body and mind, and had a strong political component: they were part of a nationwide educational project. The ideal of a Physical Education that would reach the physical, the intellectual and the moral domains of the students was part of a 'utopic integrated education,'[29] proper to the modern and civilized nation that was to be shaped in the country.[30]

Since the end of the 1830s – much before the 1896 Olympic Games – Brazilian journalists and medical doctors considered that the Greek Olympic Games were the perfect model of corporal practices. The background to affirm this ideology was their desire to implement a strong new nation, which was broadcasted numerous times in newspapers and scientific publications.[31] The reference to the Olympic Games helped to bring acceptability to the calls for nationwide physical exercise programmes. It brought the Ancient Greek model of education and health as a parameter to be followed in the pursuit of a harmonically perfect and healthy society.

A few times, though, the Ancient Games were also analyzed with critical eyes. A journalist, at the end of the nineteenth century, used his acid humour to ponder whether this idealization of Ancient Greek practices would be sustainable for a city with so many social issues like Rio de Janeiro. By using his well-known irony, he called his readers' attention to the incompatibility of the Ancient Greek lifestyles and the Rio citizens' 'modern lives', with its duties and tougher conditions:

> We have not been made for these prowesses, my friends! We should be happy with everything that our century gives to us. In terms of sports, please let [us] be pleased in betting in the runners and in the horses! The heroic times of the Ancient Olympic Games are lost! The modern era is for gambling games! I would rather lose my cash watching other people running than making some coins by running while others are amusing themselves looking at me.[32]

Despite these slight critiques, the expression 'Olympic' found a growing niche within Rio's population during the nineteenth century due to the increasing popularity of shows of gymnastics and acrobatics. These performances, which since the 1820s started to spread within circuses and theatres across the city, were the main broadcasters of terms associated with Olympism. Circus companies such as the 'Olympic Cirque' performed an acrobatic piece called 'Olympic Games' that fascinated the audience.

The allurement that such occasions brought to the audiences was a clear indication that new conceptions about embodiment were being engendered amongst Rio's society; the appreciation of certain physical capacities such as strength, balance, high energy and stamina did not transform the spectators into sports practitioners, but made them change their views on body practices. In this context, the references to the Olympic Games were linked in the social imaginary to a new aesthetic connected to virility and muscular impetus.

These notions were also present in the incipient sports arena that was taking shape in Rio's society during the second half of the nineteenth century. During that time, the term 'Olympic' started to move beyond the circuses and the health and educational fields and became part of Rio's growing sports terrain.[33]

The *Clube Olímpico Guanabarense* is a typical example of this influence. Established in 1883, this club was one of the first sports associations in the whole country to promote walking races and also cycling contests.[34] Clearly its name proudly associated the word 'Olympic' with Rio's marine landscape, the Guanabara Bay – 'Guanabarense' is the adjective of someone or something that is from 'Guanabara'.

Another example of the growing influence of the 'Olympic' ideal within sports clubs is the club Sport Federal, located in Rio as well. This club used to promote its activities in Rio's newspapers by broadcasting its 'Olympic' events, such as fencing training and competitions, walking and bike races, restaurants and 'everything that is connected to the Athletic and Olympic Games'.[35]

However, despite the increasing broadcasting of the expressions connected to the Olympic Games, the actual events held in Athens (1896) and Paris (1900) were seen by Rio's society in a distant manner. Hence, a few journalists still demonstrated certain resistance and even mistrust towards these sports events. The 'traditional' features of the 1896 Athens Games were questioned just a few days after its opening ceremony:

> Athens, 6. – The traditional Olympic Games have started ... We read this and leave the newspaper drop, we close the eyes and feel like crying. The soul starts to imagine, to dream on what we have studied, how these Games would be in the Golden Era, when the Greeks did not ... [dress] up with suits and did not eat *foie gras* ... This is my word of honour! We feel horrible when we read that on 6 April 1896, in Athens, the Olympic Games have started, with the support of the Greek royal family ... But then, I stop feeling desperate and instead, I feel an irresistible desire of laughing ... Imagining what is happening over there. And I shout and laugh.[36]

Other writers doubted that the 1896 Games would be successful, mostly because there was no betting system, which was the main point of attraction, according to them, for any sports events.[37] A similar idea brought another journalist to query another commercial enterprise in Rio, which would be predominantly connected to Olympic sports events.[38]

In fact, the International Olympic Committee (IOC) leadership had to battle to legitimate their definition of the Olympic Games that they conceived and were willing to see evolve.[39] In Brazil, as in other counties, it took some time for this legitimation to occur. The Rio's press had an important role in the construction of a valid narrative about the Olympics, shaping its boundaries and limiting every time its meanings.

Institutionalizing the Representation: The Olympic Games of the 1910s and 1920s and the Brazilian Press

During the first decade of the twentieth century, the uses of the expression 'Olympic Games' were still very diverse within the Brazilian press. The terms were still associated with political contexts, and to connections with Physical Education and Health within circus performances. However, during this decade we can also see an increasing association of 'Olympic' terms with a range of sports practices.

This slight change of focus was associated more with other international sports events than to the actual quadrennial Olympic Games themselves. Brazilian press gave more attention to sports competitions held in Athens (1906) and Montevideo (1907) than to the 1900 Paris Olympic Games and to the 1904 Saint Louis Olympic Games. The newspaper *Correio da Manhã* even sent a press correspondent to Greece and also published pictures of the event,[40] as did *O Paiz*.[41]

The Brazilian press was particularly interested in the Montevideo competition, as allegedly that was the first time the country was 'represented abroad in sports festivals'.[42] Abrahão Saliture's (from *Club de Natação e Regatas*, Rio de Janeiro) swimming victories were specially highlighted. Winning rowing athletes Ernesto Corri, Octavio Glovini and Salvador Pastore (from *Club Esperia*, São Paulo) also received special coverage from the Brazilian press. The press praised the athletics records achieved by Hermann Friese (from *Club Germania*, São Paulo) a German footballer who lived in Brazil and in the 1907 Uruguayan competition sprinted both the 1500 metres and the 800 metres races on the same night, winning both and taking second place in the 400 metres.

According to the local newspapers, the success of national sportsmen was linked to their demonstration of athletic values to the nation. During that period, the press was already promoting a sound relationship between sports practice and the country's values. Newspaper editors were clearly promoting the 'intrinsic sports values' in order to create and strengthen an imagined national community. Sports competitions were useful for this purpose as they helped to grow the rivalries against South American neighbour countries, hence increasing an 'us versus them' mentality that helped to create a nationwide patriotic ideology.

Similar journalistic reports were noticed in other South American sports events Brazil took part in during those days, such as the 1908 Pan-American Scientific Congress, the 1909 Paraguayan independence festival and during the 1910 Argentinean Republic centennial celebrations. New expectations were generated by the Brazilian athletes increasing numbers participating in those international competitions; the press coverage of the events had also been augmented, creating more public interest and making these athletes well-known public figures, adored by the population.

Santos Dumont was the first Brazilian to achieve international Olympic glory. In 1905, he received the Olympic Merit diploma due to his aeronautical prowess and records. Pierre de Coubertin was not only acknowledging Santos Dumont as an outstanding sportsman but was also trying to develop a closer relationship with South American sports stakeholders. However, Dumont's Olympic highlighting did not have any major impact within Brazilian Olympic Games press coverage.[43]

The Brazilian press coverage of the Olympics press started to grow by the 1908 London Olympic Games, as seen by the greater number of news articles highlighting the international relevance of the event.[44] On the one hand, sport was fast acquiring a larger space in Brazil's social life; on the other hand, the Games were becoming more legitimate in the international community, with positive repercussions in Brazil.

Hence, it was not a coincidence that in 1912 an initiative to organize the Olympic Games in Rio de Janeiro started to gain momentum. This enterprise had as one of its main backers the *Jornal do Brasil*, a major Brazilian newspaper.[45] The creation of the Interim Brazilian Olympic Committee was one of the main outcomes of this initiative. The Interim Committee met occasionally in the *Jornal do Brasil*'s chief officer's office.[46]

In 1913, Raul Paranhos, the Brazilian ambassador in Switzerland, was elected delegate to the IOC. This move was a clear indication that the IOC wanted to grow its South American influence. However, Paranhos was not aware that in the same period the Provisory Brazilian Olympic Committee had already been established in order to provide a better structure for Brazilian athletes. It was only a year later (1914) that Paranhos and the members of the Provisory Committee came together to create the Brazilian Olympic Committee (COB).

The COB formation was well received by the national press, as they saw it as a major sign for a better national sport structure. Local press also celebrated COB's inception as a measurement of the Brazilian people's strengths: 'A robust sport performance indicates a great future for the nation, as sports prepare next generation's vigorous bodies and minds'.[47]

However, COB's foundation did not immediately guarantee its full effectiveness. It took more than 20 years for the COB to become more active in the national scenario. Political conflicts between the old elites of the states of São Paulo and Minas Gerais, and the Federal Capital, as well as emerging powerful state public employees such as the military,[48] were undermining the progress of sport around the country. Political tensions were reflected in the sporting arena, especially within the clashes between São Paulo and Rio de Janeiro sport federations and sport club managers and owners. These local struggles were particularly damaging for the football national team's increasing participation in international competitions.[49]

These political intrigues lasted for many years and help us to understand why COB had not worked properly in the first decades of the past century. The COB only became more active in 1935 when Antonio Prado Junior, a member of an elite family and well-known politician and sportsman, became its president.[50]

Yet, Olympic news began to appear more frequently in Brazilian press from the 1910s. During this period, the expression 'Olympics' started to obtain new meanings more closely associated with internationally acknowledged sports. This is clearly stated in a note that circulated in an important weekly magazine: 'it is our duty to clarify when we talk about

Figure 1. *O Malho*, 14 August 1920

Olympic sports we mean that they are named Olympics because they are part of the Olympic Games program'.[51]

Press coverage was also paying attention to the early development of different Olympic sports in Brazil. Brazilian sportsmen were sent for the first time to compete in the 1920 Antwerp Olympic Games, representing the country in shooting, swimming, water polo, rowing and diving competitions.[52] The highlight of the Brazilian team was the shooting athletes, who secured a gold medal (Guilherme Paraense, 30 metres military pistol), a silver medal (Afrânio Costa, 50 metres free pistol) and a bronze medal (Sebastião Wolf, Dario Barbosa e Fernando Soledade in the team 50 metres free pistol).

Shooting in Brazil was already well organized, as its associations, such as the National Shooting Stand, founded in 1899 and the National Shooting Federation, established in 1906, were connected with the National Army. Therefore, the sporting prowess on this field reflected the national concern for the defence of the new Brazilian Republic.[53]

Brazilian journalists narrated with euphoria the Brazilian shooters' wins. One writer for a weekly magazine narrated the medals as a 'great merit that placed Brazil in a highest place among the nations'.[54] According to this writer the amazing performance surprised everyone, as the national team was not only unknown but lacked good training resources. He concludes by saying the win promoted an international wave of curiosity in Europe about Brazil, and closes with a nationalistic impetus: 'Honour to Brazil'.

In another analysis of the shooting outcomes, the same magazine pointed out that the positive results were evidence Brazil not only excelled in military instruction but also that Brazilian sportsmen fought their hazards with good sportsmanship. According to the analyst, national athletes had many virtues, such as 'organic resistance and accuracy'; hence, they could overcome 'the world's strongest nations'.[55] A cartoon in the same publication celebrated this new social representation (Figure 1).

In the drawing we can see Europe, the old lady, bowing in front of a Brazilian – who is represented in a winning position, carrying a 'World Champion' standard. The key in the cartoon, though, is the representation of the Brazilian without shoes, to show the poor conditions and the difficulties these athletes had to overcome to beat the rich European competitors. The *O Malho* journalist had no doubts in saying that the Olympic Games medals were 'more valuable to broadcasting the country's names than the numerous and costly diplomatic representations' that used to go to Europe during this period.

The Olympics: Political Consequences in the Early 1920s

The increasing press coverage of the Olympics with the growing use of 'Olympic' expressions associated to sporting prowess attracted the attention of the political arena. The winning 1920 shooters became instant national heroes. They were welcomed back in the country by political authorities and the general public. The 'heroes' participated in several public ceremonies where they received accolades and were praised by high authorities. The Brazilian president attended the Defence National League celebration and acclaimed the new national heroes as well.[56]

The shooter-heroes also received money for their accomplishments. The Brazilian president provided extra funding to the Ministry of War in order to reward the shooting team, 'particularly the 30 metres military pistol World Champion Guilherme Paraense'.[57]

The medals and wins were also responsible for increasing interest and broadcasting of the Olympic ideals in Brazil. National press, as evidenced above, was already covering national sportsmen competing abroad and the Olympic victories resulted in an increase of this dissemination. Furthermore, sports became part of the nation's imagination, serving both internal social cohesion purposes and external aspirations to promote the country's positive image.

However, in the early 1920s the internal political situation in Brazil became unstable. The 1922 presidential elections were controversial and in the same year the Communist Party was created. The political elites in power since the foundation of the Republic at the end of the nineteenth century were being clearly contested.[58]

The federal government then decided to create a distraction and celebrate Brazil's independence centennial anniversary. They believed the festivities would both alleviate the internal political tension and broadcast Brazil as a peaceful and organized country to the world.[59]

The chief activity for the centenary celebrations was the International Exhibition conceived as a showcasing strategy of Brazil as a major and modern nation.[60] Sport competitions were included in the programme festivities as a sign of the country's progress and integration in the modern world. Competitions occupied a key place in the 1922 events; sports rivalries and heroes were largely broadcasted by the national press; the coverage supported the government's ideals of national identity building through 'the upmost civilized sports competitions'.[61]

During the centennial celebrations, there were three types of sports events: the South American Football Championship, the International Military Games and the Latin American Athletics Games, the latter being known also as the Latin American Olympic Games. Brazilian people were, for the first time, allowed to follow the details of a real Olympic competition and their response was fantastic: these Games were by far the most popular event within the 1922 Independence centennial celebrations.

The 1922 Latin American Olympic Games was the implementation of a plan originated in 1913 by the same group that created the COB. Since their first meetings they had already talked about the potential that Rio de Janeiro had as an Olympic city. Their inspiration came from other South American neighbouring countries – such as Argentine, Uruguay, Chile and Paraguay – that had successfully organized international competitions in the past.[62]

Yet, the Brazilian group who was in charge of the 1922 Games had several struggles with the IOC. Pierre de Coubertin, despite his desire to spread the Olympic ideal around the globe, did not trust Brazil's capacity to promote anything similar to the Olympic Games. Coubertin was finally convinced by YMCA executive, Elwood Brown, an old Frenchman who shared Olympic ideals with the IOC president. Brown was also responsible for the conversations with the Brazilian authorities in order to put the Games together.[63]

The 1922 Latin American Olympic Games Organizing Committee faced various problems. First, the Brazilian Government delayed and ultimately reduced the funding to the event due to an economic crisis. Second, the country's internal political struggles were replicated within the Committee leadership, which also lacked sports management experience in such large events. These tensions nearly led to the cancellation of the Games.

However, the 1922 Latin American Olympic Games overcame all those issues and were successfully held in Brazil between August and October. Some sports venues built especially for the Games became part of Rio's sporting heritage. However, most of the time these arenas were not open for the use of the general public after the Games – and their final costings were often more expensive than the initial budget calculations indicated.

Regardless of several economic, managerial and political troubles, the 1922 Games were important to both the international Olympic movement and to Brazil's international image as well. A year later, two Brazilian representatives (Arnaldo Guinle and José Ferreira dos Santos) were elected to the IOC.[64]

Final Sprint: The 1922 Games and the 2016 Games

Using an historical lens, it can be said that the 1922 Latin-American Olympic Games were a culmination of a social process that legitimated the Olympic ideal as intrinsically associated with sports and the wider Brazilian society.

This legitimation was a slow and heterogeneous process. The Olympic ideals arrived in Brazil much earlier than the inauguration of the Modern Era Olympics in 1896. It was associated with the insertion of Ancient Greek ideals in civilizing processes, both in educational and health proposals; it was also related to the field of entertainment, where specific body skills were highlighted and promoted. At the very beginning of the Olympic legitimation process, these two sides were not linked in any aspect; however, even if they were not connected, they still expressed the ambiguities of a changing society, where the emerging elites within the new cities tried to adjust themselves to the more developed countries, a tuning practice that included the business of entertainment.

The news of the first Olympic Games of the Modern Era arrived in Brazil in the late nineteenth century without carrying enough significance to change the Olympic ideologies that were predominant in the country on those years. The ideological content of the Modern Olympics propagated by the International Olympic Movement gained true impetus in Brazilian society through a series of sports competitions across South America, where Brazilian sportsmen achieved good outcomes. These results led to an association of the country's civilizing ideals to sports prowess: the winners started to be seen as national heroes.

It was in the 1910s when values of Modern Olympism started to be introduced in the country. The first participation of a Brazilian Team in the 1920 Antwerp Olympic Games was a major impulse towards forming a proper structure for the Brazilian Olympic Movement. As the winners came back with their medals, they were elevated to the pantheon of national heroes and acknowledged across the nation for their service in propagating the positive qualities of the country around the world; moreover, these athletes and their victories were seen as indicators of a civilized Brazil that was fast moving towards gaining a place amongst the most important countries of the planet.

Hence, the Olympic Games came to be represented by the media as the ideal space to propagate the country's successes. It was with no surprise that the political elite decided to organize a regional continental competition with an Olympic profile during the country's centennial independence anniversary celebrations in 1922. Those celebrations were deemed and planned as the defining moment to celebrate the modernization of Brazil; the precise platform to showcase national interests to the world.

The mediated stimuli, which slowly enhanced in the nation's imagination a closer connection between sports and Olympism, had a clear influence in the political spheres, which facilitated the appropriation of the Olympic ideals as part of the nation's imagination. Nevertheless, these Games demonstrated the weaknesses that Brazil's sports administrators had in relation to the management of large events. They also showed that the political aspects of such events cannot be undermined and should be treated carefully.

During this period, the national press served as the platform to the building and consolidation of Olympic ideologies. As it has been shown in this paper, many of these ideals were paradoxical, and praise walked hand-in-hand with criticism of the Olympic achievements of the country.

The question posed to historians at this precise moment is whether the 1922 historical lessons will be relevant in further analyses of the 2016 Rio Olympic Games or not. Brazil's situation in 2016 is curiously very similar to that of 1922: political turmoil, with an elected president impeached by obscure forces, and economic struggles. How will these social eruptions affect the 2016 Games? Will Rio's population see a better social and educational legacy than they saw in the 1922 Games? Will the final budget reveal the same controversial numbers as it did nearly 100 years ago? Will the mainstream media vehicles display the same behaviour as the press of the 1920s?[65]

Future analysis will reveal the different meanings the 2016 Games had to the diverse populations of Rio de Janeiro. At the moment, the mediated and political representations of Olympics in the city are just reinforcing what was being built in the 1920s – if this is the only legacy that the 2016 Olympics leaves in the city, they will be remembered by most of Rio's population as a major and expensive trauma.

Notes

1. Eula Davis Siqueira and Denise da Costa Siqueira, 'Corpo, mito e imaginário nos postais das praias cariocas' [Body, myth and imaginary in the post cards of Rio de Janeiro's beaches], *Intercom: Revista Brasileira de Ciências da Comunicação* 34 (2011), 169–87.
2. Victor Andrade de Melo and Andre Schetino, 'A bicicleta, o ciclismo e as mulheres na transição dos séculos XIX e XX' [Bicycle, Cycling and Women in the 19th to 20th Centuries' Transition], *Estudos Feministas* 17, no. 1 (2009), 111–34.
3. Guilherme Nothen, 'Paving the Olympic Dream: The Politics of the 2007 Pan-American Games in Rio de Janeiro', *The International Journal of the History of Sport* 33, nos 1–2 (2016), 203–16.

4. Martin Curi, Jorge Knijnik and Gilmar Mascarenhas, 'The Pan American Games in Rio de Janeiro 2007: Consequences of a Sport Mega-Event on a BRIC Country', *International Review for the Sociology of Sport* 46, no. 2 (2011), 140–56.
5. Maurice Roche, *Mega-events and Modernity: Olympics and Expos in the Growth of Global Culture* (London: Routledge, 2000).
6. David Rowe and Deborah Stevenson, 'Sociality and Spatiality in Global Media Event', in Alan Tomlinson and Christopher Young (eds), *National Identity and Global Sports Events: Culture, Politics, and Spectacle in the Olympics and the Football World Cup* (Albany, NY: SUNY Press, 2006), 197–214.
7. Ibid.
8. David Rowe, 'Cultural Citizenship, Media and Sport in Contemporary Australia', *International Review for the Sociology of Sport* (2016), doi:10.1177/1012690216641147.
9. Rob Millington and Simon Darnell, 'Constructing and Contesting the Olympics Online: The Internet, Rio 2016 and the Politics of Brazilian Development', *International Review for the Sociology of Sport* 49, no. 2 (2014), 190–210.
10. Christopher Gaffney, 'Mega-Events and Socio-Spatial Dynamics in Rio de Janeiro, 1919–2016', *Journal of Latin American Geography* 9, no. 1 (2010), 7–29.
11. Victor Andrade de Melo and Fabio de Faria Peres, 'O corpo da nação: posicionamentos governamentais sobre a educação física no Brasil monárquico' [The body of the nation: government positions on physical education during the Brazilian monarchy], *História, Ciências, Saúde – Manguinhos, Rio de Janeiro* 21, no. 4 (2014), 1131–49.
12. David Rowe, *Global Media Sport: Flows, Forms and Futures* (London & New York: Bloomsbury Academic, 2011).
13. *O Paiz*, 5 August 1894, 2.
14. Victor Andrade de Melo, *Cidade Sportiva – primórdios do esporte no Rio de Janeiro* [Sporting City: the beginning times of Rio de Janeiro's Sporting life] (Rio de Janeiro: Relume Dumará, 2001).
15. Victor Andrade de Melo, 'De Olímpia (776 a.c.) a Atenas (1896) a Atenas (2004): problematizando a presença da antiguidade clássica nos discursos contemporâneos sobre o esporte' [From Olympia (776 BC) to Athens (1896) and to Athens (2004): problematizing the presence of the Classical Age in contemporary analysis of sport issues], *Phoinix*, Rio de Janeiro, no. 13 (2007), 350–76.
16. *O Paiz* (5 August 1894, 2) highlighted that the Congress was opened and chaired by the former Ministry of France in Berlin, the Coursel Baron and also stressed the addresses by poet Jean Aicard. Furthermore, the news reported that several countries such as Italy, Greece, Belgium, Russia, England, German, the USA and France were present.
17. *O Paiz*, 5 August 1894, 2.
18. *Jornal do Brasil*, 6 and 7 April 1896, 1.
19. *Jornal do Brasil*, 25 March 1896, 1.
20. The Olympic Games took place between 6 and 15 April in the Gregorian calendar, which was different from the one adopted in Greece at those times.
21. *Jornal do Brasil*, 2 May 1896, 2; *O Apostolo*, 10 May 1896, 2.
22. *Jornal do Brasil*, 2 May 1896, 2.
23. *Gazeta de Petrópolis*, 20 May 1896, 1.
24. *Gazeta de Petrópolis*, 20 May 1896, 1.
25. Victor Andrade de Melo and Fabio de Faria Peres, 'Primeiros ventos olímpicos em terras tupiniquins' [The initial Olympic gusts in Tupiniquim lands], *Revista USP*, 2016.
26. *Diário da Câmara dos Senadores do Império do Brasil* [The Diary of the Senators Chamber of the Brazilian Empire], 17 July 1826, 440.
27. *Correio Oficial*, 13 November 1833, 475–6.
28. *Gazeta de Notícias*, 14 October 1894, 1.
29. José G. Gondra, 'Artes de civilizar: medicina, higiene e educação escolar na Corte Imperial. Rio de Janeiro' [Civilizing arts: medicine, hygiene and schooling during the Imperial Court], *EdUERJ* (2004).

30. Victor Andrade de Melo and Fabio de Faria Peres, 'O corpo da nação: posicionamentos governamentais sobre a educação física no Brasil monárquico', *História, Ciências, Saúde* 21, no. 4 (2014), 1131–49.
31. Victor Andrade de Melo and Fabio de Faria Peres, *Gymnastica no tempo do Império* [Gymnastics during Imperial times] (Rio de Janeiro: 7 Letras 2014).
32. *A Cigarra*, 30 May 1895, 3.
33. Victor Andrade de Melo and Fabio de Faria Peres, 'Relações entre ginástica e saúde no Rio de Janeiro do século XIX: reflexões a partir do Colégio Abílio (1872–1888)' [The relationship between Physical Education and health in Rio de Janeiro in the nineteenth century: reflections based on the case of Colégio Abílio, 1872–1888], *História, Ciências, Saúde – Manguinhos* 23, no. 4 (2016), 1133–51.
34. André Schetino, *Pedalando na modernidade: a bicicleta e o ciclismo na transição dos séculos XIX e XX* [Riding in themodernity: bicycle and cycling in the transition from the 19th to the 20th Century], Rio de Janeiro: Apicuri, 2008.
35. *O Paiz*, 1 January 1890, 4.
36. *Jornal do Brasil*, 8 April 1896, 1.
37. *Gazeta de Notícias*, 17 March 1895, 1.
38. *Gazeta de Notícias*, 29 March 1896, 1.
39. Pierre Bourdieu. 'Como é possível ser esportivo?' [How is it possible to be a good sport?], in *Questões de sociologia*, ed. Pierre Bourdieu (Rio de Janeiro: Marco Zero, 1983), 136–63.
40. *Correio da Manhã*, 17 June 1906 (suplemento ilustrado); *Correio da Manhã*, 3 June 1906 (suplemento ilustrado); *Correio da Manhã*, 24 June 1906 (suplemento ilustrado).
41. *O Paiz*, 10 June 1906, 9.
42. *Gazeta de Notícias*, 27 e 28 February 1907, 2.
43. Marcia De Francesci Neto-Wacker and Christian Wacker, *O Brasil torna-se olímpico* [Brazilbecomes Olympic] (Manaus: CBAt, 2012).
44. The amount of news and articles about the 1908 London Games and the 1912 Stockholm Games were much larger than the coverage linked to former Olympic Games organized by the IOC.
45. *Jornal do Brasil*, 10 October 1912, 13. According to the newspaper *O Imparcial* (3 August 1913, 10) the idea of organizing the Olympic Games in Rio, despite facing several struggles, would turn up in the Sports Week being held in the city and in the creation of the Brazilian Olympic Committee in 1914.
46. *Jornal do Brasil*, 27 June 1913, 11.
47. *Revista da Semana*, 26 July 1913, 46.
48. Marieta de Moraes Ferreira and Surama Conde Sá Pinto, 'A crise dos anos 1920 e a Revolução de 1930' [The crisis of the 1920s and the 1930 Revolution], in Jorge Ferreira and Lucilia de Almeida Neves Delgado (eds), *O Brasil republicano: O tempo do liberalismo excludente: da Proclamação da República à Revolução de 1930* [Brazil as a Republic: the excluding liberalism, from Republic Declaration to the 1930 Revolution] (Rio de Janeiro: Civilização Brasileira, 2003), 387–415; Maria do Carmo Campello de Souza, 'O processo político-partidário na Primeira República' [Political parties in the 1st Republic], in Carlos Guilherme Mota (ed.), *Brasil em perspectiva* [Brazilunder perspective] (Rio de Janeiro: Bertrand Brasil, 1990), 162–226.
49. Carlos Eduardo Sarmento, *A regra do jogo: uma história institucional da CBF* [The game's rule: an institutional history of the Brazilian Football Federation] (Rio de Janeiro: CPDOC, 2006).
50. Renato Lanna Fernandes, *O jogo da distinção: C. A. Paulistano e Fluminense F. C. – um estudo da construção das identidades clubísticas durante a fase amadora do futebol em São Paulo e no Rio de Janeiro (1901–1933)* [A distinctive match: a study of clubs' identities construction during football amateurism in São Paulo and Rio de Janeiro – 1901–1933] (Rio de Janeiro: FGV, 2016).
51. *Revista da Semana*, 28 June 1913, 41.
52. COB, *Comitê Olímpico do Brasil 100 anos* [Centenary of the Brazilian Olympic Committee] (Rio de Janeiro: Casa da Palavra, 2015).
53. Victor Andrade de Melo, *Rio Esportivo* [Sporting Rio] (Rio de Janeiro: Casa da Palavra, 2015).

54. *O Malho*, 14 August 1920, 19.
55. *O Malho*, 14 August 1920, 25.
56. *Sport Ilustrado*, 20 August 1920, 18.
57. BRASIL. Decreto n. 15160, de 7 December 1921.
58. Marly Silva da Motta, *A nação faz cem anos: a questão nacional no centenário da independência* [Brazil turns 100: the national quest in the Independence centenary] (Rio de Janeiro: Editora FGV, 1992).
59. Ibid.
60. Sandra Jatahy Pesavento, *Exposições universais: espetáculos da modernidade do século XIX* [The universal exhibitions: shows of modernity in the 19th century] (São Paulo: Hucitec, 1997).
61. João Manuel Casquinha Malaia dos Santos, Mauricio Drumond and Victor Andrade de Melo, 'Celebrando a nação nos gramados: o Campeonato Sul-Americano de Futebol de 1922' [Celebrating the nation on the football pitches: the 1922 South American Football Championship], *História: Questões & Debates, Curitiba*, no. 57 (2012), 151–74.
62. *Jornal do Brasil*, 9 May 1913, 10.
63. César Torres, *Jogos Olímpicos Latino-Americanos: Rio de Janeiro – 1922* [The 1922 Rio de Janeiro Latin-American Olympic Games] (Manaus: Confederação Brasileira de Atletismo, 2012). See also: João M.C.M. Santos and Victor Andrade de Melo eds, *1922*: comemorações esportivas do centenário [1922: Sporting celebrations of the Centenary] (Rio de Janeiro: 7 Letras, 2012).
64. COB, *Comitê Olímpico do Brasil 100 anos* [Brazilian Olympic Committee 100 years] (Rio de Janeiro: Casa da Palavra, 2015).
65. See Gilmar Mascarenhas, Glauco Bienenstein and Fernanda Sanchez eds, *O jogo continua: megaeventos esportivos e cidades* [The game goes on: sports mega events and the city] (Rio de Janeiro: Ed. Uerj, 2011).

Acknowledgements

The authors would like to acknowledge Mr Jawed Gebrael (Centre for Education Research, Western Sydney University) for his careful proof reviewing of this manuscript. We would like also to acknowledge the anonymous reviewers for their comments that helped us to improve the quality of this paper.

Disclosure Statement

No potential conflict of interest was reported by the authors.

ORCID

Jorge Knijnik http://orcid.org/0000-0003-2578-8909

The Development of Social Media and its Impact on the Intercultural Exchange of the Olympic Movement, 2004–2012

Yinya Liu [iD]

ABSTRACT
The development of social media, in the form of Internet and mobile platforms, has rapidly flourished in the early twenty-first century. The changes in broadcasting forms of the first three Olympic Games of the twenty-first century, Athens 2004, Beijing 2008 and London 2012, have corresponded and reflected the speedy expansion of this social media. This phenomenon invites not only attention to the historical transformation of the roles of media for the Olympic Games but also reflection on the concept of culture and intercultural exchange based on this phenomenon. This paper studies the relationships between social media, cultural exchange and the Olympic Games in the context of globalization. It argues that the characteristics of social media as 'participation; openness; conversation; communities; connectedness' will meet up with the goal of the Olympic Movement and aid the realization of the Olympic Ideal.

Introduction

The importance and significance of media in the promulgation of the modern Olympic Games was recognized by Baron Pierre de Coubertin, the founder of the International Olympic Committee (IOC) at the end of the nineteenth century. Along with the development of media technology in the twentieth century, however, the use of social media in the twenty-first century has increased rapidly. In fact, the user numbers, user coverage and use frequency of social media, mainly in the forms of online and mobile telephone platforms, have changed exponentially over the span of the first three Olympic Games of the twenty-first century: the 2004 Athens Games, the 2008 Beijing Games and the 2012 London Games. It is significant to examine the roles and changes of media in the organization and promotion of these three Games because this bears witness to the major turning point of the development of media itself as it moves away from traditional media forms of newspapers, magazines, radio and television, and towards new media forms of Internet-founded social media and mobile–telephone platforms.

The aim of the paper is to explore the relationships between social media, cultural exchange and the Olympic Games in the context of globalization. The most distinguishing feature of recent social media in the context of the Olympic Games is the interactivity of different cultures in a global context. This intercultural exchange of the social users associated with the Olympic Games (2004–2012) is the main concern of this paper. The paper is divided into four sections. The first section supplies a theoretical foundation for cultural exchange, and we also evaluate various voices on the concept of culture and intercultural exchange and its most updated development. Section two addresses the development of Olympic Media and its impact on the organization of the Olympic Games. In this section, we tentatively propose that a fifth period of 'Socialympics' has arrived and explore the inside of social media and the way in which these platforms link to the Olympics and form a 'Socialympics'. Section three is a case study that examines the changes in the broadcasting and media of the Olympic Games between 2004 and 2012 and analyzes the interrelation between the Games' organization and the relevant data. In the final section, we deal in particular with the relationship between media cultural exchange and the Olympic Games in the context of globalization.

The Concept of Culture and its Development in the Context of Globalization

Before we examine cultural exchange via social media in the context of the Olympic Games as a global event, it is of importance to define the concept of 'culture' because this term can refer to many things. Eliot proposes three important conditions for defining culture.[1] The first is organic structure which emphasizes the growing characteristics of this concept. The second condition highlights the importance of local cultures. And, the last condition indicates the balance of unity and diversity in religion. Eliot reminds readers that the term culture is applied to 'the development of an individual, of a group or class, or of a whole society', but among these three categories, Eliot believes that the culture of the society is fundamental.[2] Eliot's definition of culture is mainly from the perspective of literary criticism and was proposed in 1948. He has nonetheless articulated the dynamic, geographical and plural characteristics of this concept, which are still appropriately applied to its discussion today.

With regards to the concept of media culture, this term falls under the category of cultural studies and the major influence of mass media in the way meaning is organized in the twentieth century. Kellner argues that 'media culture is now the dominant form of culture which socialises us and provides materials for identity in terms of both social reproduction and change'.[3] In our context of discussion, the broadcasting of the Olympic Games is delivered by means of images, sounds and spectacles in the form of radio and television, and now online and mobile platforms via social media. Thus, we will limit our analyses on cultural exchange of the Olympic Games in the term of media culture. The reason is that social media is now the main platform for individuals to create their national and cultural identities, which has produced a new phenomenon of a 'global village' or globalization.

The concept of globalization is also growing and has its distinctive features when it is applied to the discussion of the Olympic Games. Considering Olympic Games as media events, Roche distinguishes two paradigms of globalization, 'basic globalisation' and 'complex globalisation'.[4] These two paradigms demonstrate the development of the understanding of the concept of 'globalisation'. Globalization is not only a process of international integration but also a process to reveal the differentiation and particularization on the 'sub-national levels' and 'trans-national levels'. It is exactly this complex paradigm of globalization that inevitably invites various discussions on cultural phenomena.

Hence, we will briefly discuss the distinctions between multiculturalism, cross-culturalism and interculturalism with regard to the topic of cultural exchange in the postmodern cultural context. The discussion is limited in the range of media culture in order to distinguish its inner relationships, which are significant for further discussion. Based on this examination, we will pave the way for addressing the relationship between social media cultural exchange and Olympic Games in the context of globalization.

Multiculturalism

Multiculturalism is a broad concept that covers multiple cultural traditions in various aspects in different ethnic groups. This concept is mainly applied in political philosophy and used to respond to cultural and religious issues. Rosado articulates a definition of multiculturalism,

> Multiculturalism is a system of beliefs and behaviours that recognises and respects the presence of all diverse groups in an organisation or society, acknowledges and values their socio-cultural differences, and encourages and enables their continued contribution within an inclusive cultural context which empowers all within the organisation or society.[5]

From this definition, we can see, all diverse groups will be respected by their cultural diversity in social arrangements within a particular nation or cultural group, but the cultural interactivity between them is not a necessity.

Cross-culturalism

Cross-culturalism, by contrast, mainly deals with cultural interactivity, especially in literary and cultural studies. Compared to multiculturalism, this concept emphasizes how the diverse groups reach across cultural boundaries between nations or social groups, and thus are open to change. In the postmodern period, cross-culturalism indicates that the boundaries of human relationship would play a role of separation to clarify human existence but also could reveal deeper connections by revelation from the different other.[6]

Interculturalism

Multiculturalism defines its research objects in a particular nation or cultural group while cross-culturalism designates its objects between nations and social groups. Interculturalism refers to the interaction between people who are from different social or cultural groups when they come together. Cantle argues that 'Inter-culturalism can potentially offer a more dynamic model, capable of coping with ever changing patterns of diversity and hybrid identities'.[7]

From the brief review of these three concepts, it seems interculturalism would be the most appropriate concept for the discussion on the relationship between cultural exchanges via social media in the context of Olympic Games. However, there are controversial viewpoints on the distinction between 'multi-culturalism' and 'inter-culturalism', so we also need to clarify the controversies before we apply it to our discussion.

Cantle argues that interculturalism would replace multiculturalism as a framework because it provides a new model to support the cohesiveness of communities.[8] By comparison,

Meer and Modood give a 'no' to the question originally raised by Lentin about Cantle's argument – 'is inter-culturalism an 'updated version' of multiculturalism?'.[9] They argued that interculturalism should be able to provide a clear perspective in political discourse, otherwise, it only plays a complementary role to multiculturalism and is impossible to replace the concept of multiculturalism.[10] Levey, however, notes the distinction between 'hard' and 'soft' versions of interculturalism – hard mode emphasizes the fundamental difference between these two concepts, while soft mode accentuates the distinctive focuses between them.[11] But this 'hard-soft' dual paradigm cannot thoroughly clarify their distinction because the main distinction between these two terms lies in the political consideration behind all scenarios and both terms are semantically problematic because they 'conjure images of culturalism ruling the roots'.[12] From Levey's point of view, it is more significant to clarify the concepts and to correct confusions.[13] Thus, Bouchard has clarified the concept 'inter-culturalism' and provided some basic principles, paradigms and characteristics on it.[14] Although the main topic is intensively argued on the management of ethnocultural diversity in Quebec, this article significantly provides at great length seven characteristics of interculturalism.[15] These seven characteristics are: (1) majority/minorities duality; (2) a process of interaction; (3) the principles of harmonization: a civic responsibility; (4) integration and identity; (5) elements of *Ad Hoc* precedence for the majority culture; (6) a common culture; (7) the search for equilibriums. In addition, Bouchard also argues that interculturalism has essential roots in Europe 'as a formula for coexistence in the context of diversity'.[16] But we will maintain and extend it to the global context of Olympic Games in our discussion. In other words, interculturalism is also a formula for examining the coexistence of cultural diversity and exchange via social media for the Olympic Movement in the twenty-first century.

By means of proposing characteristics of interculturalism, Bouchard indeed provides a clearer platform for us to analyse our topic. Thus, we will concentrate on these characteristics and apply them to our study on the role of social media and the development of media culture in the Olympic context. These characteristics are particularly related to an overwhelming impact of social media on the Olympic Games. This phenomenon is named as 'socialympic'. In the next section, we will discuss the development of Olympic media and indicate how the developments affect the organization of Olympic Games.

Development of Olympic Media and its Impact on the Organization of Olympic Games

The relation between the roles of media and the organization of Olympic Games or the Olympic Movement has been discussed by several scholars since the late twentieth century.[17] Their focuses vary, from historical and commercial perspectives,[18] to cultural, international, supranational and global perspectives.[19] The Olympic Games are one of the most influential mega-events in the world, and so, they have a close relationship with various forms of media, especially in the time frame that we have set for this paper, from 2004 to 2012. During this time frame, media is not only the carrier that delivers the entire process of the Games but also an essential part of 'event-based popular cultural forms' and 'social movements'.[20] Thus, the development of Olympic media reflects the functions of media both at and in different time periods and indicates also its pattern and impact on the Olympic Games themselves in their history. The main function of Olympic media in the early twenty-first century, nonetheless, still partially follows the traditional functions of press, namely: 'to inform (the news function), to persuade (the advertising function), to entertain (the features function), and to pass on the cultural heritage (the educational function)'.[21] Therefore, we will start from the review on the impacts of these functions in traditional media.

Owing to his awareness on the importance of mass media, Baron Pierre de Coubertin devoted a considerable amount of his efforts in public relations expertise with respect to promoting the Olympic Games in the form of newspapers and magazines.[22] This is the first period of the development. From the beginning of the modern Olympic Games, for instance, 'sports writers' for 'sports pages' had been set up in order to satisfy the enthusiastic needs of the 'athletic craze' in the United States.[23] In comparison to newspapers and magazines, which would retell the Olympic performances in a heroic, historic and even mythic way, radio in its way had the capacity to deliver the major sports events '"to the world" as a "live" event at which an international audience would feel *as if* they were "present" as witnesses',[24] especially in the 1932 Los Angeles Olympics and the 1936 Berlin Olympics. At this time, the press was the main format of mass media and still dominated the sources of Olympic news until television entered the everyday life of the audience: the 'event-witness function' has overwhelmed the 'noticeboard/record-keeping function'.[25]

During the second period of 'television before satellites' (1936–1964),[26] television started to transform the nature of the organization of Olympic Games on 1 August 1936, in Berlin. It was the opening of the 'TV age of sports'.[27] This can be discussed, but is not limited to two aspects. The first is that, in this period, the Olympic Games develop into a 'media event' as television becomes increasingly popular. According to Roche, 'A criterion for qualifying as a media event is that people in many nations feel obliged to watch and feel privileged to be able to witness the event'.[28] This accessibility and popularity of television, therefore, provides the possibility for the participants to 'be there', though in the form of compensation by means of moving pictures, information and commentary, and so forth. With regard to the 'media event' features, Dayan and Katz remark that there are three partners for television events: the organizers, the broadcasters and the audiences. The main function of the organizers is to properly allocate all required elements for the Games; the main function of the broadcasters is to reproduce and deliver information about the Games to the audiences; the main function of the audiences is to receive the information from the broadcasting and to witness the event. All these partners are indispensable for completing a media event for television.[29] Roche adds that the state and market should also be taken into account when considering the 'informal social contract' of the 'negotiated partners' in a media event.[30] The analyses of these elements emphasize the significant roles of media in the context of Olympic Games. Without the development of media, especially in the form of television in this period, the scale and the influence of the Olympic Games would not be so crucially turned into such global public events that can 'make history',[31] but they would just be sporting events in the history of their time. The second aspect of the 'TV age of sports' indicates the commercial relationship between media and the Olympic Games. Slater observes that the Melbourne 1956 Games is a 'key turning point' in this relationship because, at this stage, the realization is that the 'Olympics could be a source of profit'.[32] When we analyze the Olympic Games as a 'sports-media complex'[33] or a 'complex cultural form',[34] the commercial feature of Olympic television as a hidden Olympic movement element must be acknowledged. The organizations of the Games, after all, need revenue and the sale of television rights for the

Olympic Games provides financial profit. Therefore, it is obviously exceedingly difficult to keep the balance of the leading forces between media, the market, the state and the Games.

This situation lasts and even deepens till the third period of 'Satellite Television before the Internet' (1968–1988).[35] The main change here is that satellite enables real-time broadcasting of the Olympic Games, which leads to a continuous increase in broadcasting rights fees.[36] Meanwhile, various corporate sponsorships form the major source of income of the organization of the Olympic Games, though it also decreases the dependence on television rights. Thus, it is not surprising to note that the situation of providing and maintaining an unbalanced relationship between the needs and pressure of financial support and the autonomous rights of the Olympic Committee has been a major struggle. Who, or, perhaps more accurately, what, then, is playing the leading role in the organization of the Olympic Games? At this stage, this question is no longer hidden but decisive regarding the further development of the Games.

In order to answer this question, the IOC explained a new strategy, which indicates that the development enters a fourth period, 'the era of Olympic dominance' (from around 1992 into the future):

> Included in the broadcasting agreements are the rights to broadcast Games for which host cities have not yet been chosen, a clear indication that choice of city is in no way influenced by the commercial considerations of broadcasters ... Previously there used to be extended debate over broadcasting time-zones and the value of the local market to sponsors. All of this is now of minimal importance as broadcasters and sponsors focus on the global nature of the Games.[37]

The determination of the IOC, therefore, demonstrates, on the one hand, the global influence of the Olympic Games in the Olympic television period and, on the other hand, shows a concern to maintain the significant global nature of the Olympics over the impact of media. This has been further specified in the annual Olympic Broadcasting Reports.[38]

From the foregoing discussion, the four distinct time periods have been reviewed in relation to the role of 'media event' and the role of 'commerce' in the process of the organization of the Olympic Games. The development of media, however, did not stop but reached another stage, which came into prominence for the organizers and spectators of the Olympic Games in the early twenty-first century. This phenomenon emerged from the 2008 Beijing Olympic Games and evolved into a mature form in the 2012 London Olympic Games. In the consideration of the development of a media event and its impact on the Olympic Games, I agree with Larson and Park's view that a long-term view of a media event should be taken rather than a short-term view, though their concerns were mainly on the 'Socio-Political Process'.[39] Therefore, in the next section, we will take the broadcasting of the Olympic Games (2004–2012) as a case study in order to outline and assess the interaction between the new form of media, social media with Internet and mobile platforms, and the Olympic Games. The following questions will be explored and answered: (1) What are the differences between these three Olympic Games in regard to broadcasting; (2) What is the new form of the media and its new features as distinct from the media forms in the previous four periods?; (3) What is the impact of this new media on the reception and our understanding of the Olympic Games?

A Case Study: The Opening Ceremonies and Broadcasting of Olympic Games (2004–2012)

It is both of importance and of significance to take together and analyze the broadcasting of the three Olympic Games hosted by Athens, Beijing and London from 2004 to 2012 because this time span reflects the major shifts and factors in the historical, social, cultural and economic elements that contribute to the organization of the Games and, in particular, the crucial information of the 'opening ceremonies' and the formative factors of the broadcasting. In this section, therefore, we will begin by briefly reviewing the content of the opening ceremonies of these three Games, and then compare the data of the performance of the audiences provided by Olympic Broadcast Reports, for the purpose of noting the changes in approaches and changes of audience receptions in relation to these three Games. We will further demonstrate the new form of media and its features which has emerged from the Beijing and London Olympic Games.

Athens 2004

The opening ceremony of Athens 2004 was held on 13 August 2004 and the motto of the Games was 'Welcome Home'. Athens Olympic Broadcasting, as the host broadcaster, provided high definition for the first time in Olympic Games broadcasting history.[40] The opening ceremony was directed by Greek dancer and choreographer Dimitris Papaioannou. The ceremony unfolded the nationalist sentiments on the reflections between the 'ancient Greece' and 'new Greece'.[41] The 'ancient Greece' recorded the first modern Olympic Games in history in 1896 and the 'new Greece' witnessed the postmodern Olympic Games after more than 100 years. By presenting the symbols that were used in the ceremony, both the historical significance of the Olympic spirit and the recurrence of the ancient Greek civilization recalled the audience reception on the foundation of Western civilization.

Beijing 2008

The opening ceremony of the Olympic Games in Beijing was held on 8 August 2008 and the motto of the Games was 'One World, One Dream'. This was the first time in its history that China hosted the Olympic Games and the director was Chinese filmmaker Zhang Yimou. The main theme of the opening ceremony was harmony and this theme penetrated the event by use of different patterns of manifestations, e.g. scroll painting, written characters, opera. As articulated in a report, the central ideas of this opening ceremony were peace, unity and friendship, which indicate the concept of harmony.[42] The use of symbolism is a common feature of many opening ceremonies and Zhang is famous for using symbolic images and performances to illustrate cultural elements with Chinese characteristics. Under the main theme 'harmony', a similar sub-theme is comparable to Athens 2004's opening ceremony, which is the harmonious coexistence of historical traditions and modern development.[43]

London 2012

The opening ceremony of the London 2012 Olympic Games was held on 27 July 2012 and the motto of these Games was 'Inspire a Generation'. This was the fourth time in its history

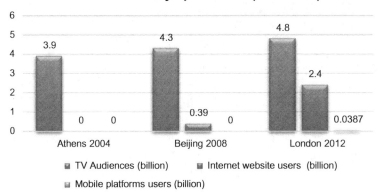

Chart 1. Source: Chart 1 is tabulated according to the 'Athens 2004 Olympic Broadcast Report', '(Beijing 2008) Global Television and Online Media Report' and '(London 2012) Global Broadcast Report'.[63]

that the United Kingdom hosted the Games in London. It was directed by Danny Boyle, who is famous for winning an Academy Award. The opening ceremony also prolifically collected representative symbols and cinematic images to show the British history of struggles, political change, literary tradition, cultural movements and the British sense of humour. Children and young people featured in the ceremony reflected the motto for inspiring a generation, which also shared the theme of 'the past versus the future' with the previous two opening ceremonies.

Analysis

By analyzing the opening ceremonies as significant 'mega-events' and 'media-events', the motivation of the directors, which represented the organizers and producers, as well as reviewing the main content of the ceremonies regarding the embedded cultural elements, we will move to the third partner of a television event, the data analyses of broadcasting for the whole process of these three Olympic Games.

By comparing data from these three reports provided by Olympic Game organizers, especially in relation to the changes of 'Media forms' and 'Data of Internet and mobile platform', we can see the dramatic evolution of the media form towards the newly emerging social media via the Internet and mobile platforms. Though the television coverage and the number of the audiences, as traditional mass media have kept expanding stably, online and mobile platforms have shown a momentum of rapid development. This raises important questions: For instance, can we still define these online and mobile platform users as 'audiences' in a traditional way? Can we say that broadcasting must now be understood in a broader sense because the idea regarding whether or how to view the Games will be decided by individuals at hand, and not exclusively in the hands of broadcasting networks? The interaction on the Olympic topics has obviously been extended from one-sided communication to reciprocal communication. This raises the question: What kind of social, cultural and economic impact on the organization of the Games will occur with the change from the traditional television to online and mobile platforms?

With regard to the analyses on the traditional mass media, firstly we will look at MacAloon's later work. He analyzes four genres of the contemporary Olympic Games: 'festival', 'ritual', 'spectacle' and 'game',[44] which are intensively presented in the opening ceremony, and certainly, in the competitions. The analyses will mainly target the opening ceremony because this worldwide-witness event has already displayed the first three genres of the Olympic Games, as a prologue of the Olympic Games. And in the context of the 'TV age of sports' or 'Olympic TV', the spectacle genre from these four has taken over the priority of the other genres,[45] especially the development of technology has provided a high-tech platform to realize the request of both the organizers and the audiences.

The content of the opening ceremony specifically reflects the inner connections between the organizers or producers and the audiences. Since commercial elements, however, have become inextricably related to the organization of the Olympic Games, the entire process of the Games necessarily becomes part of the Olympic industry. And opening ceremonies, as the most important symbols of this industry, are cultural and political festivals to demonstrate the Olympic meanings and values from both national and international perspectives. The organizers convey the echo of national history, popular culture, symbols and identities of the tradition, and, in a word, all the aspects that represent the essence of the host countries along with their understanding and expression of peaceful internationalism by means of mixtures of images and messages. The audience reception of watching both the opening ceremony and games can be discussed, at least, in two aspects. The first is the local audience who would receive the sense of national and historical identity, national pride and cultural citizenship, etc. The second is the audience from all over the world, who would receive new national and new 'post-national' conceptions from the ceremony in the context of globalization.

During the time period of 2004–2012, these three Olympic Games were held in a postmodern period, but they still maintained the mythic and ritual elements in the opening ceremony, while at the same time, strengthened the 'consumer culture', notably, with the development of mobile devices, which has maximized the autonomous roles of the ordinary audience and sports fans in the Olympic Movement. In other words, from these three Games, we have seen major, real and significant changes in the interaction between the organizers and audiences (individually, nationally and internationally) both from the opening ceremonies as well as in the competitions. It is, nonetheless, difficult to obtain a clear evaluation of the exact impact of this change precisely because it is developing so rapidly. We can say, however, that the fifth period of the relationship between the media and the Olympic Games has arrived – the period of 'Socialympic'.

It has been pointed out that the 2012 London Olympic Game was the most connected Olympics because of the overwhelming use of social media which, in turn, brought in 'Socialympics'. Various forms of social media contributed to this new wave, for example, Twitter, YouTube, Facebook, live blogs and so forth. As indicated in Chart 1, social media unofficially connected to the Beijing Olympics in an experimental way, but four years later the advancement of social media broke into the field of everyone's vision.

This can be proved by a statistic which demonstrates more detailed information about this change. Facebook only had less than one million members at the 2004 Olympics in Athens. The number of members increased to 90 million at the 2008 Beijing Olympics and by the time of the London 2012 Olympics Facebook had nearly 1 billion members.[46] According to the most updated statistics from Facebook.com, '[there are] 1.09 billion daily active users on average for March 2016; 989 million mobile daily active users on average for March 2016; 1.65 billion monthly active users as of March 31, 2016; 1.51 billion mobile monthly active users as of March 31, 2016; Approximately 84.2% of our daily active users are outside the US and Canada'.[47] The situation of Twitter is similar. Twitter started in 2006 and there were around 3 million active users during the Beijing Games.[48] Today, there are 310 million monthly active users and 1 billion unique visits monthly to sites with embedded Tweets. 83% of active users are on mobile facilities and 79% of accounts are outside the US. Twitter also supports more than 40 languages.[49]

The statistics of Facebook and Twitter, as examples, show the trend of future expansion of social media on the Olympic Games. The legislation issues of Socialympics have also been noted.[50] Accordingly, we can summarize some characteristics of Socialympics: (1) it is an online Olympic Hub to connect fans with athletes via social media accounts. Traditional media is no longer the only source to access the news as well as the comments of the players and winners of the Games. (2) Sponsors on social media are more flexible and extensive. This will bring in more career opportunities to individuals who work online for the Games. (3) The social media connects the digital world to the physical world,[51] for example, offline activities organized by online groups. There are also negative voices on the role of social media, which mainly concern athletes' personal privacy.[52]

In sum, social media provides opportunities for individuals not only to witness the Olympic Games, by viewing the opening and closing ceremonies or competitions but also for them to contact athletes both from their own nations and from other countries. The organizers can offer more feature materials and instant news online; audiences can express their comments and exchange information. In this sense, social media realizes the idea of 'desiring to see the local (self) as part of the global (Olympics)'.[53] Social media users, therefore, have achieved the situation of 'being-there' with the athletes globally, technically speaking.

Thus, we can answer the questions raised earlier in this section. Regarding the first question, it is no longer appropriate to define the online and mobile platform users as traditional 'audiences'. According to the characteristics of Socialympic, the users would not just listen to or watch particular television or radio programmes. They would also leave comments at various platforms. The users' comments would be published widely and instantly through these platforms, which would not only be received by other users, but also by athletes who attend the Games and the organizers of the Games. Given this background, the relation between users, the relation between users and athletes and the relation between users and organizers implicate the features of interculturalism. All these relations carry duality and interaction in the global sense. Although the host city or country would highlight its majority culture, the global nature of the Games and the international nature of the social media provide a platform or space for other cultures to speak and communicate with ongoing communication on the same topic (the Olympic Games), which also have been deepening cultural exchange.

For the second question, Socialympic, as an emerging and developing phenomenon, decides that the spreading of information is no longer unidirectional but bidirectional or multidirectional. Socialympic is not only about information sharing but more about creating communities or networks for processing interaction on specific topics. These features of Socialympic indicate that, nowadays, broadcasting has to be understood in a broader sense because social media includes the technologies of delivering information as well as the functions of generating new approaches of sharing. For example, hashtag or metadata tag is a type of label used on social networks for efficiently spreading and sharing hot topics on particular events. Individuals could use hashtag to process 'deep mining' for searching most relevant information about the topic, e.g. the Olympic Games. In this way, social networks are multilayers; the structures of information are diverse and media culture are inclusive to users from different backgrounds.

With reference to the last question, at the current stage, there is no confirmed answer on the social, cultural and economic impact brought forth by the Socialympic because Socialympic itself is still a developing phenomenon. However, we can anticipate that issues of interculturalism will be embedded in all these impacts. Our review on the complex paradigm of globalization in section two indicates that globalization has developed into another stage where standardization or integration has been withdrawn while differentiation and particularization have been accentuated. Social media platforms are exactly the places for the audiences to express their comments in the 'sub-national levels' and 'trans-national levels' on Olympic related issues. This is a paradoxical situation: social media is a powerful approach to accelerate the process of international integration, while it also provides platforms for users to express their individual voices. This mechanism interestingly matches with the organization of the Games. As Roche argued, the Olympic Games is a global event as well as a media event. In this global event, the achievement of the Olympic Moto 'Swifter, Higher, Stronger' can only be realized by athletes' continuous breakthroughs. Successful organization of this event brings active participation of people from all over the world, in the past, by means of traditional media and today, social media connects organizers, audiences and athletes.

In this regard, as channels of communication, the social media platforms bring Game organizers, audiences and athletes from around the world together producing a highly globalized phenomenon which impacts socially, politically and economically on various aspects of our daily life. Yet, it is cultural exchange in particular that is arguably the first and foremost element which is embedded in these impacts. Thus in the next section, we will discuss cultural exchange via social media in the context of globalization.

Media Cultural Exchange and Olympic Games in Globalization

After we reviewed the development of Olympic media and its impact on the organization of the Olympic Games and work on the case study of the changes of the broadcasting of the 2004–2012 Olympic Games, we tentatively proposed that the fifth period of 'Socialympics' has arrived. In order to examine the theoretical foundation for cultural exchange under a new form of cultural exchange via social media, we also evaluated various voices on the concept of culture and its most updated development. In this section, therefore, we will intensively deliberate on media cultural exchange and Olympic Games in the context of globalization.

When MacAloon commented on 'the spectacle dimension of Olympics in the television age', he intimated that there would be both negative and positive implications for the ritual dimension of the Games but that there would consistently be a negative impact for the festive character of the Games.[54] The reason he gives is that the Olympics on television would bring in 'inequalities and hierarchies of sport 'stars'.[55] According to Roche, 'Olympic TV addresses itself to presenting just such a unitary event, prioritising some (dominant, official) perspectives and narratives over others'.[56] Yet the emerging worldwide use of social media has changed the forms of exchange, most of which are embedded in the background of cultural exchange with the characteristics of interculturalism. For people who can afford the relevant electronics, social media has been a platform for life, or even a way of their daily life. Cultural exchange via social media has been boosted in every corner of our life to search for the right of individuals' voices, which includes the Olympic Games – an event that invites the host country to manifest its tradition, history and current development; an event that invites athletes from all over the world to compete in a fair play environment; an event that invites audiences from every country to witness achievements of human physical ability via athletic performances and exchange their excitements and opinions with the most convenient approach through social media.

Therefore, the mechanism of social media instinctively shuns 'inequalities and hierarchies', of sport 'stars' (social users can follow their favourite athletes' social media account to express their support) or of sport 'types' (social media would avoid the issue of the coverage rate of the unitary broadcasting system, for example, traditional broadcasting usually gives more coverage of the more popular sports type according to audience rating and sponsors' interest). We argue that this change is significant for both the users of social media and the organizers of the Olympic Games. The geographical and climatic factors of the participating countries determine the fact that athletes from each country would have different types of sports that they are competent in. The different populations of the participating countries will also influence the broadcasting rate of various sports competitions. Olympic TV presents the Olympic Games as a unitary event with a unitary approach but social media offers multi-layered platforms for users to be aware of all these deeper factors existing in every aspect of the Olympic Games, when they search their favourite athletes or sports from these platforms, when they share their comments on the platforms and when they communicate with the users from completely different backgrounds. In this sense, an Olympic event is not only a media event, but also a cultural event. It is an event that links people together, deepening their understanding of sport and the Olympic Idea.

Therefore, we argue that by means of social media, the Olympic Idea can be delivered in the most efficient and original way. This ideal is stated in the first fundamental principle of Olympism,

> Olympism is a philosophy of life, exalting and combining in a balanced whole the qualities of body, will and mind. Blending sport with culture and education, Olympism seeks to create a way of life based on the joy found in effort, the educational value of good example and respect for universal fundamental ethical principles.[57]

The goal of the Olympic Movement also reflects this ideal,

> The goal of the Olympic Movement is to contribute to building a peaceful and better world by educating youth through sport practiced without discrimination of any kind and in the Olympic spirit, which requires mutual understanding with a spirit of friendship, solidarity and fair play.[58]

The characteristics of the social media can be seen as containing five aspects: (1) participation; (2) openness; (3) conversation; (4) communities; (5) connectedness.[59] And interactivity, which is a defining feature of social media, connects these five characteristics as an essential factor.[60] Thus, these characteristics of social media meet the requirements of the goal of the Olympic Movement and the ideal, which the Olympics seeks.

Conclusion

The main concern of this paper is the intercultural exchange of social media users on the Olympic Games. From the foregoing discussion, the social media users, not in the traditional sense of audiences, can connect directly with their favourite sports stars, participate in online events, join online communities and have instant conversations with athletes or other users. These are entirely based on the premise that social media costs very little, is easy to manage and is quicker for updates and communication. If the Olympic Games provides the opportunity for a regular venue to set up 'a global village' every four years, social media now has become a tool of cultural transformation within this village.[61] The presentation of local and cultural structures of the host nations can be detected instantaneously from the opening to the closing ceremonies. In the competition of the Games, we also can see and find cultural traces of other countries from the presentation of their athletes. And, by virtue of online means of social media individuals from many different cultures can 'be there' and 'be with' athletes and audiences interacting interculturally at the global village of the Olympic Movement.

All these elements of the Olympic Games, as global media events, reflect the characteristics of globalization. As we have mentioned in the second section, Roche distinguishes two paradigms of globalization, 'basic globalisation' and 'complex globalisation'.[62] He argues that the Olympics should be considered in a complex context, while Olympic television, as a global 'media event', shows the perspective of 'basic globalisation' because the way that television delivers information is standardized and uniform with a deterministic process and audiences, in a traditional sense, view the ceremonies or competitions from nearly the same angle. The comments from the interpreters mainly represent the national guidance of public opinion. The examination of cultural exchange via social media of the Olympics, as we argue, should adopt the complex paradigm. The complex paradigm emphasizes the duality of individual and collective effort, national and international organizations, which implicate differentiation and particularization. Furthermore, the complex paradigm recognizes the temporal and spatial differences on sub-national and transnational levels. The complex paradigm characteristics of social media correspond to the interculturalism formula, which we have already discussed above, when we further studied the coexistence of cultural diversity and exchange in the Olympic Movement.

Social media has been growing rapidly in an unpredictable way since it first stepped on the stage of the 2008 Beijing Olympic Games. The 2012 London Olympics brought the word Socialympics' into our vision, but it is just at a starting point or an early stage for researches on the topic of this paper. Further research requires more specific data and interdisciplinary support for collecting necessary information. Faced with these changes and challenges, our research interest is and will be on the cultural exchange issue of the Olympic Games, especially in relation to the intercultural perspective and paradigms since this is a dynamic process happening in our daily life.

Notes

1. T.S. Eliot, *Notes Towards the Definition of Culture* (London: Faber & Faber 2010), xv.
2. Ibid., 1.
3. Douglas Kellner, *Media Culture: Cultural Studies, Identity and Politics between the Modern and the Post-Modern* (London: Routledge, 1995), i.

4. Maurice Roche, 'Olympic and Sport Mega-Events as Media-Events: Reflections on the Globalisation Paradigm', in Kevin Wamsley, Bob Barney and Scott Martyn (eds), *The Global Nexus Engaged: Past, Present, Future Interdisciplinary Olympic Studies* (London, ON: International Centre for Olympic Studies, University of Western Ontario, 2002), 2–3, The differences between Basic paradigm and Complex paradigm can be summarized as four perspectives, respectively. Basic paradigm: (1) globalization is a deterministic process; (2) it requires the promotion of standardization and uniformity in all spheres of life. (3) Globalization involves a historically unprecedented experience of 'one world' and of 'compression' of social space and time. (4) Globalization impacts are mainly felt at the national rather than sub- or transnational levels. Complex paradigm: (1) it also involves the possibility for collective agency and influence by political and cultural collectivizes such as nations and international organizations and movements. (2) It also involves differentiation and particularization; (3) it also involves the reconstruction of temporal and spatial distance and differences; (4) it also involves the sub-national levels and transnational levels.
5. Caleb Rosado, *Toward a Definition of Multiculturalism, for Change in Human Systems*, 1997, http://rosado.net/pdf/Def_of_Multiculturalism.pdf (accessed 27 June 2016), 2.
6. Yoshinobu Hakutani, *Postmodernity and Cross-Culturalism* (Madison: Fairleigh Dickinson University Press, 2002), 14. Hakutani comments, 'human existence can be achieved in ways that do not necessarily assert self by excluding other: truth is often a revelation from other'.
7. T. Cantle, *Interculturalism: The New Era of Cohesion and Diversity* (London: Palgrave Macmillan, 2012), 32.
8. Ibid., 2.
9. A. Lentin, 'Replacing "Race", Historizing the "Culture" in the Multiculturalism', *Patterns of Prejudice*, 39, no. 4 (2005), 379–96.
10. Nasar Meer and Tariq Modood, 'How Does Interculturalism Contrast with Multiculturalism?' *Journal of Intercultural Studies* 33, no. 2 (2012), 175. Original comments, '… until interculturalism as a political discourse is able to offer a distinct perspective, one that can speak to a variety of concerns emanating from complex identities and matters of equality and diversity in a more persuasive manner than at present, interculturalism cannot, intellectually at least, eclipse multiculturalism, and so should be considered as complementary to multiculturalism'.
11. Geoffrey B. Levey, 'Interculturalism vs. Multiculturalism: A Distinction Without a Difference?' *Journal of Intercultural Studies* 33, no. 2 (2012), 218.
12. Ibid., 223.
13. Ibid.
14. Gérard Bouchard, 'What is Interculturalism?' *McGill Law Journal* (2011), 437–68.
15. Ibid., 445–62.
16. Ibid., 437.
17. See, John Slater, 'Changing Partners: The Relationship Between the Mass Media and the Olympic Games', *Fourth International Symposium for Olympic Research* (Ontario: University of Western Ontario, 1998), 49–68; Also Maurice Roche, *Mega-Events and Modernity: Olympics and Expos in the Growth of Global Culture* (London: Routledge, 2000); Roche, 'Olympic and Sport Mega-Events as Media-events'; Bruce Kidd, 'The Olympic Movement and the Sports-Media Complex', *Sport in Society: Cultures, Commerce, Media, Politics* 16, no. 4 (2013), 439–48.
18. Slater, 'Changing Partners'.
19. Roche, *Mega-Events and Modernity,* and Roche, 'Olympic and Sport Mega-Events as Media-Events'.
20. Roche, *Mega-Events and Modernity*, 159.
21. Slater, 'Changing Partners', 51.
22. Ibid., 51.
23. Ibid. See also John J. MacAloon, *This Great Symbol: Pierre de Coubertin and the Origins of the Modern Olympic Games* (Chicago: University of Chicago Press, 1981).
24. Roche, *Mega-Events and Modernity*, 162. Emphasis added.
25. Ibid.
26. Four time periods were proposed by Slater.

27. Slater, 'Changing Partners', 53. Also, 'Olympics Lead in Appeal for Sports Experts: Dempsey-Schmeling Title Bout is Next Choice', *New York Times*, 22 January 1932, 23.
28. Roche, *Mega-Events and Modernity*, 164.
29. Daniel Dayan and Elihu Katz, *Media Events: The Live Broadcasting of History* (Cambridge: Harvard University Press, 1994), Chapter 3, especially page 54.
30. Roche, *Mega-Events and Modernity*, 164.
31. Ibid., 163.
32. Slater, 'Changing Partners', 53.
33. Sut Jhally, 'The Spectacle of Accumulation: Material and Cultural Factors in the Evolution of the Sport/Media Complex', *The Insurgent Sociologist* 12, no. 3 (1984), 41–57, also Kidd, 'The Olympic Movement and the Sports-Media Complex', 439–48.
34. John MacAloon, ed., *Rite, Drama, Festival, Spectacle* (Philadelphia: The Institute of Human Issues, 1984).
35. Slater, 'Changing Partners', 54.
36. Ibid. According to Slater, ibid., 55, 'In 1960, television provided only one of every four hundred dollars of the cost of hosting the summer Olympics. In 1972, one of every fifty dollars was provided by television; in 1980, one of every fifteen dollars; by 1984, one of every three dollars of Olympic host costs were paid for from television revenues'.
37. 'Olympic Marketing Agenda Established for New Millenium', *Marketing Matters: The Olympic Marketing Newsletter*, no. 8 (Spring 1996), 2. Also Slater, 'Changing Partners', 60.
38. For an example, see the original statement: 'To ensure the widest possible television audience for the Olympic Games, Olympic broadcast rights are sold to broadcast networks that can guarantee the broadest free-to-air coverage throughout their respective territories' in 'Athens 2004 Olympic Broadcast Report', 78, https://stillmed.olympic.org/media/Document%20Library/OlympicOrg/IOC/How_We_Do_It/Broadcasters/EN_Athens_2004_Broadcast_Report.pdf.
39. Roche, *Mega-Events and Modernity*, 187. Also J. Larson and H-S Park, *Global Television and the Politics of the Seoul Olympics* (Oxford: Westview Press, 1993).
40. 'Athens 2004 Olympic Broadcast Report', 77.
41. Jilly Traganou, *Designing the Olympics: Representation, Participation, Contestation* (New York: Routledge, 2016), 137.
42. Kim Bissell and Stephen Perry, *The Olympics, Media and Society* (New York: Routledge, 2015), 61; also Y. Tang, 'Beijing Olympic Opening Ceremony: Zhang Yimou Keeps Everyone Guessing', *China Today*, 3 (March 2008), 52–5.
43. For instance, the presentations on the four great inventions of ancient China and the hi-tech symbol of modern China. Luo Qing and Giuseppe Richeri, *Encoding the Olympics: The Beijing Olympic Games and the Communication Impact Worldwide* (London: Routledge, 2013), 189.
44. Roche, *Mega-Events and Modernity*, 165. See also Dayan and Katz, *Media Events*, 142–5.
45. Roche, *Mega-Events and Modernity*, 165.
46. Alpha Digital, http://alphadigital.com.au/socialympics-social-media-at-the-olympics/ (accessed 27 June 2016).
47. Source: Facebook, http://newsroom.fb.com/company-info/ (accessed 27 June 2016).
48. Alpha Digital, http://alphadigital.com.au/socialympics-social-media-at-the-olympics/ (accessed 27 June 2016).
49. Source: Twitter, https://about.twitter.com/company (accessed 27 June 2016).
50. Daniel McLaren, http://digitalsport.co/the-socialympics (accessed 27 June 2016).
51. Neil Vidyarthi, 'Social Times', http://www.adweek.com/socialtimes/the-london-2012-socialympics-infographic/103811 (accessed 27 June 2016).
52. Alpha Digital, http://alphadigital.com.au/socialympics-social-media-at-the-olympics/ (accessed 27 June 2016).
53. Roche, *Mega-Events and Modernity*, 191. See also M. de M. Spa, N. Rivenburgh, and J. Larson, *Television in the Olympics* (Luton: John Libbey Media, 1995), 248.
54. Roche, *Mega-Events and Modernity*, 166.
55. Ibid.

56. Ibid.
57. International Olympic Committee, 'Olympic Charter', 2015, 13.
58. Ibid., 17.
59. S.R. Veil, T. Buehner, and M.J. Palenchar, 'A Work-in-Process Literature Review: Incorporating Social Media in Risk and Crisis Communication', *Journal of Contingencies and Crisis Management* 19, no. 2 (2011), 110–22. See also Angle Tesorero, 'The Characteristics of Social Media', Home of Service, 2013, http://homeofservice.com/blogs/21/the-characteristics-of-social-media/#.V3E5nvkrK70 (accessed 27 June 2016).
60. W. Timothy Coombs, *Ongoing Crisis Communication: Planning, Managing, and Responding*, 4th ed. (California: Sage, 2014), 19.
61. Marshall McLuhan used the term 'global village' in 1962 in his book, *The Gutenberg Galaxy: The Making of Typographic Man* (Toronto: University of Toronto Press, 1962), 31: 'But certainly the electro-magnetic discoveries have recreated the simultaneous "field" in all human affairs so that the human family now exists under conditions of a "global village"'.
62. Roche, 'Olympic and Sport Mega-Events as Media-Events', 2–3.
63. 'Olympic Broadcast Reports' (2004–2012).

Disclosure Statement

No potential conflict of interest was reported by the author.

ORCID

Yinya Liu http://orcid.org/0000-0002-9406-4384

A Game for the Global North: The 2018 Winter Olympic Games in Pyeongchang and South Korean Cultural Politics

Jung Woo Lee

ABSTRACT
The South Korean region of Pyeongchang will host the 2018 Winter Olympic Games. Using Wallerstein's world system theory and Collins's notions of zones of prestige and emulation as a conceptual framework, this paper examines the South Korean Government's intention to stage the winter sporting spectacle. As the Winter Olympics is arguably considered a game for the relatively affluent global north, South Korea, as a semi-core state, attempts to elevate its position to a global economic and cultural powerhouse through being a host of this winter sports mega-event. However, it should be noted that the Winter Olympic Games is an event through which white supremacy and Western cultural hegemony are continuously reinforced. Therefore, the South Korean ambition to enhance its international standing by staging the Winter Olympic Games paradoxically reflects Western cultural imperialism and Orientalism embedded in South Korean cultural politics associated with the winter sporting contest.

Introduction

A sports mega-event has become one of the most discussed academic topics in the field of sport studies today. With the notion of globalization emerging as a major conceptual framework, many social scientists have paid their attention to political, cultural and economic implications of a global mega sporting event.[1] In terms of global politics, major international competitions such as the Olympic Games or the FIFA World Cup Finals are seen as an effective diplomatic instrument, often linked to the concept of soft power, for enhancing the international reputation of host countries.[2] Also, a range of political activist groups and non-governmental organizations utilize these sporting occasions as a platform to demonstrate their causes to the world audiences.[3] Concerning global culture, a sports mega-event offers dynamic cultural space wherein the interface between globalism and nationalism is actively at work within which various social identities are represented and contested.[4] Moreover, a regular occurrence of international championships has facilitated a global diffusion of modern sport which is arguably the most universal form of global culture.[5] With regard to the global economy, a global sporting spectacle functions as an ideological apparatus that reinforces a neoliberal sense of global capitalism and consumerism.[6] Additionally, transnational companies also attempt to maximize their business interests by taking part in sport event sponsorship programmes and by implementing advertising campaigns associated with global sporting festivals.[7] These are all indicative of the fact that while sports mega-events are essentially an athletic contest, this sporting dimension alone cannot fully explain their operating mechanisms.

In July 2011, the International Olympic Committee (IOC) declared that the 2018 Winter Olympic Games will be held in the South Korean region of Pyeongchang. The South Korean media unanimously celebrated the IOC's decision, and this media frame led to a sudden eruption of the mood of joyfulness and triumph in South Korean society.[8] Given that Pyeongchang had failed in its two previous Winter Olympic bids with only minor differences, such a feeling of excitement emerging in the country can be understandable. The perplexities are the reasons why this relatively humble mountainous district has been so eagerly willing to stage the massive winter sporting spectacle. As indicated above, promotion and performance of winter sports themselves do not provide sufficient explanation for more than a decade of Pyeongchang's Olympic 'dream'. It is also necessary to take into account political, cultural and economic circumstances wherein South Korea is located in order to understand the motivation and rationale behind a series of the uncompromising Winter Olympic bidding campaigns. This study, therefore, undertakes a social scientific and historical inquiry into the South Korean intention to host the Winter Olympic Games. Through this research, it aims at identifying major political goals that the South Korean Government tries to achieve by hosting this winter sports mega-event.

This type of research requires a comprehensive examination of the social changes that South Korea has undergone, and of the role that a sports mega-event plays in the process of political and economic development in this region. The paper adopts this holistic approach. As this study is primarily concerned with the Pyeongchang Olympics, it first critically evaluates the sociocultural meaning of the Winter Olympic Games in general. After this, it will look at the structure of global politics and economy so that the current status of South Korea within the system of the global political economy can be identified. Then, this paper reviews major sports mega-events held in South Korea from the 1986 Summer Asian Games to the 2018 Winter Olympic Games with specific reference to the political and economic environment that affect the organization of these events. This is followed by an investigation into the Pyeongchang Winter Olympics with the aim of uncovering the underlying political and cultural undertone of this winter sport festival. Finally, a critical reading of the South Korean desire for hosting the Winter Olympics is offered.

The Winter Olympics: The 'White' Games?

The Winter Olympic Games may not be regarded as a so-called first-order sporting event in terms of an economic impact, global media interests and the number of participating countries.[9] When considering these objective measures, this quadrennial winter sport competition is a smaller scale event in comparison with the Summer Olympic Games and the FIFA World Cup Finals. However, this international contest of snow and ice sports has unique cultural implications. In principle, it is a sporting competition through which Western hegemony and a discourse of white supremacy are continually represented and reproduced.[10] Unlike its summer counterpart, where athletes from various parts of the world with diverse cultural and ethnic identities compete for Olympic medals, the Winter Olympic

Games is largely dominated by Western white competitors. In the almost hundred years of its history, only six nations, namely Russia (the Soviet Union), Germany, Norway, the United States, Austria and Finland have won nearly two-thirds of the awarded medals at the Winter Olympics.[11] In addition, Olympic medal winners still have predominantly been Caucasian athletes although the presence of East Asian skaters has recently challenged this almost complete white exclusiveness. With regard to equity in sport, the paucity of black athletes both in the North American and European national teams and in African and Caribbean countries' delegates is particularly problematic in this winter sport championship.[12]

This overt representation of white athletes from Western countries at the Winter Olympic Games implies the existing practice of racial segregation in this global sporting event. Unequal racial relations in sport are nothing new. Yet, at the Winter Olympic Games, the structural exclusion of non-white athletes appears to be a more taxing problem.[13] It seems that both economic and cultural factors influence these asymmetrical racial differences at the Winter Olympic Games. Obviously, taking part in winter sports such as skiing and snowboarding requires a significant amount of financial resources, and only relatively small groups of elites in society can afford such sporting luxuries. If this logic is applied to a global context, it can be argued that those in the relatively rich area of the global north which includes mainly North America and Europe have more opportunities to participate in these winter sporting activities. This also means that people in the relatively less developed region of the global south, which encompasses Sub-Saharan Africa, South America and South-East Asia, are unlikely to enjoy snow and ice sports. The factors concerning geography and climate may also affect this global north and south division. Yet, as Farhi aptly points out, such differences are mostly related to economic issues given that there are a plenty of snow-covered high mountains in Ethiopia, Nepal, Peru and Afghanistan.[14] Because equipment, facilities and training for winter sporting events cost much more than most summer Olympic sports, relatively poor countries in the global south have only a limited chance to partake in the Winter Olympic Games.

At the same time, the Winter Olympics is also a cultural domain in which discourse of white supremacy prevails.[15] It should be noted that both winter and summer editions of the Olympic Games contain Western-centric elements from the outset.[16] However, at the Summer Olympic Games, at least in the sporting fields, Western white hegemony has been increasingly challenged, although non-white dominant events such as athletics and basketball are ideologically exploited to construct a false stereotypical image of a specific racial group.[17] At the Winter Olympic Games such a challenge hardly exists. In fact, this winter sporting competition offers one of the few occasions where white elite athletes exclusively display their sporting prowess. As noted earlier, white athletes from the West have won a disproportionately large number of Winter Olympic medals and some snow sports, particularly snowboarding, are regarded as a culturally exclusive space for the white middle-class youth, the consequence of which raises a bar that prevents non-white individuals from joining this mainstream winter sporting culture.[18] Therefore, it is no surprise to see that when black athletes enter this field of 'white' sport, the media tend to pay attention to their peculiar characteristics instead of focusing on their sporting ability and athletic identity, with John Turteltaub's 1993 film *Cool Runnings* being a good example.[19] After all, this winter sporting festival functions as a cultural bastion of white privilege.

These observations suggest that every four years during the winter time relatively affluent North Americans and Europeans hold an exclusive cultural ritual to celebrate the white supremacy so that Western cultural hegemony and privilege are continually reaffirmed. The fact that the most editions of Winter Olympic Games have taken place in the West thus far also underpins the status of the Winter Olympics as the games for the global north.[20] Regarding this, one journalist rightfully wrote that the Olympic winter edition is Westerners' 'expensive sports festival' which glorifies 'elitism, exclusion, and the triumph of the world sporting haves over its have-nots'.[21] Recently, a few skaters from South Korea, China and Japan have begun to list their names on the Olympic medal tables. Moreover, the next two editions of the Winter Olympic Games have been awarded to the South Korean province of Pyeongchang and the Chinese capital city, Beijing. That said, it is legitimate to ask a question about why these East Asian cities, particularly Pyeongchang, had so much desired to win the Winter Olympic bid for more than 10 years, even if this winter sporting spectacle is mainly a party for the West. The following section attempts to find a clue to this question.

The Structure of Global Economy and Cultural Politics

In order to understand the motivation behind the South Korean desire to host the Winter Olympic Games, it is important to examine the economic and cultural transformation that the country has undergone since the 1980s. Wallerstein's world systems theory,[22] and Collins's notion of zones of prestige,[23] offer useful conceptual tools for a systematic investigation of the characteristics of Korean society. The world system theory is mainly concerned with unequal power relations between the nations within the economic structure of the international division of labour.[24] More specifically, it divides the world into three distinctive blocs according to an economic role that each nation plays within the global production network. These are the core, the semi-periphery and the periphery. In this world system, the core countries are positioned at the centre of the global capitalist market. They accumulate a disproportionately large amount of financial capital, and the major cities within the global core region function as a node of international economic flows.[25] Their economic growth is primarily sustained by the operation and investment in knowledge and information industry. The concentration of the experience and knowledge-based technology in the core countries gives rise to the information inequality amongst the three areas in the world system, and this difference results in widening the economic and knowledge gap between them.[26] Such an unequal access to information technology, which is the fundamental component of the global economy today, brings more power and hegemony to the core in the system of global capitalism.[27] In a geographical term, North America and Western Europe are considered the global core in the world system.

The periphery indicates a comparatively less developed part of the world whose economic growth primarily relies on exporting raw materials.[28] The nature of society in this marginalized area is still largely agricultural and it shows a relatively low level of industrialization. Because the peripheral countries usually do not have a sustainable means of income generation, their development depends heavily on the trade with the global core countries and the economic assistance from them. This dependency gives rise to the unequal power relations between the core and the periphery. In this circumstance, it is not uncommon to see that the core countries exploit labour forces and natural resources in the periphery in order to maximize their profit.[29] The most nations in sub-Saharan Africa, South-East Asia and South America display the characteristics of the periphery.

The semi-periphery refers to the countries that are positioned between the core and the periphery. These are nations whose society is undergoing rapid industrialization including the construction of infrastructure for information and knowledge-based economies. While the semi-peripheral countries usually have a competitive domestic market, their industry is still largely export-driven where labour-intensive manufacturing industry constitutes one of the major economic driving forces.[30] Additionally, the semi-peripheral nations also attempt to attract foreign direct investment mainly from the global core in order to facilitate their economic growth.[31] This means that moderate economic dependency to the core still exists. At the same time, the semi-periphery also establishes economic ties with the periphery which supplies relatively cheap raw materials to the manufacturing industry of the former.[32] This builds mutually interdependent relations between the two blocs. Generally, newly emerging states such as the Asian Tigers in the 1980s and the BRICS in 2010s can be categorized as the semi-periphery in the global economic structure.

South Korea has undergone a process of the compressed capitalist industrialization from one of the poorest in the 1950s to the one of the richest in the present time.[33] With reference to the world system theory, the country is now arguably located between the core and the semi-periphery. As one of the emerging economic powerhouses in the East Asia in the 1980s, South Korea exemplified a typical semi-peripheral country at that time.[34] Today, South Korea has become an even more important economic player whose main strength lies in information and high-tech industry. Still, the country shows the characteristics of an export-driven economy. Yet, it no longer entirely relies on exporting manufactured products. South Korea is now one of the leading developers of information and communication technology, which provides this East Asian country with major leveraging forces in its international trade.[35] In that sense, in economic terms, the nature of South Korean society is similar to that of the core countries. Nevertheless, South Korea is not yet fully recognized as the core advanced economy, and the reason being so is arguably the permeation of Western hegemony in the sphere of global culture.

With regard to global cultural politics, Collins's notion of zones of prestige provides a valuable theoretical tool for conceptualizing the relation between the Western hegemony and the South Korean aspiration to join the global core. Zones of prestige can be defined as 'multiple and singular centre where culturally impressive activities are produced, displayed and consumed'.[36] According to this theory, those countries whose cultural heritage and legacies significantly influence other nations can be seen as the established in the global power relations.[37] By contrast, those nations, the cultural products of which are not as much attractive and sought after as those in the established, are featured as outsiders.[38] Amongst these outsiders, some countries tend to emulate the cultural practice of the established with aspirations to obtain a more privileged cultural resource that the nations in the zones of prestige hold. Places, where this cultural imitation occurs, are called zones of emulation. Of course, it should be highlighted that the relations between zones of prestige and emulation are a clear reflection of existing cultural hegemony which presumes a specific cultural form, particularly Western culture, is somewhat superior, or at least more attractive, to that of the outsiders. Thus, this conceptual division is rightfully a subject for critical interpretation as it simply reinforces the concept of Western cultural imperialism. Nevertheless, a realistic snapshot of cultural politics today suggests that amongst others Western cultural products are the most widely circulated and most extensively consumed commodities.[39] Hence, it can be argued that the notions of the zones of prestige and emulation more or less objectively describe hegemonic cultural relations between different cultural zones in the world.

Some elements of sport are considered as the culturally impressive activities which help enhance the prestige of the nation. In the realm of cultural politics, sport becomes a useful resource simply because it constitutes a significant part of the contemporary popular culture industry.[40] Moreover, commodities associated with sports are globally circulated cultural currencies to which a desirable symbolic value is ascribed.[41] Additionally, sport products in some countries often turn into attractive cultural capital which can be strategically exploited for maximizing the country's soft power.[42] Yet, sport as a cultural utility is not equally distributed in the world. Rather, almost every valuable asset in the global sport industry either mainly reflects sporting culture in the West or is largely owned by Western stakeholders. In other words, culturally important sporting capital has its roots in the zones of prestige. English Premier League, Major League Baseball and Nike to name but a few exemplify these dominant forms of global sport commodities.

A global sports mega-event, especially the right to host it, is also one of the valuable resources in the global sport industry.[43] In fact, a major sporting spectacle works as a useful vehicle for reinforcing the privileged status of the established core state.[44] For the outsider states, a mega sporting event offers an opportunity to emulate the cultural and economic prowess of the established.[45] As explained in the previous section, the Winter Olympics functions as an important ritual which celebrates the cultural domination of the West. In addition, it is also highlighted that the Winter Olympic Games is a party exclusively for the affluent Western countries. In this light, South Korea's willingness to host the Winter Olympic Games can be understood. This country is currently positioned in the zones of emulation and it has aspirations to be recognized as a global core. By staging this game for the global north, it appears that this semi-peripheral or semi-core country emulates the cultural practice of the West with the hope that a successful delivery of the event will assist South Korea to enter the zones of prestige. In the following section, the relation between sports mega-events and cultural politics of South Korea will be discussed in more detail.

Sports Mega-Events in South Korea

To date,[46] South Korea has hosted a diverse range of international sports competitions. Whenever they occurred, these sporting events had significant political implications for the host country.[47] A brief review of the historical development of cultural politics associated with sports mega-events in South Korea needs to be provided so as to understand a political mechanism linked to the 2018 Winter Olympic Games more accurately. While each competition unfolded separately, a pattern and continuity can be observed also concerning sociopolitical ramifications.[48] When examining the social and political history of the mega sporting events held in South Korea, three distinctive periods can be identified.[49] These are a Cold War period, a reconciliation period and a cultural diplomacy period.

In the 1980s, South Korea hosted two major international sport competitions: the 1986 Summer Asian Games and the 1988 Summer Olympic Games. South Korea planned to stage these events because of the two major reasons: (1) to display its remarkable economic development and modernization to the world; and (2) to secure an advantageous position in the ideological conflict with North Korea.[50] Firstly, it was the time when the country was seen as rising economic power. It should be noted that South Korea was one of the poorest in the 1950s. Yet, from the late 1960s its industry began to gather momentum, and in the 1980s South Korea became an emerging Asian economic centre. This fast-track transition from the peripheral nation to semi-peripheral country was so noticeable that this development was often featured as a miracle of the Han River.[51] The Asian Games and the Olympic Games in Seoul were certainly occasions through which South Korea celebrated its outstanding economic achievement within and showed off its economic strength to the international audience.[52] In other words, by staging these two international sporting events this East Asian nation effectively directed a coming out party.

Internationally, the 1980s was the period when the Cold War political structure divided the world into three parts: the capitalist side, the communist bloc and the non-affiliated third world. As an ideologically partitioned nation, the tension between North and South Korea was particularly high during this period. In this circumstance, the two premier international sporting contests awarded to the South functioned as a useful instrument to highlight the superior quality of its economic and political system over that of the North.[53] At the same time, the world observed the mood of détente being developed in the late 1980s. In the midst of this changing world order, China and the Soviet Union's satellite states intended to establish economic relations with South Korea given the growing importance of its industry.[54] Equally, building economic ties with these communist states, including China brought impactful political leverage to South Korea, especially its relations with North Korea. Under this changing world order, most communist countries decided to send their delegates to the Asian Games in 1986 and the Olympic Games in 1988.[55] In effect, these two sporting events lubricated the process of formal recognition between South Korea and the communist states, the outcome of which subsequently led to the opening of their diplomatic and economic ties.[56]

In 2002, South Korea delivered the FIFA World Cup Finals and the Busan Asian Games. In these two events, reconciliation came to be a major theme. In addition, the reconstruction and re-imagination of Korean national identity were another important development occurring during and post mega-event settings. South Korea co-hosted the FIFA World Cup with Japan. Given these two nations made notorious East Asian old foes whose rivalry originated from the history of Japanese invasion and its colonial domination over Korea,[57] the amicable collaboration between the two nations had been hardly imaginable. Yet, the fact that Korea and Japan accepted the FIFA's offer to stage the major football championship together to some extent signalled a gesture of mutual respect and understanding between them. It is certainly an exaggeration to claim that this cooperation between the two resolves sensitive issues around historical controversies and mistrust in Korea–Japan relations. Yet, it is equally difficult to dismiss some constructive changes to which this collaboration has given rise, such as a visa waiver agreement and the promotion of cultural relations between South Korea and Japan.

The 2002 Busan Asian Games represents reconciliation between North and South Korea.[58] For the first time in its history, the North Korean delegates took part in an international sport competition held in South Korea. Also, almost 300 North Korean cheerleaders crossed the border with the athletes. It marked the largest number of North Korean nationals landed on South Korean soil since the Korean War. South Korean people welcomed the visitors from the north and the friendly relations between the two Koreas lasted throughout the competition. In fact, since 1998, the South Korean Government had implemented a policy of engagement in order to improve its relations with the northern siblings. The 2002 Asian Games epitomized this policy, symbolizing the reconciliation between North and South Korea.

Another important issue concerning sport mega-events in the 2000s was the South Korean football team's unexpected success at the FIFA World Cup. In the history of international football, South Korea had always been an underdog. Yet, the team which had never won any single match at the World Cup Final managed to advance to the semi-finals in 2002, beating the top-notch Spaniards and Italians. Such a dramatic event unfolding on home soil brought a feeling of pride and glory to the Korean people.[59] Because of this remarkable sporting success, the South Koreans experienced a new sense of an empowered nationhood.[60] Additionally, after the event the South Korean Government and its media arm initiated a campaign for encouraging its citizens to have a more confident group mentality such as a 'Can-do spirit' and 'Great Koreans'.[61] This nationalistic mood forged in South Korea mainly through football gradually led to the situation where the country began to consider hosting another symbolic event, the Winter Olympics, to show off the nation's new cultural identity in the near future, and this development will be discussed further later in this paper.

The 2014 Asian Games in Incheon and the 2018 Winter Olympic Games in Pyeongchang must be understood in relation to the South Korean Government's cultural diplomacy programme. The most distinctive feature in this period is that South Korean cultural products such as films, television shows and music have begun to dominate in the Asian entertainment industry.[62] Subsequently, the South Korean Government has been strategically utilizing these increasingly popular cultural commodities as part of its cultural relations.[63] As noted earlier, an economic factor alone is insufficient to transform its status from the semi-core to the core. Rather, it is culturally impressive and attractive activities that provide a nation with an international privilege. This implies that economic and cultural factors must be developed simultaneously so that a country in the zones of emulation lays a path to enter the zones of privilege. Arguably, for the Korean Government, the 2014 Asian Games mainly functioned as a theatre that represented its growing cultural power.[64] For instance, a famous film director choreographed the opening and closing ceremonies of the Incheon. Asian Games, and the appearance of Korean pop stars was the major attraction during these spectacular shows. In addition, a famous Korean actress was selected to be the final runner of the Asian Games torch relay who lit the cauldron. The performance of Korean pop artists can be seen as 'culturally impressive' activities, and by harnessing this sought-after Korean show business during the Asian Games, South Korea attempted to affirm its cultural privilege in Asia.

The nature of the 2018 Pyeongchang Winter Olympic Games will not be dissimilar to the 2014 Asian Games apart from the fact that it will be a larger scale event, targeting the global audiences. It is difficult to expect exactly how this premier winter sport festival will unfold because the commencement of this event is still two years away from the time of this writing. Nonetheless, it can be estimated that the Winter Olympic will be yet another occasion to show off its contemporary culture in an attempt to gain recognition as an emerging cultural powerhouse globally. As noted earlier, the Winter Olympics itself emanates a specific cultural meaning as a game for the global north. By winning the right to stage such a value-laden event and an eventual delivery of the 'white' Olympics, South Korea aims to accumulate a good amount of cultural capital which moves up its international status and reputation. For the Korean political elites, the Winter Olympics is perceived as an occasion that brings a global core position to their home nation. The relation between South Korean cultural politics and the Winter Olympics deserves a more comprehensive sociohistorical analysis, and this is the topic with which the following section deals.

The Winter Olympic Games and South Korean Cultural Politics

The Pyeongchang Winter Olympics, as a game for the affluent nations, may produce cultural capital that the South Korean Government can harness to improve its standing. Now, it is appropriate to consider the reason why South Korea so much strives for acquiring a more prestigious status in international relations. Put simply, why is relocating its position to zones of cultural privilege so crucial for the country? Such a South Korean aspiration may be derived from a series of unfortunate historical events which severely interferes with the sovereignty and political autonomy of the nation. The Korean Peninsula had been occupied by the Japanese imperialists from 1910 to 1945, and during this period Korean people suffered from highly exploitative and intensely brutal Japanese colonialism.[65] While there had been a fierce independent struggle by the nationalists, Korea was emancipated from Japan, thanks primarily to the Japanese emperor's unconditional surrender to the United States at the end of the Second World War. And then the Korean Peninsula was divided into two by the United Nations' mandate, and the two Korean sides were under Washington's and Moscow's trusteeship against the Korean nationalists' willingness to establish a unified independent government. Shortly after this, as ideological tension between the North and the South sharply escalated, the Korean War broke out which almost devastated the entire nation. The three years of civil war only halted with an armistice in 1953. Here, the important fact is that the armistice was signed not between the two Koreas but between North Korea and the United Nations on behalf of South Korea. Since then the US army has been stationed in the South until today. While South Korea reclaimed its sovereignty after the Korean War, its defence heavily relied on American military power throughout the Cold War period. This military reliance, though less severe, still exists today. Under this circumstance, frequent American political interference in internal and foreign affairs of South Korea was almost inescapable.

This historical development indicates that the fate of South Korea was largely controlled and determined by external forces against internal actors' will power. This experience of political domination and intervention which seriously limited the autonomy of the nation has left huge emotional scars on the South Korean collective mentality. Subsequently, the reclamation of its full sovereignty and the liberation from foreign political dependency constitute major components of Korean national consciousness. In recent years, the display of such nationalistic elements becomes more visible because the nation has gained more political confidence with its flourishing economy. Yet, South Korea's cultural prominence is not as much appreciated globally as its economic power, and as explained earlier, it is the realm of culture that the nation must foster in order to relocate its position to the zones of prestige. The South Korean devotion to secure a place in the circle of global cultural elites is, in fact, its struggle to overcome the memory of its unfortunate past. Hosting the Winter Olympic Games as a cultural ritual that only an affluent few are able to afford to stage, therefore, is a symbolically significant political project to show South Korea's intention to join the global core.

With regard to the Winter Olympic Games more specifically, it should be noted that the South Korean Government first conceived the idea of tendering for the right to host Winter Olympics in the early 2000s.[66] It was the time when the South Korean economy was booming after the East Asian financial crisis in 1997, and when winter sport activities, particularly skiing and snowboarding were becoming increasingly popular.[67] It was also the time when Korean peoples observed the South Korean football teams' remarkable performance, defeating European football superpowers during the World Cup matches on home soil. This brought South Korean citizens to more confidence in expressing their national identity, and made them feel more proud of being a Korean.[68] At this juncture, having experienced the delivery of the two top-tier global sporting events which were the 1988 Summer Olympics and the 2002 FIFA World Cup finals, government officials began to articulate the view that it is beneficial for the country to host the Winter Olympics, which is arguably the third largest sporting event with a unique cultural value as mentioned earlier. It seems that the political initiative to host a sports mega-event as a vehicle for promoting the merit and prowess of the nation resumed its operation. In 2011, the IOC declared that the South Korean region of Pyeongchang would host the 2018 Winter Olympic Games. In fact, the right to stage this winter sporting spectacle was awarded to Pyeongchang after the two unsuccessful bidding campaigns for the 2010 and 2014 Winter Olympics. This continuous effort to win the Winter Olympic bid is indicative of South Korean stubborn willingness to recover its pride.

In the South Korean Winter Olympic campaign, Yuna Kim, a South Korea female figure skater, played a crucial role. She won an Olympic gold at the 2010 Winter Olympics in Vancouver, and in the next edition in Sochi, Yuna Kim also gained a silver medal. Given that figure skating was conventionally a West-dominated event, and that it includes not only a sporting dimension but also artistic and musical elements, this specific sport displays a unique cultural aura as a symbol of Western elitism.[69] Hence, when she became an Olympic champion, the whole nation celebrated as if they overcame the collective mental block of Western dependency. Moreover, during the figure skating contest, the South Korean media highlighted a fierce sporting rivalry between Korean Yuna Kim and Japanese Asada Mao.[70] When the Korean defeated the Japanese, the media constructed the narrative of a post-colonial duel, featuring as if it was symbolic revenge on the former colonizers. This nationalistic representation offered Korean audiences additionally cathartic euphoria. Furthermore, the media also note that the body image of Yuna Kim was seen as a Westernized and an efficient sporting body which is distinctive from a somatic composition of an average Korean woman.[71] This body politics represents a nationalistic heroine who has enough strength and shows no fear in the competition against the Westerners at the global sporting stage. In that sense, Yuna Kim was an individual who symbolically eliminated the nation's collective psychological burdens, and who, as a result, embodies South Korea's aspirations to be recognized as a prominent and privileged state. Therefore, it is no surprise to see this sporting heroine acting as one of the core members of the 2018 Winter Olympic bidding team. Yuna Kim was also appointed as the Winter Olympic Ambassador after it secured the right to host the major event. Therefore, it can be argued that the figure skater encapsulates the South Korean desire to enhance its cultural prowess and prominence through being a host of the winter sport festival.

Critique: Is It True Empowerment?

Thus far, this paper clarifies the following: (1) The cultural meaning of the Winter Olympics; (2) The South Korean ambition to become a cultural powerhouse with the reference to the world system and the zones of prestige and emulation; and (3) The social and historical background of South Korean desire to host sports mega-event, with particular attention to the 2018 Winter Olympic Games. While the instrumental use of the Winter Olympics by the Korean Government as a vehicle for improving its status is an understandable strategy of cultural relations, this tactic also poses a number of problems. First, the idea that South

Korea attempts to enhance its reputation and to claim its privilege by hosting the Winter Olympic Games reveals the situation where Western cultural imperialism is deeply rooted in the cultural landscape of the Far East country. Basically, South Korea is the nation which belongs to an East Asian civilization zone to which the country has contributed distinctive cultural legacies. It is also the nation that has a long cultural and historical tradition which provides Korean people with valuable resources to build its unique national identity. Nevertheless, South Korea has been making a devoted effort to emulate Western winter sporting practice which primarily sustains American and European cultural hegemony in order that the value of the contemporary Westernized South Korean culture is appreciated by the international audiences. This South Korean reliance upon the Western cultural products to improve its international standing is indicative of cultural imperialism at work which may gradually perish, or at least weaken, distinctive Korean elements in a global cultural spectrum.[72] It is paradoxical, therefore, that this non-white nation has a strong intention to display its cultural prowess by staging the 'white' Olympics. Hence, it is not too illogical to anticipate that the Pyeongchang Winter Olympic Games is likely to be an event that simply reproduces the West-centric world view, actively endorsing Western cultural hegemony at the expense of a peculiar Korean historical legacy.

Second, it is problematic to find an orientalist mentality embedded in South Korean attitudes towards cultural politics associated with the Winter Olympics. Put simply, Orientalism refers to a perspective to see the world on the presumption of the superiority of the West.[73] It also postulates that non-Western others tend to be weak, irrational and vulgar. Hence, this perception naturalizes the proselytization of the Orient by introducing the cultural logic of the Occident. This orientalist sensitivity can be detected in the way in which the South Korean Government strives for overcoming the country's mentality of subordination which is constructed through its unfortunate historical trajectory mentioned earlier. Of course, it is understandable that the country, whose fate has been largely determined by powerful neighbouring states in the previous century, aspires to foster more cultural power to enhance its status. However, the South Korean strategy to empower its position by hosting the Winter Olympics fundamentally assumes the notion that the more Western culture the nation embraces, the more prestigious status it will gain. There is no need to reiterate the fact that the winter sport contest is basically a party for white Western athletes. Concerning an Olympic champion Yuna Kim, this South Korea figure skater comes to be a national heroine largely because Kim symbolizes a westernized female body which is physically fit and psychologically strong to fight against Western and former colonialist competitors. This way of thinking implies that the principle of conventional Korean culture, however valuable, is not forceful enough to overcome its historical misfortune. Instead, it suggests that South Korean cultural capital can only be strengthened by actively adopting and subsequently internalizing the cultural logic of the West. Hence, while South Korea may be able to earn a ticket to enter the zones of privilege by hosting the Winter Olympic Games, such a sense of enhancement can only be justified within the paradigm of Orientalism.

Third, the Winter Olympic Games will be an event that appropriates an unreasonably large amount of the nation's natural and financial resources. This point may be less theoretical than the previous two arguments, but it is closely related to the notions of cultural imperialism and Orientalism. It should be noted that the Winter Olympic Games often involves the destruction of the natural environment to build winter sport facilities, the construction of which also requires a huge amount of public expenditure.[74] With regard to the Pyeongchang

Winter Olympics, the Organizing Committee has decided to bulldoze five-century-old primitive forests in order to make an Olympic standard ski slope even if it had a more sustainable option.[75] The Committee also has a plan to build a new stadium that only stage the opening and closing ceremonies during the Olympic Games in a small country town in the region of Pyeongchang whose population is no more than 4000 people. Especially, this town is encircled by untouched mountains which include natural habitat for a diverse range of wildlife. Thus, building this large stadium in this small town inevitably disturbs the surrounding natural environment. These are only a few examples of controversial building projects directly related to the Olympic Games. The key rationale for constructing these new facilities can be found arguably in the host nation's willingness to impress the visitors mainly from the West. Because the major motivation for staging the Winter Olympic Games include, rather ironically, boasting about a Korean way of appreciating and representing Western culture, it is crucial to arrange the best possible winter sport facilities for the 15 days of the event. It appears that the Korean Government is so much concerned with pleasing the guests largely from North America and Europe that it is justifiable, for this specific purpose, to sacrifice its own natural settings, which is also an important element of traditional Korean identity. Here again, Westernized contemporary Korean values prevail over a conventional component of Korean culture.

Conclusion

The Winter Olympics is the game for the global north through which Western 'white' cultural hegemony and privilege is continuously re-enacted. It is also a sporting contest that clearly distinguishes the division between the global haves and have-nots. In other words, the Winter Olympic Games engenders global cultural capital to be used for making a distinction between the global established and outsiders. The winter sporting spectacle to be held in the South Korean region of Pyeongchang clearly mirrors South Korea's aspirations to be recognized as a member of the global core. Economically, the nation has already passed the stage of the semi-periphery industry, and is now considered as one of the leading economic powers.[76] Culturally, South Korea is still positioned in the zones of emulation with the strong ambition to promote its standing. By hosting the game for the global haves, South Korea attempts to make its identity more visible on the map of global cultural geography. In South Korea, the right to host this sports mega-event appears to be seen as a badge of honour and a ticket to enter the zones of privilege. In that sense, this edition of the Winter Olympic will be a highly political game.

However, it is paradoxical to see that this project of empowering the cultural merit of South Korea may also entail weakening its unique cultural tradition. It should be noted that the level of empowerment will only be measurable by a Western cultural barometer. The idea that this East Asian nation tries to gain a more prestigious status through staging the Winter Olympic Games fundamentally means that the country relies on the instrumental use of Western cultural products. Therefore, in order that South Korea materializes its vision to be a cultural powerhouse more effectively, the Winter Olympics needs to be a show that mainly represents the image that imitates mainstream Western cultural values. The more Western modernity (or post-modernity) South Korea displays at this winter sporting spectacle, the more privileged cultural capital the country is likely to accumulate. In this formula of South Korean cultural politics, there will be only a marginal place where a conventional Korean heritage stands. More problematically, this political and cultural project involves the sacrifice of the Korean natural landscape. This is the consequence of cultural imperialism embedded in the practice of the Winter Olympic Games and of the widespread Orientalism in Korean culture.

Some commentators note that, given the South Korean region of Pyeongchang won the right to host the Winter Olympics only after the failure of the two previous Olympic bids, it is 'third time lucky' for the Korean host.[77] This paper does not completely dismiss a potential political opportunity that this premier winter sporting competition offers to the host city and the nation. Yet, while South Korea may be able to materialize the plan to upgrade its international standing, it should be noted that such an improvement is not without expenses. Basically, the Winter Olympic Games is the event that reinforces the inequality between the global core and periphery. This implies that in an attempt to attain a more privileged position, South Korea inevitably underpins the current political and economic structure which fortifies the gap between the global north and south. Moreover, it is anticipated that the Pyeongchang Winter Olympics will be a cultural spectacle which exhibits a Westernized, or proselytized, Korean identity to the international audiences. In so doing, a conventional Korean cultural legacy is likely to be marginalized. When balancing out all these features together, cultural and political values of the 2018 Winter Olympic Games will be more objectively calculated.

This anticipation may prove wrong because the opening of this winter sporting event is still more than a year away at the time of writing. It is possible that the host can project its unique cultural value in harmony with the Western legacies of the Winter Olympics. Additionally, Pyeongchang's 'Dream Program' initiative, which aims to assist the development of winter sports in developing countries, can potentially make a valuable contribution to reducing the gap between the global north and south in the snow and ice sporting arenas. Nevertheless, given the nature of South Korean cultural politics which embraces a Western sense of (post) modernity without critical reflection, and given the characteristic of the international winter sport development programme which can be seen as a rather strategic cultural diplomatic tool to win the Winter Olympic bid, it is somewhat uncertain whether the Pyeongchang Olympic Games will leave genuine and sustainable positive legacies. In this view, a more careful approach is necessitated before having an optimistic vision such as 'third time lucky' because it is equally possible that the sporting occasion turns into the omen of bad luck. More importantly, unless this Western-centric political and economic structure is deconstructed which eventually leads to a paradigm shift in global sporting culture, the possibility to observe a more multicultural Winter Olympics for the global humanity is only few and far between.

Notes

1. John Horne, 'The Four "Knowns" of Sports Mega-Events', *Leisure Studies* 26, no. 1 (2007), 81–96; Jonathan Grix (ed.), *Leveraging Mega-Event Legacies* (Abingdon: Routledge, 2016); and Andrew Smith, 'Leveraging Sport Mega-Events: New Model or Convenient Justification?', *Journal of Policy Research in Tourism, Leisure and Events* 6, no. 1 (2014), 15–30.
2. Jonathan Grix and Paul M. Brannagan, 'Of Mechanisms and Myths: Conceptualising States' "Soft Power" Strategies Through Sports Mega-Events', *Diplomacy & Statecraft* 27, no. 2 (2016), 251–72.

3. Jean Harvey et al., *Sport and Social Movements: From the Local to the Global* (London: Bloomsbury, 2013).
4. Jung Woo Lee and Joseph Maguire, 'Global Festivals through a National Prism: The Global and Local Nexus in South Korean Media Coverage of the 2004 Athens Olympic Games', *International Review for the Sociology of Sport* 44 (2009), 5–24.
5. Joseph A. Maguire, 'Power and Global Sport: Zones of Prestige, Emulation and Resistance', *Sport in Society* 14, nos 7–8 (2011), 1010–26.
6. John Horne, *Sport in Consumer Culture* (Basingstoke: Palgrave, 2006).
7. John Davis, *The Olympic Games Effect : How Sports Marketing Builds Strong Brands*, 2nd ed. (Chichester: Wiley, 2012).
8. Udo Merkel and Misuk Kim, 'Third Time Lucky!? PyeongChang's Bid to Host the 2018 Winter Olympics–Politics, Policy and Practice', *The International Journal of the History of Sport* 28, no. 16 (2011), 2365–83.
9. Dennis Coates, 'Not So-Mega Events', in Wolfgang Maenning and Andrew Zimbalist (eds), *International Handbook on the Economics of Mega Sporting Events* (Cheltenham: Elgar, 2012), 401–33.
10. C. Richard King, 'Staging the White Olympics: Or, Why Sport Matters to White Power', *Journal of Sport and Social Issues* 31, no. 1 (2007), 89–94.
11. Paul Farhi, 'Where the Rich and Elite Meet to Compete', *Washington Post*, 5 Feburary 2006, B01.
12. Reihan Salam, 'White Snow, Brown Rage: The Racial Case Against the Winter Olympics', *Slate*, 15 Feburary 2006, http://www.slate.com/articles/sports/fivering_circus/2006/02/white_snow_brown_rage.html (accessed 14 June 2016).
13. To find out the mechanism of racial identity politics and racial inequality at the Winter Olympic Games necessitates a systematic sociological investigation, and certainly it is an extremely important research subject. Yet, such a close examination is beyond the remit of this paper which is mainly concerned with the South Korean desire to host the Winter Olympic Games. For this specific research focus, it may be sufficient to provide a preliminary observation on the elements of white supremacy embedded in the practice of the Winter Olympics.
14. Farhi, 'Where the Rich and Elite Meet'.
15. David J. Leonard, 'To the White Extreme in the Mainstream: Manhood and White Youth Culture in a Virtual Sports World', in Michael D Giardina and Michele K Donnelly (eds), *Youth Culture and Sport: Identity, Power, Politics* (New York: Routledge, 2008), 91–112; and King, 'Staging the Winter White Olympics'.
16. Susan Brownell, 'The View from Greece: Questioning Eurocentrism in the History of the Olympic Games', *Journal of Sport History* 32, no. 2 (2005), 203–16; and King, 'Staging the Winter White Olympics'.
17. Ellis Cashmore, *Making Sense of Sport*, 5th ed. (Abingdon: Routledge, 2010).
18. Leonard, 'To the White Extreme in the Mainstream'.
19. Salam, 'White Snow, Brown Rage'.
20. It should be noted that the 1972 and 1998 Winter Olympic Games were held in the Japanese city of Sapporo and Nagano, respectively. Yet, while it is geographically located in the Far East, Japan emerged as a modern advanced nation in the early twentieth century. In that sense, Japan had already joined this global rich club when it hosted the Winter Olympics.
21. Farhi, 'Where the Rich and Elite Meet'.
22. Immanuel Wallerstein, *World-System Analysis: An Intoduction* (Durham, NC: Duke University Press, 2004).
23. Randall Collins, 'Civilizations as Zones of Prestige and Social Contact', *International Sociology* 16, no. 3 (2001), 421–37.
24. Thomas R. Shannon, *An Introduction to the World System Perspective*, 2nd ed. (Boulder, CO: Westview Press, 1996).
25. Manuel Castells, *The Rise of Network Society*, 2nd ed. (Oxford: Willy-Blackwell, 2010).

26. Jan A.G.M. van Dijk, *The Deepening Divide: Inequality in the Information Society* (London: Sage, 2005).
27. Leslie Sklair, *Globalization: Capitalism and Its Alternatives*, 3rd ed. (Oxford: Oxford University Press, 2002).
28. Shannon, *An Introduction to the World System Perspective*.
29. Peter Dicken, *Global Shift: Mapping the Changing Contoyr of the World Economy*, 6th ed. (London: Sage, 2010).
30. Robin Cohen and Paul Kennedy, *Global Sociology*, 3rd ed. (London: Palgrave Macmillan, 2103).
31. George Ritzer, *Globalization: A Basic Text* (Chichester: Wiley-Blackwell, 2010).
32. Shannon, *An Introduction to the World System Perspective*.
33. Kyung S Chang, *South Korea Under Compressed Modernity: Familial Political Economy in Transition* (Abingdon: Routledge, 2010).
34. Wallerstein, *World-Systems Analysis*.
35. James F. Larson and Jaemin Park, 'From Developmental to Network State: Government Restructuring and ICT-led Innovation in Korea', *Telecommunications Policy* 38, no. 4 (2014), 344–59.
36. Maguire, 'Power and Global Sport', 1021.
37. Ibid.
38. Ibid.
39. Mark Dyreson, 'The Republic of Consumption at the Olympic Games: Globalization, Americanization, and Californization', *Journal of Global History* 8, no. 2 (2013), 256–78.
40. David L. Andrews, 'Sport in the Late Capitalist Moment', in Trevor Slack (ed.), *The Commercialisation of Sport* (Abingdon: Routledge, 2004), 2–28.
41. Jung Woo Lee, 'The Meaning of Sport: Sociolinguistic Analysis of Sport and Energy Drink Brands' Advertising Messages', *International Journal of Sport Communication* 8, no. 2 (2015): 174–92.
42. Joseph S. Nye, *Soft Power: The Means to Success in World Politics* (New York: Public Affair, 2004).
43. Jonathan Grix and Barrie Houlihan, 'Sports Mega-Events as Part of a Nation's Soft Power Strategy: The Cases of Germany (2006) and the UK (2012)', *British Journal of Politics and International Relations* 16 (2014), 572–96.
44. Maguire, 'Power and Global Sport'.
45. Jonathan Grix and Donna Lee, 'Soft Power, Sports Mega-Events and Emerging States: The Lure of the Politics of Attraction', *Global Society* 27, no. 4 (2013), 521–36.
46. For a more comprehensive review of political implications of sport mega events held in Korea, see Jung Woo Lee, 'The Politics of Sports Mega Events in South Korea: A Diachronic Approach', in Alan Bairner, John Kelly and Jung Woo Lee (eds), *Routledge Handbook of Sport and Politics* (Abingdon: Routledge, 2017), 471–82.
47. Victor D. Cha, *The Beyond the Final Score: The Politics of Sport in Asia.* (New York: Columbia University Press, 2009).
48. Jung Woo Lee, 'Do the Scale and Scope of the Event Matter? The Asian Games and the Relations Between North and South Korea', *Sport in Society* 20, no. 3 (2017), 369–83.
49. Lee, 'The Politics of Sports Mega Events'.
50. Cha, *The Beyond the Final Score*.
51. Brian Bridges, 'The Seoul Olympics: Economic Miracle Meet the World', *The International Journal of the History of Sport* 25, no. 14 (2008), 1939–52.
52. Sandra Collins, 'East Asian Olympic Desires: Identity on the Global Stage in the 1964 Tokyo, 1988 Seoul and 2008 Beijing Games', *The International Journal of the History of Sport* 28, no. 16 (2011), 2240–60.
53. Lee, 'The Politics of Sports Mega Events'.
54. Charlesk Armstrong, 'South Korea's "Northern Policy"', *Pacific Review* 3, no. 1 (1990), 35–45.
55. Within the communist bloc, only North Korea and Cuba boycotted these events.
56. Cha, *The Beyond the Final Score*.

57. Gwang Ok and Kyoungho Park, 'Cultural Evolution and Ideology in Korean Soccer: Sport and Nationalism', *The International Journal of the History of Sport* 31, no. 3 (2014), 363–75.
58. Lee, 'Do the Scale and Scope Matter?'
59. Rachael M. Joo, *Transnational Sport: Gender, Media, and Global Korea* (Durham, NC: Duke University Press, 2012).
60. Ibid.
61. Hyundai Research Institute, *Post World Cup ei Baljeon Jeonryak gwa Jungchack Gwajae* [Post World Cup developmental strategy and policy implication] (Seoul: Hyundai Research Institute, 2002).
62. Woongjae Ryoo, 'Globalization, or the Logic of Cultural Hybridization: The Case of the Korean Wave', *Asian Journal of Communication* 19, no. 2 (2009), 137–51.
63. Seung H Kwon and Joseph Kim. 'The Cultural Industry Policies of the Korean Government and the Korean Wave', *International Journal of Cultural Policy* 20, no. 4 (2014), 422–39.
64. Lee, 'The Politics of Sports Mega Events'.
65. Bruce Cumings, *Korea's Place in the Sun: A Modern History*. Updated. (New York: W.W. Norton & Company, 2005).
66. Merkel and Kim, 'Third Time Lucky!?'
67. KOLE, *Leisure Baekseo* [White paper on leisure industry] (Seoul: KOLE, 2003).
68. Joo, *Transnational Sport*.
69. Jung Woo Lee, 'Yuna Kim in Television Advertising and Her Celebrityhood: Representation of a Nationalist Ideology and a Gender Identity', *Korean Journal of Sociology of Sport* 22, no. 3 (2009), 1–18.
70. Hee Jin Seo and Ok Hyun Kim, 'Analysis of Media Frames in the Composition of "Yuna Kim vs Asada Mao" Appeared in the Korean Press', *Korean Journal of Physical Education* 54, no. 3 (2015), 127–39.
71. Jae H. Hong, 'Kimyuna Sanghache biyul 1:2 shin-e-nae-rin monmae' [A gift from God: The 2:1 ratio of Yuna Kim's body], *Sports Donga*, 3 Februrary 2014, http://sports.donga.com/3/01/20140202/60528582/3 (accessed 15 June 2016).
72. John Tomlinson, *Cultural Imperialism: A Critical Introduction* (London: Pinter, 1991).
73. Edward W. Said, *Orientalism* (London: Penguin, 1995).
74. Helen J. Lenskyj, *Olympic Industry Resistance: Challenging Olympic Power and Propaganda* (Albany: State University of New York Press, 2008).
75. Julian Cheyne, 'Destruction of Mount Gariwang forest for Pyeongchang2018 Winter Olympics', *GamesMonitor: Debunking Olympic Myth*, 25 September 2014, http://www.gamesmonitor.org.uk/node/2203 (accessed 19 June 2016).
76. Uk Heo and Terence Roehrig, *South Korea's Rise: Economic Development, Power and Foreign Relations* (Cambridge: Cambridge University Press, 2014).
77. Merkel and Kim, 'Third Time Lucky!?'; Jeremy Laurence, 'Olympics-Third Bid is Pyeongchang's Best Yet, IOC Team Say', *Reuters*, 19 Februrary 2011 http://www.reuters.com/article/olympics-pyeongchang-idUSTOE71I00J20110219 (accessed 14 June 2016); and 'Third Time Lucky', *Korea Herald*, 20 March 2010, http://www.koreaherald.com/view.php?ud=20090425000009 (accessed 14 June 2016).

Disclosure Statement

No potential conflict of interest was reported by the author.

The Development of the Olympic Narrative in Chinese Elite Sport Discourse from Its First Successful Olympic Bid to the Post-Beijing Games Era

Richard Xiaoqian Hu and Ian Henry

ABSTRACT
As a phenomenon exogenous to China, the Olympics have been proactively interpreted in the local context since China's entry (and subsequent re-entry in 1984) into the Olympic movement. With China's increasing involvement in promoting three bids to host the Olympic Games, two of which were successful, respectively, in 2001 and 2015, the nature of the discourse of key stakeholders in relation to Chinese elite sport has both reflected and reshaped the meaning of the Games to Chinese elite sport. This paper examines the discursive construction process of the Olympics in the Chinese elite sport system by key stakeholders through analyzing statements of political figures on sport and Olympic phenomena, Chinese elite sport policy documents, and the commentaries of leading Chinese sport academics. The analysis of discourse highlights two main features in the construction of the Games in official accounts during the period under investigation. The development of these two themes reflects the nature of the Chinese Olympic discourse, manifests the political power over the interpretation of the Olympics in Chinese context, and continues to characterize the on-going major themes in Chinese elite sport policy.

Introduction

Even though Chinese society had traditionally shown limited enthusiasm for physical activities, particularly competitive sport, and had experienced a century of humiliation since the Anglo-Chinese War in 1839, it has recently demonstrated an increasing interest in modern sport, and in particular the Olympics, subsequently forming its own 'Olympic dream'.[1]

Rather than simply 'translating' Western versions of the doctrine of the Olympic ideology, key groups in China's political and sports administration world have proactively interpreted and reconstructed the Olympics, in order to advocate a competitive culture in Chinese society and to provoke the restoration of the Chinese nation through promoting modern sport, particularly elite sport.[2] Elite sport and the Olympics are hence closely associated with political elements since its introduction to Chinese society. Instances can be seen from the relationship between the promotion of competitive body culture and the requirement of the salvation of China in the nineteenth century,[3] to Changchun Liu's endeavour to become the first Chinese, rather than Japanese, Olympian in 1932 during Japan's invasion of China.[4]

The communist regime of the People's Republic of China (hereafter PRC), established in 1949, was fully aware of the political significance of the Olympics. Less than a month after its official establishment, the PRC initiated the reform of the Chinese Olympic Committee (hereafter, COC), which has then become another banner of the governmental organ in sport.[5] Even though only one athlete of the first PRC Olympic delegation which was sent to Helsinki in 1952 actually competed in the Games, the then Prime Minister, Zhou Enlai highly valued China's first Olympic appearance as 'a victory for [communist] China, even if we could do nothing but just fly our flag in the Olympic village'.[6]

Six years later, there was another political matter, i.e. the 'Two-China' issue.[7] In this case, the PRC terminated its relationship with the International Olympic Committee (IOC) in 1958, a relationship which was not re-built until the Nagoya IOC session in 1979.[8] Thanks to significance associated with the Olympic Games and elite sport performance in the Chinese context, the reinstatement of the PRC's position in the IOC has resulted in a strong emphasis on elite sport and a considerable increase in its Olympic performance since then.[9]

Since the last decade of the twentieth century, China's interest in being involved with the Olympics has increased from participation to another level, to the point where it has bid for the hosting of the Olympic Games on three occasions, two of which were successful, namely 2001 and 2015, respectively. In this context, the political significance of the 2008 Beijing Games to China has been thoroughly investigated by academics.[10]

Given the significance of the 2008 Beijing Olympics to China[11] and the traditional close association between the Olympics and elite sport in a Chinese context,[12] this research seeks to explore the development of the Olympic discourse in the Chinese elite sport system since China was awarded the 2008 Olympic Games in 2001, and to identify discourse themes defining the nature and significance of Olympics to Chinese elite sport. Accordingly, Fairclough's Critical Realism-Based Critical Discourse Analysis framework is employed in the research to investigate those documents that strategically focus on the overall development of Chinese elite sport and other supporting material.

Methodology

The research question revolves around the way the Olympics has been (continuously or differently) constructed in the Chinese elite sport system since China won its first Olympic bid, through to the post-2008 era. The period chosen for the research starts from the year 2001, in which China was awarded the 2008 Olympic Games and published its first Olympic Glory Plan that covers a full decade,[13] and ends with the current Chinese President Xi Jinping's speech in 2014 to the Chinese delegation for the Sochi Winter Olympics.[14] The year 2008 is recognized as a watershed dividing the period, because of not only the Beijing Olympic Games in that year but also the then Chinese president Hu Jintao's speech at the Awards Ceremony for the 2008 Olympics and the Paralympics,[15] which provides a new mission for Chinese sport.

Wodak and Meyer suggests that discourse analysts must focuses on 'a dialect relationship between a particular discursive event and the situation(s), institution(s) and social

Table 1. List of key policy documents and speeches.

Government documents	Author	Year
The SPCSC's Opinion on Deepening the Reform of Sport System	The SPCSC	1993
The Sport Law of the PRC	National People's Congress	1995 2009
The Olympic Glory Plan	The SPCSC The GAS	1994 2001 2011
The Central Committee of the CPC and the State Council's Guidelines for Further Strengthening and Improving Sporting Affairs in the New Era	The Central Committee of the CPC and the State Council	2002
Speeches by political leaders		
Jiang Zemin's speech to the Chinese delegation of the XXVII Olympics	The then-President of China	2000
Hu Jintao's Speech at the Awards Ceremony for the 2008 Olympics and the Paralympics	The then-President of China	2008
Hu Jintao: The Chinese People are Capable of Making More Contribution to the Human Race	The then-President of China	2008
Xi Jinping's Speech at the Chinese camp in the Sochi Olympics	The President of China	2014
Speeches by top sport officials		
Yuan Weimin's Report in the Ceremony of Beijing's Successful Olympic Bid	The then-Sport Minister	2001
Hezhenliang's Report in the Ceremony of Beijing's Successful Olympic Bid	The former President of COC	2001
Sport Minister's report at the All States Sports Minister Conference	The Sport Minister	2001–2013
The Speech of Deputy Sport Minister at All States Sports Minister Conference	The Deputy Sport Ministers	2001–2013

Table 2. Protocol of CDA.

Chronology	Pre-2008	Post-2008
Genre	The action implied in discourse (relationship with, and attitudes towards, others; action over others)	
Discourse	The perspective and presentation of topics (knowledge about event & structure; control over things)	
Style	How the identity is constructed (knowledge about, relations with self, e.g. Zhuanye system and reformists)	

Modified from Norman Fairclough, 'Discourse Analysis in Organization Studies: The Case for Critical Realism', *Organizational Studies* 26, no. 6 (2005), 915–39; Norman Fairclough, 'A Dialectical-Relational Approach to Critical Discourse Analysis in Social Research', in Ruth Wodak and Michael Meyer (eds), *Methods of Critical Discourse Analysis* (London: Sage, 2009), 162–186.

structure(s), which frame it', as discourse is a multi-aspect social phenomenon.[16] In his CDA framework, Fairclough furthers this point and identifies discourse as a manifestation and regulation of social identity, social practice, and social representation/construction.[17] He states that 'discourse' embraces not only the *linguistic* and *semiotic term*, but also embodies a dialectical social process and with three aspects: a way of *being, acting* and *materializing*. Thus, through employing Fairclough's CDA framework for a cross-language discourse analysis,[18] this research seeks to unveil social actors' constructive activities and their relationship with Chinese elite sport, while scrutinizing 'real' social structures, which facilitate and constrain the discursive construction.

Table 1 provides a list of the main documents analyzed for this research. As the first step, all publicly accessible Chinese elite sport policies and speeches of Chinese political leaders and top sport officials announced during the period that is investigated in the research were reviewed. Those documents and speeches that strategically focus on the overall development of Chinese elite sport were selected as the main documentary source subject to the analysis, which sought to concentrate on the influence of Olympic discourse on the construction of the general development of Chinese elite sport. In addition, supporting references also include other documents concerning concrete practices, for example the ideological education of Chinese elite athletes, and academic and media material from institutions, such as Beijing Sport University, the China sport press and the Chinese sport daily, which are directly affiliated to, and controlled by governmental sport organs and thus are a part of the Chinese elite sport system.[19]

As shown in Table 2, the data is analyzed following Fairclough's concept of the *order of discourse*, namely *genre*, *discourse* and *style*, which are three textual elements that 'reflect structural feature in a certain society'.[20] Fairclough indicates that *genre* which constructs relationships between the respective sides of a discursive construction, can be identified at different levels of abstraction. These include those at an abstracted level, i.e. argument, discussion and statement; those at more concrete level, i.e. interview, advertisement and report; and those at micro level, which construct relationships in communication through conveying different concrete active meanings via terms such as 'to promote' or 'to implement'.[21] It is the *genre* at micro level that is investigated in this research, which aims to explore purposes of communication, the relationship with, and attitude towards others constructed in the discursive 'actions over others'.[22]

The objects that fall into the column of *discourse* include not only representation of discourse, but also the perspectives of representation and interpretation (e.g. the diverse and/or consistent ways in which the Olympics are framed). These diverse perspectives of construction compose a 'panoramic view' of Chinese Olympic discourse and its relationship with elite sport development. They also reflect the structural elements, facilitating or constraining the actors' knowledge of events (the Olympic Games, especially the 2008 Games) and of social structure (Chinese elite sport and political elements).

Style symbolizes the discursive facet of identity,[23] in other words, how actors view and construct their own and others' social identity. For example, being a sport official requires not only certain managing behaviours, but also certain discursive 'manners', such as speaking like other administrators do. Through investigating the style constructed with Chinese Olympic discourse, the research explores the different/consistent role of the Olympics within the development of Chinese elite sport overarching the 2008 Games.

The Pre-2008 Chinese Olympic Discourse Themes: Politicizing the Games, Emphasizing Performance

Extrinsic Functions of the Olympics

As stated in the introduction, the Olympics, and modern sport in general, are often associated with political elements in the Chinese context, which could be argued are a consequence of the original purpose for which these Western phenomena were introduced to China. The political, economic and cultural implications of the Olympics are recognized as its 'extrinsic function'; while the 'intrinsic functions', which is common to all types of sport, refer to its impacts on education, health promotion and entertainment.[24]

Among all its 'extrinsic functions', the political implications of the Olympic movement and Olympic Games are often directly and positively stated in elite sport policies, and are recognized as an essential motivation for China's involvement with the international Olympic movement. And after Beijing was awarded the 2008 Olympics, these political implications were then explicitly associated with the Beijing Olympics. For instance, *the Olympic Glory Plan 2001–2010*, which was published in 2002, comments that:

> Winning the bid of the 2008 Games ... will have significant impact on the economic and social development [of China] in the new century, on the establishment of an 'all-dimensional', multi-tiered and wide-ranging 'opening-up' of our country, as well as on enhancing its international status.[25]

In the same year, the Central Committee of the Communist Party of China (hereafter, the CPC) and the State Council indicate that:

> Winning the bid of the 2008 Games fully reflects the great accomplishments that have been achieved through the reform and opening-up ... It is a mutual duty of all Party members, governments at various levels and Chinese people of all ethnicities ... to try their best to make the 2008 Olympic Games the most outstanding Olympics in history ... in order to promote the development of the socialist material progress, and cultural and ethical progress, of our country.[26]

The political implications of the Olympic movement are emphasized in both quotations from key elite sport policy publications by the GAS and the core of the PRC regime. These official discourses not only stress the political function of the Olympics, but also indirectly regulate the means for realizing this function, i.e. the 2008 Olympic Games, through explicitly acknowledging the political significance of the Beijing 2008 Games.

This accentuation of the Olympic Games per se is not only evidenced in the quoted policy statement but also in the two original documents, in which, the term 'Olympic' is only mentioned once without being directly linked with terms such as 'Games' or 'strategy'. It is in the 2001 Summary that it is stated '[we should] utilise the opportunity of the Beijing Games ... to energetically promote the Olympic spirit, [in order to] make the whole society emphasize and support the Olympic strategy'. Nonetheless, even in this solely exceptional case, the Olympic strategy was still identified as the ultimate goal for promoting the Olympic spirit. In contrast to the overwhelming emphasis on the Games per se in these two important documents, terms such as 'the Olympic spirit', 'the Olympic Movement', etc. are employed more frequently in the previous edition, i.e. the 1994 edition of the Olympic Glory Plan.[27]

The emphasis on the political significance of the Olympics and on elite sport performance in the Olympic Games is evidenced not only in the Olympic discourse in policy documents, but also in the interpretation of the Olympic movement in other resources.[28] For instance, Douyin Xiong, a renowned Chinese sport scholar, indicates that:

> We experienced a 27-year conflict with the IOC fighting about the 'two-Chinas' [issue], during which it was obviously impossible to promote the Olympic movement, let alone to have Olympic education [in China], therefore it is natural that Chinese people, even sport personnel and media have not had abundant knowledge about the Olympic [movement] ... [and] regard the Olympic [movement] merely as a sport competition, for winning gold medals, which is a superficial understanding.[29]

The political interests of the PRC, which are related to the 'two Chinas' issue in its political conflict with the IOC, are identified as the principal, if not the sole, concern of the communist regime in promoting the Olympic movement (including Olympic education) in China. This account implicitly acknowledges that the guarantee of meeting its interests was a condition of the PRC's involvement with the international Olympic movement. Such prioritization of the political interests is consistent with Xuanjian Ma's argument that 'Chinese Olympic policy is essentially an important part of the diplomatic policy of China. Diplomacy relates to core national interests, to which sport affairs [therefore] have to be subordinate and serve'.[30] For Xiong and Ma, who are both internal researchers of the GAS, the Chinese government's influence on the Chinese Olympic movement is embraced, or more precisely internalized, as the condition and premise of the establishing of the Chinese Olympic movement.

In addition, it is also worth noting that Xiong normalizes the sole emphasis on Olympic performance in China as a consequence of the political conflict. Even though Xiong criticizes this exclusive attention paid to the competition side of the Olympic movement as a 'superficial understanding', this account indirectly endorses the accentuation on the Olympic performance, at least in elite sport policies, through portraying it as a consensus that is 'natural' for Chinese people.

Nonetheless, it is important to address that this suggests neither that the political usefulness of the Olympic Games had been the sole motive of the PRC government for hosting it, nor that the discourse of the 2008 Games, particularly those in relation to performance in the Beijing Games, had replaced all other Olympic discourses in China after 2001. However, we would argue that the political features, and the focus, of the Chinese Olympic discourse do reflect the Chinese government's emphasis on the political implications of the Olympic Games, which is in line with its political interests. While the emphasis on elite sport performance structures the way in which the key impact of the 2008 Games should be achieved, and thus increases the significance of Olympic performance, particularly of the performance in the 2008 Games, which was officially recognized as the premier political task for Chinese elite sport.

In addition to the positive portrayal of the impact and political function of the Olympics in the official discourse, the negative side is also normally stated in policy documents, which follows and reflects a dialectical materialist style of discussion (which might be said to have its roots in the Marxist origins of the PRC regime). To contrast with the explicit acknowledgement upholding the national interests and political features in the positive portrait, the negative implications are usually stated vaguely, for example, portraying the 2008 Games as 'a rare historical opportunity, as well as a new challenge'.[31]

Several years after Beijing's first successful bid in 2001, Xuanjian Ma, an official/researcher in the GAS, provided further details of both the potential positive and negative political impacts of the Beijing Games on China in his work, stating that:

> Hosting the 2008 Games in Beijing ... we will be able to have more communication with the IOC, IFs and NOCs ... to make more friends ... The ... challenges are that the increase of interaction ... may result in more problems and conflicts. Therefore, we have to hold the dialectical materialist and historical materialist stance, in order to understand, maintain and develop the Olympic policy of our country, [we have to] analyse and adjust relevant policies for the Beijing Olympiad as soon as possible.[32]

A protective attitude is constructed in the above quotation through employing a number of conservative terms, such as 'have to hold', 'in order to ... maintain'. This defensive perspective is associated with the construction of the identities of different parties, for example, international organizations are portrayed as those with whom China would have 'more problems and conflicts' as a result of the increase in their interaction. By contrast, the mainstream political 'dialectical materialist and historical materialist' ideology of the PRC is acknowledged as the foundation to react in these potential 'problem-provoking' interactions associated with the opportunity of hosting the 2008 Olympic Games.

We may argue that the conservative tone and terms illustrate the nature of 'analysis and adjustment [of] relevant policies for the Beijing Olympiad' is to address the greater occurrence of 'problems and conflicts'. In other words, from a negative perspective, Ma's prediction of the potential challenges in the Beijing Games and the 'defensive' suggestions further emphasize the political significance and implication of the Beijing Games and ultimately promotes the political interests of the socialist regime.

Thus, on the one hand, there was a growth in the quantity of activities in relation to the Olympic movement in China and an increase in China's interaction with the international communities, especially the IOC and other international organizations,[33] during the preparation for the Beijing Olympics. And China was also confronted with fierce, if not more, criticisms coming from the international community in relation to various areas, including its sport system.[34] On the other hand, a conservative tone, which was in line with political mainstream of the Chinese society, was carefully maintained, at least, in the Chinese elite sport system, which was mainly based in a socialist planned economy and was seen as 'a reserve field' in China's market-oriented reform for the conservative attitude and limited achievement in terms of reform in this area.[35]

It is worth noting that due to the importance of the socialist character of the PRC, we choose to leave further investigation of its function in, and impacts on, Chinese Olympic discourse to a specific section. We now turn to the other two major political features of the Chinese Olympic discourse, i.e. nationalism and patriotism.

Nationalism and Patriotism in Olympic Discourse

In their encyclopaedia, *Nations and Nationalism*, Herb and Kaplan view nationalism as 'the process that defines, creates, and expresses the essential loyalty … holding people's allegiance … to a nation'.[36] Bairner indicates that the nationalist elements in sport, such as representing one's nation in international event, are closely related to cultural nationalism.[37] And patriotism, which sometimes is relatively politically influenced, is also evidenced in the sport domain, for example, in the desire to express national identity.

Due to the PRC government's concerns with the ethnic denotation of the concept of nationalism, which might have a negative impact on the minority ethnicities, the communist regime consistently employs 'patriotism', associating with its conflicts with imperialism and colonialism, and avoids using the term 'nationalism' (particularly its ethnic denotation).[38] The government also redefines the nature of the concept of 'Chinese nationalism' based on political criteria, i.e. the communist notion of the revolutionary class, and vague cultural principles.[39] Therefore, the concepts of patriotism and nationalism, in the Chinese context, are naturally associated with the Marxist 'class struggle' theory and an international narrative of independence in the Third World, and commonly overlaps each other for their political connotation.

As indicated in the previous section, elite sport and the Olympics are closely associated with political significance in Chinese narratives, thus both of the concepts, nationalism and patriotism, are regarded as integral features of Chinese elite sport and the Chinese

Olympic movement.[40] For example, a typical narrative in the Chinese Olympic discourse constructing the linkage between western Olympism and the Chinese nation is the notion of the 'Olympic dream' of China.[41] The speech of Weimin Yuan, the then-Minister of Sport,[42] in the ceremony of Beijing's successful bid in 2001 provides a good example of the 'Olympic dream' narrative and the politicization of this national aspiration. He states that:

> Hosting an Olympic Games in China is a dream of generations of Chinese people, and is also a common wish of the 1.3 billion Chinese people. As early as the 1950s, and 1960s, the leaders of the Party and of the country had repeatedly stated that China would host an Olympic Games.

Yuan also reminds the audience that this suggestion or aspiration was repeated by Deng Xiaoping in February 1972, and again in July 1990, and he went on to argue:

> ... Now, we are able to give consolation to the older generations of revolutionaries that under the leadership of the CPC Central Committee with Comrade Jiang Zemin at the core, thanks to the endeavours of Chinese people and of BOBICO as well as the support and understanding of the IOC members and international community, Beijing was finally awarded the 2008 Olympic Games.

Yuan portrays the opportunity of hosting an Olympic Games not only as a national dream which had lasted for generations, but also an expectation, particularly, of the political leaders of the PRC, despite the fact that the first three Chinese Olympic delegations were sent by its rival during the Chinese civil war, i.e. the Republic of China.[43] Through quoting statements of the top PRC leaders, Yuan emphasizes the role of these political leaders in the 'realisation of the Olympic dreams' and subtly mixes their identity with 'the Chinese people' in terms of the Olympic dream. These politicians then represent, if not replace, the Chinese people as those who have finally been able to realize their Olympic dream and to achieve their Olympic goals. This transformation of the subjects of the Olympic dream manifests a way in which a nationalist discourse, i.e. the realization of Chinese Olympic dream, is shaped as synonymous with the Party's Olympic dream, and is therefore utilized as an endorsement of the regime. This is similar to the function of the previous quotation crediting the 2008 Games to 'the great accomplishment that has been achieved in the reform and opening-up of society'.[44] Such an account reflects the political power over Olympic discourse exerted by the regime, which regulates the way in which the Chinese Olympic dream should be interpreted and to whom the achievement should be credited.

This national 'Olympic dream' is recognized as a 'part of the project to reinsert China into an international narrative of history and progress'.[45] As with the relationship between political implications of the Olympics and Olympic performance in the Chinese context, this connotation of national restoration and salvation is also often associated with Olympic performance, especially victories, which is recognized as 'the political task' of Chinese elite sport. And thus, the features of nationalism and patriotism, particularly the latter, are normally employed in the narrative of the ideological education for Chinese elite athletes. Taking the scenario of the speeches of Peng Liu, the Sport Minister, in All States Sport Minister Conferences before the Beijing Games, Mr Liu indicates in 2007 that:

> It is pointed out by comrades in the leading core [of the CPC] that, the spiritual character ... of [how] the Chinese female volleyball team and Chinese table tennis team worked tenaciously to win glory for the country ... is the foundation of the [Chinese] elite sport to prepare for the battle of the 2008 Games ... the victory of the Long March was achieved by the Red Army due to their recalcitrant spirit under the tough conditions; preparing the battle of the Olympic Games also needs the same recalcitrant spirit.

> Winning glory for the country is the eternal topic of the ideological and political work of elite sport teams. Facing the Beijing Games, [we] have to make our athletes realize that winning glory for the State is not only a slogan, but also a heavy responsibility and an honourable mission.[46]

One year later, the Sport Minister reinforces that:

> The construction of the ideology and the sportsmanship [and positive behaviour] of elite sport teams is as important as training ... in the battle-preparation [for the 2008 Games]. All Centres ... have to regard the education of patriotism ... the honing of [an appropriate] mentality as important elements in the battle - preparation [for the 2008 Games].[47]

In both quotations, patriotism, as an element of the ideological education of Chinese athletes, is portrayed as a crucial factor for the preparation of the 2008 Beijing Games. Chinese elite sport and athletes, in return, had also been utilized and internalized as a metaphor of patriotism, such as in the case of the Chinese female volleyball team and Chinese table tennis team in the above quotation. Because of the victories of Chinese table tennis players and female volleyball players in the pre-reform era and the early stage of China's reform, these two sports are not only closely associated with national pride, but also well recognized as incentives for patriotic feelings with socialist hints and symbols for China's restoration from the damage of Cultural Revolutions.[48]

Thanks to the traditional ideological education and political portrait of Chinese elite sport, 'winning glory for the country' in international events has been recognized as an innate and essential duty of Chinese elite sport.[49] Moreover, this heavily used patriotic phrase is not only linked with Chinese elite athletes, but also associated with political metaphors, such as the revolutionary spirit of the Red Army. In addition to the notion of the Red Army, other revolutionary spiritual concepts or phrases, such as 'recalcitrant spirit' and 'working tenaciously to win glory for the country', are also portrayed as essential content of the ideological education of Chinese elite athletes in their striving to achieve Olympic success. This linkage between Chinese Olympic discourse and the features of the socialist regime is also illustrated in the previous quotation from the speech of the then Minister of Sport, Yuan Weimin, and is analysed in the following section looking at socialism narratives in Chinese Olympic discourse in the elite sport system.

Socialism in Olympic Discourse

As one of not many countries that remain labelled (by itself or others) as a socialist one, China has embraced and merged its socialist character into the Olympic discourse in two principal ways. On the one hand, it associates China's achievements in the Olympics (in terms of both its successful bid and elite sport performance) with the fact of its socialist characteristics as a means of legitimating its political system. On the other hand, socialism provides the ideological foundation on which it bases its interaction with the international community.

The socialist character of the PRC is associated with Chinese Olympic victories both in the Olympic stadia and during its bidding procedure for hosting Olympic Games. For instance, the successful bid for the 2008 Games was officially identified as a victory that 'fully reflects the great accomplishments that have been achieved through the reform and opening-up ...' in a number of policy documents and official publications.[50] Given the strong political connotation of 'the reform and opening-up', symbolizing the socialism with Chinese characteristics, we would maintain that such official rhetoric, which was commonly employed in Chinese society in the pre-2008 era, portrays the successful bid of 2008 as an endorsement of the socialist regime and its development route, albeit there is no direct reference to socialism.

The speech of He Zhenliang, the former President of the COC, which is recognized as another title of the GAS,[51] in the celebration ceremony for the successful 2008 bid in 2001 provides a more obvious example, stating that:

> This [winning the 2008 bid] is the [IOC's] recognition of our achievement in the reform and opening-up, and of the support of our government and Chinese people [to the bid] ... Genuinely speaking, I would ascribe [the successful bid] to the leadership of the Party, to our achievement in the reform and opening-up, to the People's support.[52]

In the above quotation, the successful bid is not only identified as a product of the socialism with Chinese characteristics (represented by the terms 'reform and opening-up') but also portrayed as a symbol of the international recognition of this development route. Given He's ambiguous expression, ignoring the difference between the accomplishments of the reform of China in different domains, for example the economy and politics, we would suggest that this account, implicitly generalizes the nature of the international recognition and thus subtly endorses the political theme of the PRC.

It is also worth noting that in the second part of the above quotation, He identifies the domestic factors leading to the successful bid. In contrast to his interpretation from the international perspective, the Party's leadership is explicitly indicated as the leading and foremost factor. This feature of He's account in relation to the role of the Party's leadership is in line with a pattern of embracing political rhetoric in Chinese Olympic discourse, in which the socialist character of the regime is normally portrayed as the foundation for excellence in Olympic performance in terms of both resource and ideology.

At the same time the excellent Olympic performance of Chinese athletes, in turn, embodies the superiority of socialism. For instance, it is stated by the Central Committee of the CPC during the preparation for the 2008 Olympics that:

> Drafting the Plan for Winning Olympic Glory in the new era ... [we should] further utilize the superiority of socialism, [we should] insist and refine Juguo Tizhi ... [and] better integrate sport resources from the whole country.[53]

The phrase of '[the capability of] concentrating all national resources for a major task' is acknowledged as an embodiment of the 'superiority of socialism' by Hu Jintao, the former President of China.[54] This is also consistent with the main feature of Juguo Tizhi,[55] the support of the whole nation for the elite sport system, and with the notion of 'integrat[ing] sport resources from the whole country' in the above quotation. Given the close relationship, constructed by the core of the CPC, between the socialism and Juguo Tizhi and *the Olympic Glory Plan*, we would argue that this promotion of the socialist features of Chinese elite sport officially reinforces and endorses the status of Juguo Tizhi and the significance of excellent Olympic performance in the PRC.

In ideological terms, the account in relation to the ideological education of elite athletes for the preparation of the Olympics provides another good example of the socialist elements in Chinese Olympic discourse. It is stated in a GAS document that is specifically published in 2006 for the ideological education of elite athletes preparing for the Beijing Olympic Games:

> Further strengthening the ideological education of the national teams is an urgent need in the preparation for the Olympics, and is an important means to guarantee the effectiveness of the preparation of the 2008 Games.

> It is worth addressing specifically that some athletes ... have even behaved in libertarian, hedonistic, ways exhibiting extreme individualism and materialism [money-worship] ... [because] they have abundant opportunities for competing overseas, they are susceptible to Western ideology, values, cultural products and unhealthy practices ...
>
> All of the new members of the national teams have to be given [ideological education] tutorials ... [We] must educate [athletes] about the history of the [Communist] Party ... the 'Socialist concept of honour and disgrace' ... [which should be] reflected in their love of the country and the organizations [to which they belong] ... in order to let them clearly understand the essential task of, and the significance of, the preparation for the 2008 Olympic Games.[56]

In the above quoted statement from *The Opinions on Further Strengthening and Improving the Ideological Education of National Teams*, the ideological education of the elite athletes is identified as compulsory and a necessary condition for Chinese elite athletes to win Olympic glory, especially for 2008. In other words, education in the socialist ideology is legitimated by the significance of Olympic victory in Chinese society.

As exemplified in the above quotation, such ideological education is consistent with the patriotic character of Chinese Olympic discourse, 'love of the country and the organizations'; and with the political character of China, i.e. socialism of the PRC, education in 'the history of the [Communist] Party ... [and] the "socialist concept of honour and disgrace"'. From a counter perspective, the 'misbehaviour' of elite athletes, which is identified as a result of the influence of other, i.e. Western, ideologies, is portrayed as the target of the ideological education. Given the close relationship with the term 'Western' and capitalism in the Chinese context, the socialist features of this ideological education are subtly promoted through criticizing capitalist and Western values. This is consistent with previous quotation from Ma, accentuating the importance of maintaining the 'dialectical materialist and historical materialist' stance in dealing with 'problems' caused by the increased interaction with international organizations for the staging of the Beijing Games.[57]

As previously demonstrated, providing satisfactory Olympic performance is recognized as the essential duty of Chinese elite sport, especially of those relying on government funds. We would thus argue that the ideological education is, to a degree, consistent with the interests of the Chinese elite system and the individual interests of elite athletes, given that it is designed to promote Olympic performance. In other words, even though it is the collective and national interests that are ultimately promoted in the socialist discourse advocating ideological education for Chinese Olympians, this does not necessarily lead to a full rejection of the interests of the individual. To a certain extent, the collective and individual interests are consistent with each other in the ideological education to which Chinese elite athletes are subjected. Thus, through fulfilling the collective and national interests, certain individual interests have been satisfied and vested interest groups have subsequently been formed. Such groups proactively promote the national and their own interests, which are to be realized through providing satisfactory Olympic performance, and thus reject the pursuit of 'extreme' individual interests threatening the preparation for the Olympics.

Even though the conflicts between some 'Western ideology' and socialist philosophy are well recognized, the socialist development of the country remains portrayed as a beneficiary of the Western-origin Olympics, particularly through the 2008 Beijing Games. As indicated in the previous quotation from the documents of the Central Committee of the CPC, the Beijing Games is portrayed as an opportunity 'to promote the development of the socialist material progress, and cultural and ethical progress, of our country'.

As a brief conclusion of this section, we would argue that the Chinese Olympic discourse is influenced by the 'superficial understanding' of the nature of the Olympics in the Chinese context. Along with imminence of the Beijing Games, the political significance of the Olympics was projected to, and was employed in, the accentuation of the significance of the Olympic performance. These two themes of the official Olympic discourse, i.e. the emphasis on the political significance of, and on the performance in, the Olympics, are in line with the interests of the government and of the Chinese sport authority, which is also a state organ. It also reflects its dominant power over discourse, regulating both the perspective of constructing the nature of the Olympics in Chinese elite sport systems and the approach of realizing the significance of the Olympics through Chinese elite sport.

The Post-2008 Olympic Discourse: Constant Political But Declining Performance Rhetoric

After realizing the 'century-long Olympic dream', the interpretation of the experiences and implication of the expected 'opportunities and challenges' of the Beijing Games became one of the most important parts of the post-2008 Chinese Olympic discourse.[58] Despite this change in the content of the Chinese Olympic discourse, the emphasis on the political implications of the Beijing Games and of the Olympics in general is continuously evidenced in the post-2008 era. For example, as with the manner of 'politicizing' the successful bid of the Beijing Games, the staging of the 2008 Olympics is interpreted as a communication opportunity conveying the restoration of the national status of China, and/or linked to the political character of the communist regime. For instance, in the officially-published summary of the 60-year development of Chinese elite sport, Hua Li, a senior sport official states that:

> In 2008, one year before the 60-year anniversary of the PRC, Beijing hosted the XXIX Olympiad, [by which] the Chinese nation fulfilled its century old wish. From a suffering and humiliated 'sick man of Asia', to [a country that is] ... capable of hosting a 'truly exceptional' Olympics, to the number 1 in gold medals, China's tremendous change has surprised and convinced the world ... [which] show [their] respect and admiration, representing international appreciation for the magnificent 30-year reform ...[59]

In the above quotation, the Beijing Games is explicitly associated with the development of the PRC, and is recognized as a symbol of one stage of the development of China from the humiliating past to the glorious present. China's peak performance in the 2008 Games is portrayed as a means by which China was able to 'surprise and convince' the international community, which is consistent with the pre-2008 Chinese Olympic discourse linking satisfactory Olympic performance with the extrinsic functions of the Olympic Games.

This account implies the success of the Beijing Games in fulfilling its expected extrinsic function of constructing a positive image of the re-establishment of the Chinese nation to the world. It also indirectly constructs the identity of the world in the Beijing Games, as witness to the development of China. Thus, through associating the Beijing Games with 'the magnificent task of the 30-year reform' of China, the author also frames the world's acceptance of the Beijing Games as a recognition and an endorsement of development of China and thus of the achievement and the reign of the socialist regime.

Peng Liu's speech at the 2009 All States Sports Minister Conference provides a more explicit example of this linkage constructed between the 2008 Olympics and global recognition of the communist regime. The Sport Minister indicates that:

> The successful Beijing Games and the outstanding results of Chinese [elite] sport are a true reflection of the PRC's glorious procedure of striving [to become] prosperous and strong; is a showcase of the great achievement of the reform and opening-up of Chinese society and the modernization of China; is a successful practice of a mode of sport development with a Chinese character that is consistent with the Chinese context … 2009 is the 60-year anniversary of the PRC, is a new beginning for Chinese elite sport; [Chinese elite sport] experienced its glory in the Beijing Games … is facing the future, is working around the clock, tirelessly and continuously striving to transcend [its former success].[60]

The Beijing Games is explicitly framed by the Sport Minister as a 'reflection' and a 'showcase' of the accomplishment of the PRC since its establishment. Implying the nature of the information 'reflected' and 'shown' via the 2008 Olympics, these two terms indirectly construct the international connection, and the exogenous origin, of the Olympics in the Chinese context. Thus, Liu suggests that the success in the Beijing Games should be interpreted not only as positive images conveyed to the world; but also a proof via an international means of the appropriateness of the socialist route that is implied in terms, such as 'PRC's glorious procedure' and 'the great achievement of the reform and opening-up'.

Furthermore, the top Chinese sport bureaucrat also identifies the general success of the Beijing Games as 'a successful practice of the mode of sport development with a Chinese character'. In other words, not the successful performance of Chinese elite sport in the Beijing Games, but 'the successful Beijing Games' is portrayed as an endorsement of the effectiveness of the Chinese elite sport system. Therefore, in order to 'continuously transcend' the successes in the Beijing Games, which would constantly reflect the 'great achievement of the reform and opening-up', the current direction and means of elite sport development, i.e. Juguo Tizhi and Zhuanye sport, have to be maintained after this 'new beginning of Chinese elite sport'.

More than simply maintaining this political feature of Chinese Olympic discourse, we would argue that there is a more explicit knowledge in terms of the extrinsic function of the Olympics constructed in the post-2008 Chinese Olympic discourse. For example, during Jinping Xi's visit to Sochi, the President of China emphasized in his speech to the Chinese delegation that:

> We have realized the Olympic dream through successfully staging the Beijing Games. At the moment, we are closer to the target of the rejuvenation of the Chinese nation than ever before. Everyone's dream, the dream of [being] a Sport Power is closely associated with the China Dream.[61]

Two significant phenomena, 'China Dream' and 'Sport Power' are employed in Xi's statement. The first, 'China Dream', is a political idiom Xi promoted himself, and is 'a strategic thought in relation to realize the rejuvenation of the Chinese nation'.[62] Secondly, the current Chinese President links his political idea to his predecessor's mission assigned to Chinese sport, i.e. 'becoming a Sport Power'.[63] The concept of 'becoming a Sport Power' was identified as 'the new outline and objective for the future development of Chinese sport' and was immediately embraced within Chinese elite sport discourse as its main slogan of development.[64] For example, in the latest version of *the Olympic Glory Plan*, i.e. the 2011 Plan, it is identified as the 10-year goal of the development of Chinese elite sport in the section *Guiding Theory and Principle*.[65]

It could be argued that through associating the concept of the 'China Dream', which embraces traditional nationalist connotation (i.e. the rejuvenation of the Chinese nation), into his interpretation of the Olympics, President Xi indirectly re-emphasizes the nationalist connotation of the 'Olympic Dream'. And his reference to 'Sport Power' subtly endorses the consistency of both political rhetoric of Chinese Olympic discourse and the political task of Chinese elite sport, which was assigned by President Jintao Hu, in the post-2008 era. Subsequently, as with the concept of 'Sport Power', this high-profile speech has been seriously 'studied' by Chinese elite sport authorities, has received a great amount of positive feedback, and has been embedded in Chinese elite sport discourse.[66]

From an international perspective, the changes in the policy statements of three editions of *the Plans* provide a good example of the development in the Chinese understanding of the Olympics. There are two brief statements relating to the social impact of the Olympics in the *1994 Plan*.[67] The first focuses on the Olympic performance and its impact on 'the socialist material progress, and cultural and ethical progress'. The second emphasizes the benefit of 'promoting the Olympic ideology and [of] advocating the Olympic spirit … for stimulating the opening-up of our country and its international communication'.

For the second (2001–2010) edition of this series of documents, thanks to the successful bid of the 2008 Games, the *2001 Plan* focuses solely on the social influence of the Beijing Olympic, such as its 'significant impact on the economic and social development … the "opening-up" … and international status of the country'.[68]

Compared to the brief statements in the *1994 Summary* and the 2008-focused account in the *2001 Summary*, the authors of the *2011 Summary* not only assign the significance of the Olympics to different international events but also associate these sporting events with various strategic practices of states. It is stated that:

> International sport events, represented by the Olympic Games, [could be used as a means for] international comparison, [performance in which] is the benchmark and character of progress [towards becoming a] 'Sport Power' … Elite sport and the Olympic strategy will remain its significant role and implication in the economic, social and cultural development [of China] in the following decade … the Olympic Games … has become an important platform for international communication, competition and cooperation as well as a shop window for the image of the general strength of nations.[69]

Straightforwardly, it could be argued that the above quotation from the second section of the *2011 Summary*, the majority of which focuses on the extrinsic function of the Olympics, provides a more detailed account than the statements, covering the same topic, in the previous two versions. From an international perspective, terms that imply national practices associated with the Olympics, including 'competition', 'cooperation', 'international comparison' etc., are employed in the above quotation. We would argue that these terms implying different practices of states not only suggest an increased Chinese understanding of the extrinsic function of the Olympics; but also construct various relationships between, and/or the different identities of, the participant countries of the Olympics Games.

Even though there is no direct mention of elite sport performance in the above quotation from the 2011 *Plan*, given the high media exposure and thus public attention to the Olympic medal table, it could be argued that the notions of 'international comparison', 'competitions' among different states and the 'benchmark' of being a 'Sport Power' subtly constructs elite sport performance as the criterion of 'comparison' between delegations from different NOCs. Thus, in order to realize this role as a 'Sport Power', it is subtly suggested in the policy from the GAS that elite sport performance, and consequently Juguo Tizhi and the Zhuanye sport system, needs to be maintained.

This association between Olympic performance, Olympic strategy and Juguo Tizhi is also evidenced in the official interpretation of the concept of 'Sport Power', which was made by a group of renowned Chinese sport scholars summoned by the GAS and led by its researching institution.[70] It is stated that:

> Given the scarce resources of China and the unbalanced development among elite sports, maintaining Juguo Tizhi ... [and] implementing Olympic strategies is a necessary and inevitable choice ... After the Beijing Games, as evidenced by the general strength of elite sport, there is no doubt that China has become a Sport Power in elite sport ... Reinforcing and maintaining this advantaged position in elite sport is the primary requirement of the implementation of the strategy of becoming a Sport Power, [which aims to] lead the overall development of Chinese sport with the development of elite sport.[71]

In the above quotation, the authors portray the sustaining of excellent performance as a requirement for maintaining the position of China as a 'Sport Power'. This account utilizes this powerful statement, i.e. 'Sport Power', from the top leader of China to legitimize the maintenance of Juguo Tizhi, at a time when it has been identified as a target of Chinese elite sport reform.[72] Besides stressing the importance of maintaining the 2008 success through linking it with the notion of 'Sport Power', Hu, the author, also associates the implementation of Juguo Tizhi with the character of Chinese society, i.e. 'the scarce resources' and 'the unbalanced development among elite sports', which is a supporting narrative that is also evidenced in the pre-2008 discourse.

However, the *comprehensive* development of Chinese sport is also identified as a crucial feature of 'Sport Power', which accentuates the development of mass sport and the sport industry and thus, to a degree, deemphasizes elite sport performance and the Olympic strategy.[73] In line with this feature of this significant narrative introduced to the post-2008 Chinese Olympic discourse, Hu also identifies 'the overall development of Chinese sport' as the ultimate goal of developing elite sport in the above quotation.

In contrast to the brief, and to a degree indirect, account in relation to the development of other parts of Chinese sport, i.e. mass sport and the sport industry, the Sport Minister's speeches in the All States Sports Minister Annual Conference in the post-2008 era provide a more explicit illustration of the decreasing emphasis on elite sport. For instance, straightforwardly from a quantitative perspective, the terms of 'the Olympic Games' and 'Juguo Tizhi' were, respectively, mentioned 27 and 13 times in the 2009 version; and the number was reduced to 12 and three references, respectively, in the 2013 edition.[74]

In sum, the further emphasis on, and more explicit reference to, the extrinsic functions of the Olympics (including both the 2008 edition and other Olympic Games) is the defining character of post-2008 Chinese Olympic discourse. The peak performance of Chinese elite athletes in the Beijing Olympic Games is recognized in the Chinese context as a significant characteristic of the 2008 Games. As a consequence, this excellent performance is employed as an endorsement of the effectiveness and success of Juguo Tizhi and the Olympic strategy. Nonetheless, though the importance of Olympic performance to Chinese elite sport has been consistently acknowledged in official discourse, it has been gradually deemphasized in Chinese society. This characteristic of the post-2008 Chinese Olympic discourse, especially that within Chinese elite sport policy documents and official publications, is in line with the narratives emphasized by core actors of the PRC regime, and reflects the consistent political power over the Chinese elite sport system and discourse.

Conclusion

Consistent with the original purpose for which modern sport and the Olympics were introduced to China by the national elite, these Western phenomena have accumulated remarkable political significance in the Chinese context. The Chinese Olympic discourse has thus been associated with nationalist and patriotic rhetoric, such as the restoration of the Chinese nation from its century of humiliation; and with socialism and other related ideologies, such as collective interests and values.

Olympic success has been identified as an important approach through which these 'extrinsic functions' of the Olympics are to be realized. Such emphasis on Olympic performance is consistent with the portrait and understanding of the nature of the Olympics in the Chinese context, for competition among individual athletes is recognized as an embodiment of international competition and is thus accentuated as a symbol representing the rejuvenation of the Chinese nation and the superiority of the socialist regime. The great attention paid to outstanding Olympic performance is also in line with the interests of those within the Zhuanye sport system of Chinese elite sport, whose essential duty is to provide successful Olympic performance in order to realize these 'extrinsic functions'.

Thus, in the official Olympic discourse, especially that from the Chinese elite sport authorities, the significance of successful Olympic performance is what was accentuated. This reflected the role of the sporting elite in terms of its 'power over' Olympic discourse in the pre-2008 and the hosting era, laying down the nature of Olympic success and the approach to realizing it, and promoting the notion of a politically significant sport event in which successful performance should be prioritized.

With China's increasing involvement with the international Olympic movement, especially after the Beijing Games, there is a more explicit account in relation to the extrinsic function of the Olympics evidenced in the construction of the concept of 'Olympic' in the Chinese context. The political connotation of, and political influence on, Chinese Olympic discourse (reflecting the political 'power over' discourse) have been maintained in the post-2008 era. However, the thrust of the discourse has changed. Powerful political terms have been added into the post-2008 Chinese Olympic discourse, including the notion of China as a 'Sport Power' and the 'China Dream'.

In contrast to the extreme emphasis on Olympic performance during the run up to the Beijing Games, the new addition to Chinese sport discourse, to a degree, decreases the significance of Olympic performance in Chinese society. Thus, even though Olympic performance remains an important factor, if not the important factor, to Chinese elite sport, and is continuously stressed in policy documents, there has been a declining trend in the emphasis given to Olympic performance in Chinese sport policies. It could be argued that although these changes at discursive level influence the value of, and vested interests within, Juguo Tizhi and Zhuanye sport, whose core duty is to 'win glory for the country', the discourse of the party elite is consistently and proactively supported by the administrators of these sporting bodies, because the Chinese sport bureaucrats are still actors within state organs and the Chinese sport system remain dependent upon the support of the party elite.

Notes

1. Susan Brownell, *Beijing's Games: What the Olympics Mean to China* (Lanham: Rowman & Littlefield, 2008); Jingxia Dong and J.A. Mangan, 'Beijing Olympics Legacies: Certain Intentions and Certain and Uncertain Outcomes', *The International Journal of the History of Sport* 25, no. 14 (2008), 2019–40; Hong Fan, Ping Wu, and Huan Xiong, 'Beijing Ambitions: An Analysis of the Chinese Elite Sports System and its Olympic Strategy for the 2008 Olympic Games', *The International Journal of the History of Sport* 22, no. 4 (July 2005), 510–29; and Guoqi Xu, *Olympic Dreams: China and Sports 1895–2008* (Cambridge, MA: Harvard University Press, 2008), 23.
2. Brownell, *Beijing's Games*; and Xu, *Olympic Dreams*.
3. Shi Wang, *Yan Fu Ji* [Collection of Yan Fu's Work] (Beijing: Zhonghua Shuju, 1986); and Zhang, 'Quan Xue Pian' [Encouragement to Learning], in Junmei Xue (ed.), *Xingshi Congshu* [Waking Lion Series] (Henan: Zhongguo Guji Chubanshe, 1998).
4. Wenxue Yuan, *Liu Changchun: The First Chinese Athlete in Olympics* (Liaoning: Dalian ligong daxue chubanshe [Dalian Sci-Tech University Press], 2008).
5. Yuanwei Li et al., 'Guanyu Jinyibu wanshan Woguo Jingji Tiyu Juguo Tizhi de Yanjiu', [Research on the Further Perfection of Juguo Tizhi of Elite Sports of China], *China Sport Science and Technology* 39, no. 8 (2003), 1–5.
6. Shaozu Wu, 中国体育史 [The History of Sport in the People's Republic of China] (Beijing: China Book Press, 1999); and Luzeng Song, 'Jianchi Wei Guojia Zhengti Liyi Fuwu de Woguo Tiyu Waishi Gongzuo' [Serving the General National interests: Sport in the Diplomacy of China], in GAS (ed.), *60 Years of New China's Sport* (Beijing: People's Press, 2009).
7. The conflict focuses on whether the PRC government in Mainland China or the ROC government in Taiwan should be the legitimate representative of China in the IOC.
8. Douyin Xiong, 'Beijing Aoyunhui Yu Zhongguo Tiyu Fazhan' [The Beijing Olympic Games and the Development of the Sport in China], *Journal of Sports and Science* 23, no. 6 (2002), 9–12.
9. Peng Liu, 'Cong Xiri "Dongya Bingfu" Dao Shengshi Tiyu Huihuang' [From the 'Sickman in East Asia' to the Glory], in GAS (ed.), *60 Years of New China's Sport* (Beijing: People's Press, 2009); Jiandong Yi, *Olympic History in 100 Years* (Jiangxi: Baihuazhou Wenyi Chubanshe [Baihuazhou Literature and Arts Press], 2008); and Bin Long, 'Zhongguo Aoyunhui Chengji Tanyin: Yi Bajie Xiaji Aoyunhui Weili' [Researches on the Chinese Olympic Performance in Eight Summer Olympics], *Hubei Sport Science and Techonology* 32, no. 2 (2013), 141–4.
10. Kevin Caffrey, 'The Beijing Olympics as Indicator of a Chinese Competitive Ethic', *The International Journal of the History of Sport* 28, no. 2 (2009), 1122–45; Jingxia Dong, 'Woman, Nationalism and the Beijing Olympics: Preparing for Glory', *The International Journal of the History of Sport* 22, no. 4 (2005), 530–544; Xiaoqian Hu, 'An Analysis of Chinese Olympic and Elite Sport Policy Discourse in the Post-Beijing 2008 Olympic Games Era' (PhD thesis, Loughborough University, 2015); Glos Ho, 'Attitudes Towards Mainland China Beijing Olympics Under "One Country Two Systems": An Ethnographic Study of Hong Kong Students' Attitudes towards Mainland China', *The International Journal of the History of Sport* 27 (2010), 570–87; Susan Brownell and Kevin William, 'The Beijing Olympics as a Turning Point? China's First Olympics in East Asian Perspective', *YALE CEAS Occasional Publications* 3, no. 23 (2011), 185–204; Monroe Edwin Price and Daniel Dayan, *Owning the Olympics: Narratives of the New China*; Susan Brownell, *Beijing's Games: What the Olympics Mean to China* (Ann Arbor: University of Michigan Press, 2008); and Victor Cha, *Beyond the Final Score: The Politics of Sport in Asia* (New York: Columbia University Press, 2009).
11. Jintao Hu, 'Hu Jintao's Speech at the Awards Ceremony for the 2008 Olympics and the Paralympics' (China News Agency, 2008), http://news.sina.com.cn/c/2008-09-29/125116381584.shtml (accessed 4 November 2011).
12. Xiong, 'Beijing Aoyunhui Yu Zhongguo Tiyu Fazhan' [The Beijing Olympic Games and the Development of the Sport in China].
13. GAS, *The Summary of the Olympic Glory Plan 2001–2010* (2002).

14. Tong Qian and Chen Zhi, 'Xi Jinping Qinqie Kanwang Suoqi Dongaohui Zhongguo Daibiaotuan' [Xi Jinping Visits the Chinese Delegation for the Sochi Winter Games], *Xinhua News* (2014).
15. Hu, 'Hu Jintao's Speech at the Awards Ceremony for the 2008 Olympics and the Paralympics'.
16. Ruth Wodak and Micheal Meyer, 'Critical Discourse Analysis: History, Agenda, Theory and Methodology', in Ruth Wodak and Michael Meyer (eds), *Methods of Critical Discourse Analysis* (London: Sage, 2009), 5–6.
17. Norman Fairclough, 'A Dialectical-Relational Approach to Critical Discourse Analysis in Social Research', in Ruth Wodak and Michael Meyer (eds), *Methods of Critical Discourse Analysis* (London: Sage, 2009), 162–186.
18. Ibid.
19. Fan, Wu, and Xiong, 'Beijing Ambitions'; GAS, *The Political Affairs of the General Administration of Sport*, 2016, http://www.sport.gov.cn/n315/index.html (accessed 6 April 2016); and Fan Wei, Fan Hong, and Lu Zhouxiang, 'Chinese State Sports Policy: Pre- and Post- Beijing 2008', *The International Journal of the History of Sport* 27, nos 14–15 (2010), 2380–402.
20. Norman Fairclough, *Analysing Discourse: Textual Analysis for Social Research* (London: Routledge, 2003), 37; Norman Fairclough, 'Discourse Analysis in Organization Studies: The Case for Critical Realism', *Organizational Studies* 26, no. 6 (2005), 915–39; and Fairclough, 'A Dialectical-Relational Approach to Critical Discourse Analysis in Social Research'.
21. Fairclough, *Analysing Discourse*; and Fairclough, 'A Dialectical-Relational Approach to Critical Discourse Analysis in Social Research'.
22. Ibid.
23. Fairclough, *Analysing Discourse*.
24. Douyin Xiong, 'Beijing Aoyunhui Yu Zhongguo Tiyu Fazhan' [The Beijing Olympic Games and the Development of the Sport in China], *Journal of Sports and Science* 23, no. 6 (2002), 9–12.
25. GAS, *The Summary of the Olympic Glory Plan 2001–2010*, 2002, 1. It is worth noting that *The Olympic Glory Plan* (hereafter *The Plan*), which is the source of the first quotation, is a periodically renewed Chinese elite sport policy. There have been three editions, respectively covering 1994–2000, 2001–2010, 2011–2020 (hereafter, *The 1994 Plan*, *The 2001 Plan* and *The 2011 Plan*). Though specifically named after the Olympics, *The Plans* are regarded as essentially the most representative political guidelines for the development of Chinese elite sport [see Hao, Qin, and Hai Ren, 'Lun "Juguo Tizhi" Yu Aoyun Zhengguang Jihua de Guanxi' [Discussion on the Relationship between 'Juguo Tizhi' and the Strategic Plan for the Winning Olympic Glory], and *Tiyu Wenhua Daokan* [Tiyu Culture Guide] 12 (2003), 3–6; Xiong, Xia, and Tang, *Woguo Jingji Tiyu Fazhan Moshi de Yanjiu* [Studies on the Developing Model of Elite Sport of Our Nation]], and 'the strategic blueprint guiding Chinese elite sport for its steady development, [and] the programmatic document directing the development of Chinese elite sport and the implementation of Olympic strategy' [see GAS, *The Summary of the Olympic Glory Plan 2011–2020*, 1].
26. The Central Committee of the CPC, *Zhonggong Zhongyang Guowuyuan Guanyu Jinyibu Jiaqiang He Gaijin Xinshiqi Tiyu Gongzuo de YIjian* [The Central Committee of the CPC and the State Council's Guidelines for Further Strengthening and Improving Sporting Affairs in the New Era] (PRC, 2002), 1, http://www.sport.gov.cn/n16/n1092/n16849/127397.html.
27. SPCSC, *The Summary of the Olympic Glory Plan*, 1994–2000, 1.
28. Luzeng Song, 'Jianchi Wei Guojia Zhengti Liyi Fuwu de Woguo Tiyu Waishi Gongzuo' [Serving the General National Interests: Sport in the Diplomacy of China]; Zhenliang He, 'Aolinpikeyundong de Pubian Jiazhi Yu Duoweihua Shijie' [The Universal Value of the Olympics and Multi-Cultural World], *Tiyu Wenhua Daokan* [Tiyu Culture Guide] no. 2 (2002); Weimin Yuan, *Yuan Weimin Zai Beijing Shenao Chenggong Baogaohui Shang de Baogao* [Yuan Weimin's Report in the Colloquium of Beijing's Successful Olympic Bid] (Beijing, China, 2001), http://sports.sohu.com/64/76/sports_news163357664.shtml; and Xiong, 'Beijing Aoyunhui Yu Zhongguo Tiyu Fazhan' [The Beijing Olympic Games and the Development of the Sport in China].

29. Xiong, 'Beijing Aoyunhui Yu Zhongguo Tiyu Fazhan' [The Beijing Olympic Games and the Development of the Sport in China], 11.
30. Xuanjian Ma, 'Lun Zhongguo de Aolinpike Zhengce' [Discussion on the Olympic Policy of China], *Tiyu Wenhua Daokan* [Tiyu Culture Guide] 11 (2005), 27–31.
31. The Central Committee of the CPC, *Zhonggong Zhongyang Guowuyuan Guanyu Jinyibu Jiaqiang He Gaijin Xinshiqi Tiyu Gongzuo de YIjian* [The Central Committee of the CPC and the State Council's Guidelines for Further Strengthening and Improving Sporting Affairs in the New Era], 1.
32. Xuanjian Ma, 'Lun Zhongguo de Aolinpike Zhengce' [Discussion on the Olympic Policy of China], *Tiyu Wenhua Daokan* [Tiyu Culture Guide] 11 (2005), 27–31.
33. Cha, *Beyond the Final Score*.
34. Minky Worden, *China's Great Leap: The Beijing Games and Olympian Human Rights*, 1st ed. (New York: Seven Stories Press, 2008); and Dong and Mangan, 'Beijing Olympics Legacies'.
35. Xinping, Zhang, *China's Sport in Post-2008 Era* (Guangzhou: Zhongshan University Press, 2009).
36. Guntram Herb and David Kaplan (eds), *Nation and Nationalism: A Global Historical Overview (Volume 3, 1945–1989)* (Santa Barbara, CA: ABC-CLIO, 2008), xi.
37. Alan Bairner, 'Sports and Nationalism', in Guntram Herb and David Kaplan (eds), *Nation and Nationalism: A Global Historical Overview* (Santa Barbara, CA: ABC-CLIO, 2008), 998.
38. Orion Lewis and Jessica Teets, 'China', in Guntram Herb and David Kaplan (eds), *Nation and Nationalism: A Global Historical Overview* (Santa Barbara, CA: ABC-CLIO, 2008), 1190–200.
39. William Callahan, 'National Insecurities: Humiliation, Salvation, and Chinese Nationalism', *Alternatives* 24 (2004), 199–218; and Lewis and Teets, 'China'.
40. Duan Shijie, *Guojia Tiyu Zongju Fujuzhang Duan Shijie Zai 2007 Nian Quanguo Tiyu Juzhang Huiyi Shang de Zongjie Jianghua* [The Conclusion Speech of Deputy Sport Minister Duan Shijie for 2007 All States Sports Minister Conference] (2008); Brownell, *Beijing's Games*; Dong and Mangan, 'Beijing Olympics Legacies'; and Xu, *Olympic Dreams*.
41. Hu, 'Hu Jintao's Speech at the Awards Ceremony for the 2008 Olympics and the Paralympics'; Zhenliang He, *He Zhenliang Zai Beijing Shenao Chenggong Baogaohui Shang de Baogao* [Hezhenliang's Report in the Colloquium of Beijing's Successful Olympic Bid] (2002); Yuan, 'Yuan Weimin Tongzhi Zai 2001 Nian Quanguo Tiyu Juzhang Huiyi Huiyi Shang de Jianghua' [Comrade Yuan Weimin's Speech at the Conference of All-State Sports Ministers]; Tong Qian and Chen Zhi, 'Xi Jinping Qinqie Kanwang Suoqi Dongaohui Zhongguo Daibiaotuan' [Xi Jinping Visits the Chinese Delegation for the Sochi Winter Games], *Xinhua News* (2014); Yan Tang. 'Dui Woguo "Aoyun Zhengguang Jihua" de Duowei Shenshi' [A Multi-Dimensional Analysis of Chinese Olympic Gold Medal Winning Program], *Journal of Wuhan Institute of Physical Education* 41, no. 2 (2007), 17–21; Liqun Xu. 'Liu Peng: Juguo Tizhi Will Be Carried on and Consummated', *People's Daily* (2008), http://politics.people.com.cn/GB/1027/7830416.html; and Peng Liu, *Guojia Tiyu Zongju Juzhang Liu Peng Zai 2007 Nian Quanguo Tiyu Juzhang Huiyi Shang de Jianghua* [The Speech of Sport Minister Peng Liu for 2007 All States Sports Minister Conference] (2007), http://zhuanti.sports.cn/07tiyujuzhang/fy/2007-01-18/1024430.html.
42. Weimin Yuan, 'Yuan Weimin Zai Beijing Shenao Chenggong Baogaohui Shang de Baogao' [Yuan Weimin's Report in the Colloquium of Beijing's Successful Olympic Bid], 1.
43. The PRC was established in 1949. Thus, Yuan subtly isolated those politicians of the Republic of China (hereafter the ROC. It is the regime that lost the Chinese civil war to the Communist Party and retreated to Taiwan. The Olympic delegation of the ROC is now officially known as Chinese Taipei) from the realization of the national dream through explicitly indicating the date, i.e. 1950s. Mingxin Tang, *The History of the Republic of China's Participation in the Olympic Games* (Taipei: Chinese Taipei Olympic Committee, 1999).
44. The Central Committee of the CPC, 'Zhonggong Zhongyang Guowuyuan Guanyu Jinyibu Jiaqiang He Gaijin Xinshiqi Tiyu Gongzuo de YIjian' [The Central Committee of the CPC and the State Council's Guidelines for Further Strengthening and Improving Sporting Affairs in the New Era].

45. Brownell, *Beijing's Games*; Andrew Morris, *Marrow of the Nation: A History of Sport and Physical Culture in Republican China* (University of California Press, 2004), 3; and Xu, *Olympic Dreams*.
46. Liu, 'Guojia Tiyu Zongju Juzhang Liu Peng Zai 2007 Nian Quanguo Tiyu Juzhang Huiyi Shang de Jianghua' [The Speech of Sport Minister Peng Liu for 2007 All States Sports Minister Conference], 1. The Long March (October 1933–October 1935) was a military retreat of 9000 km by the Red Amy, the CPC military force which was being chased by the KMT army. It has been constantly used as a theme of propaganda, delineating the fighting spirit and spirit of stubborn determination under tough conditions of the Chinese people, a spirit accredited to the leadership of the CPC. Zhang and Vaughan, *Mao Zedong as Poet and Revolutionary Leader: Social and Historical Perspectives* (Lexington Books, 2002).
47. Peng Liu, 'Guojia Tiyu Zongju Juzhang Liu Peng Zai 2008 Nian Quanguo Tiyu Juzhang Huiyi Shang de Jianghua' [The Speech of Sport Minister Peng Liu for 2008 All States Sports Minister Conference] (2008), 1.
48. Kevin Latham, *Pop Culture China!: Media, Arts, and Lifestyle* (Santa Barbara, CA: ABC-CLIO, 2007).
49. Wu, *The History of Sport in the People's Republic of China*; Duan Shijie, 'Guojia Tiyu Zongju Fujuzhang Duan Shijie Zai 2007 Nian Quanguo Tiyu Juzhang Huiyi Shang de Zongjie Jianghua' [The Concluding Speech of Deputy Sport Minister Duan Shijie for 2007 All States Sports Minister Conference] (2008); and Long, 'Zhongguo Aoyunhui Chengji Tanyin: Yi Bajie Xiaji Aoyunhui Weili' [Research on Chinese Olympic Performances in Eight Summer Olympics].
50. The Central Committee of the CPC, 'Zhonggong Zhongyang Guowuyuan Guanyu Jinyibu Jiaqiang He Gaijin Xinshiqi Tiyu Gongzuo de YIjian' [The Central Committee of the CPC and the State Council's Guidelines for Further Strengthening and Improving Sporting Affairs in the New Era], 1; Jianjun Guo, 'Weiguo Zhengguang Zhuzaohuihuang – Xin Zhongguo Jingjitiyu 60 Nian' [60 Years of Chinese Elite Sport], in GAS (ed.), *60 Years of New China's Sport* (Beijing: People's Press, 2009); Liu, 'Guojia Tiyu Zongju Juzhang Liu Peng Zai 2007 Nian Quanguo Tiyu Juzhang Huiyi Shang de Jianghua' [The Speech of Sport Minister Peng Liu for 2007 All States Sports Minister Conference] (2007); and He, 'Zhenliang Zai Beijing Shenao Chenggong Baogaohui Shang de Baogao' [Hezhenliang's Report in the Colloquium of Beijing's Successful Olympic Bid], 1.
51. Li et al., 'Guanyu Jinyibu Wanshan Woguo Jingji Tiyu Juguo Tizhi de Yanjiu' [Research on the Further Perfection of Juguo Tizhi of Elite Sports of China].
52. He, 'Zhenliang Zai Beijing Shenao Chenggong Baogaohui Shang de Baogao' [Hezhenliang's Report in the Colloquium of Beijing's Successful Olympic Bid], 1.
53. Ibid.
54. Jintao Hu, 'Zhongguo Renmin You Nengli Wei Renlei Zuochu Gengda Gongxian' [The Chinese People are Capable of Making More Contribution to the Human Race] (Beijing: PRC, 2008), 3, http://news.sina.com.cn/c/2008-09-29/125116381584.shtml.
55. *Juguo Tizhi*, often used as a byword for the system of Chinese elite sport, is normally translated and elaborated as 'whole-country support for the elite sport system'. However, we would argue that Juguo Tizhi should also be understood as a framework that administers and operates Chinese sport affairs as a whole, especially the planned-economy based and government-controlled-and-governed elite sport system, i.e. Zhuanye sport. Fan, Wu, and Xiong, 'Beijing Ambitions', 215; Tien-chin Tan and Barrie Houlihan, 'Chinese Olympic Sport Policy: Managing the Impact of Globalisation', *International Review for the Sociology of Sport* 48, no. 2 (2012), 131–52; and Fan Wei, Fan, and Lu, 'Chinese State Sports Policy'.
56. GAS, 'Jinyibu Jiaqiang He Gaijin Guojiadui Sixiang Zhengzhi Gongzuo Yijian' [Opinions on Further Strengthening and Improving the Ideological Education of National Teams], (Beijing: 2006), 1.
57. Ma, 'Lun Zhongguo de Aolinpike Zhengce' [Discussion on the Olympic Policy of China].
58. Hu, 'Hu Jintao's Speech at the Awards Ceremony for the 2008 Olympics and the Paralympics'.

59. Hua Li, '60 Nian Fenji, 60 Nian Rongyao – Xinzhongguo Youyong Shiye de Fanzhan Yu Chengjiu' [60 Years of Development, 60 Years of Glory, the Development and Achievement of the Diving of the New China], in GAS (ed.), *60 Years of New China's Sport*, 1st ed. (Beijing, PRC: People's Press, 2009), 242.
60. Peng Liu, 'Guojia Tiyu Zongju Juzhang Liu Peng Zai 2009 Nian Quanguo Tiyu Juzhang Huiyi Shang de Jianghua' [The Speech of Sport Minister Peng Liu for 2009 All States Sports Minister Conference] (Beijing, 2009), 1.
61. Tong Qian and Zhi Chen, 'Xi Jinping Qinqie Kanwang Suoqi Dongaohui Zhongguo Daibiaotuan' [Xi Jinping Visits the Chinese Delegation for the Sochi Winter Games] (Beijing: Xinhua News, 2014), 1, http://news.xinhuanet.com/world/2014-02/07/c_119234468.htm.
62. Qiangan Wang, 'The Origin of the Words "China Dream"', *Contemporary China History Studies* 20, no. 6, 110–7; Wang, 'The Chinese Dream: Concept and Context', *Journal of Chinese Political Science* 19, no. 1 (2014), 1–13; and The Centre for Studies and Researches of the Socialism with Chinese Characteristics, 'Shenke Bawo Zhongguomeng de Fengfu Neihan He Tezhi' [Profoundly Comprehending the Rich Content and Charactersitics of 'China Dream'], *People's Daily*, http://theory.people.com.cn/n/2014/0606/c40531-25111271.html (accessed 2 August 2015).
63. Hu, 'Hu Jintao's Speech at the Awards Ceremony for the 2008 Olympics and the Paralympics'. The notion of a 'Sport Power', representing the future target of Chinese elite sport, is combined by Hu with the term 'Sport Giant' in his speech, which refers to the status of China after the Beijing Games. These two terms are also translated as 'Strong Sporting Nation' and 'Major Sports Nation'. Research Group of the Studies on Theory and Practice of Stepping from a Major Sports Nation to a Strong Sporting Nation (eds), *Strategic Research on Strong Sporting Nation*, 1st ed. (Beijing: Renmin Tiyu Chubanshe [People' Sport Press], 2010).
64. Liu, 'Guojia Tiyu Zongju Juzhang Liu Peng Zai 2009 Nian Quanguo Tiyu Juzhang Huiyi Shang de Jianghua' [The Speech of Sport Minister Peng Liu for 2009 All States Sports Minister Conference]; GAS, *The Strategic Plan for the Winning Olympic Glory 2011–2020* (Beijing, 2010), http://www.sport.gov.cn/n16/n1152/n2448/1917247.html; Peng Liu, 'Guojia Tiyu Zongju Juzhang Liu Peng Zai 2010 Nian Quanguo Tiyu Juzhang Huiyi Shang de Jianghua' [The Speech of Sport Minister Peng Liu for the 2010 All States Sports Minister Conference] (Beijing, 2010); Jianjun Guo, 'Weiguo Zhengguang Zhuzaohuihuang – Xin Zhongguo Jingjitiyu 60 Nian' [60 Years of Chinese Elite Sport], in GAS (ed.), *60 Years of New China's Sport* (Beijing: People's Press, 2009); and Research Group of the Studies on Theory and Practice of stepping from a Major Sports Nation to a Strong Sporting Nation (ed.), *Strategic Research on Strong Sporting Nation*, 1.
65. GAS, 'The Strategic Plan for the Winning Olympic Glory 2011–2020'.
66. Li Li, Peng Gao, and Haoming Wang, 'Zhuanjia Jiedu Xijinping Suoqi Dongao Jianghua', *Xinhua News*, 10 February 2014, http://sports.qq.com/a/20140210/017339.htm.
67. SPCSC, 'The Summary of the Strategic Plan for the Winning Olympic Glory 1994–2000', 1.
68. GAS, *The Summary of the Strategic Plan for the Winning Olympic Glory 2001–2010* (Beijing, 2002), 1, http://tyj.xinjiang.gov.cn/zcfg/2012/33947.htm.
69. GAS, 'The Strategic Plan for the Winning Olympic Glory 2011–2020'.
70. Research Group of the Studies on Theory and Practice of Stepping from a Major Sports Nation to a Strong Sporting Nation (ed.), *Strategic Research on Strong Sporting Nation*.
71. Lijun Hu, 'The Strategic Research of Elite Sports in Strong Sporting Nation', in Research Group for the Theory and Practice of Stepping from Major Sporting Nation to Strong Sporting Nation (ed.), *Strategic Research on Strong Sporting Nation* (Beijing: People's Sport Press, 2010), 45.
72. SPCSC, *Guoajia Tiwei Guanyu Shenhua Tiyu Gaige de Yijian* [The SPCSC's Opinion on Deepening the Reform of Sport System] (Beijing, 1993), http://china.findlaw.cn/fagui/p_9/97826.html; SPCSC, *The Summary of the Strategic Plan for the Winning Olympic Glory 1994–2000*; GAS, *The Summary of the Strategic Plan for the Winning Olympic Glory 2001–2010*; and GAS, *The Summary of the Strategic Plan for the Winning Olympic Glory 2011–2020*.
73. Research Group of the Studies on Theory and Practice of Stepping from a Major Sports Nation to a Strong Sporting Nation (ed.), *Strategic Research on Strong Sporting Nation*.

74. Liu, 'Guojia Tiyu Zongju Juzhang Liu Peng Zai 2009 Nian Quanguo Tiyu Juzhang Huiyi Shang de Jianghua' [The Speech of Sport Minister Peng Liu for 2009 All States Sports Minister Conference]; and Peng Liu, 'Guojia Tiyu Zongju Juzhang Liu Peng Zai 2013 Nian Quanguo Tiyu Juzhang Huiyi Shang de Jianghua' [The Speech of Sport Minister Peng Liu for 2013 All States Sports Minister Conference], http://sports.people.com.cn/n/2013/1224/c22176-23935760.html.

Disclosure Statement

No potential conflict of interest was reported by the authors.

Xi Jin-Ping's World Cup Dreams: From a Major Sports Country to a World Sports Power

Tien-Chin Tan, Hsien-Che Huang, Alan Bairner and Yu-Wen Chen

ABSTRACT
Football is among the world's most popular sports. It is also one which China has sought to develop in the field of global professional sport. Nevertheless, the professionalization of football in China has not to date actually improved China's Olympic achievement in the sport. In stark contrast to the glory of being the country that won most gold medals at the 2008 Olympics, China's poor football performance has been troublesome for the country's leader. In 2009, newly elected Xi Jin-Ping made a public statement about promoting elite football and expressed his personal hope that China would be capable of both qualifying for the final stages and winning the FIFA World Cup. With such concern on the part of the state leader, attention turned to football, with many private enterprises beginning to echo government policy by demonstrating a willingness to promote elite football. In addition, to accelerate football development, the Chinese Government promised to take action on the separation of government football associations. Research on this process was based on the theoretical framework of state corporatism derived from Schmitter's work of 1974. Semi-structured interviews were conducted as the method of data collection aimed at helping us understand how Chinese Government either integrated or controlled relevant stakeholders such as NGOs and private enterprises, and further, to discuss the interactions between them.

Introduction

Football is one of the most popular sports in the world. It was also the first sport to be professionalized in China. Nevertheless, the professionalization of football has not brought about a marked improvement in the standard of China's elite football. Compared with China's prominent achievement of winning the most gold medals with 51 (100 in total) at the 2008 Olympic Games in Beijing, the outcome of its investment in elite football seemed to have brought shame to the then president of the People's Republic China (PRC), Hu Jin-Tao. As a result, after the 2008 Olympics, Hu demanded further actions in order to fulfill China's sports policy goal of going 'from a major sports country to a world sports power'. Moreover, during an official visit to Germany in 2009, Xi Jin-Ping, the then vice-president and now the current president of the PRC, also expressed the country's determination to put considerable effort into China's elite football development. At an official meeting with the president of the Korea Democratic Party in 2011, Xi had highlighted his three World Cup dreams of 'participating in the World Cup', 'hosting the World Cup', and 'being the World Cup champions'. In light of China's leaders' concerns about the future of the country's elite football, the once-neglected 'campus football' has attracted increased attention in the wider society. Private corporations have echoed the national leaders' proclamations by starting to support the development of elite football in China. Meanwhile, the government promised to speed up the reform of the football administration system in China so as to promote elite football. This research aims to investigate China's strategies for its elite football development after the 2008 Beijing Olympics and to understand the power relations and interactions among the stakeholders in Chinese elite football.

Analytical Framework and Methodological Issues

According to Schmitter and Lehmbruch, corporatism is

> a system of interest representation in which the constituents are organized into a limited number of singular, compulsory, non-competitive, hierarchically ordered and functionally differentiated categories, recognized or licensed (if not created) by the state and granted a deliberate representational monopoly within their respective categories in exchange for observing certain controls on their selection of leaders and articulation of demands and supports.[1]

Corporatism has been traditionally associated with authoritarianism, and often adopted to help explain the political and economic development of Portugal, Spain, Italy, and various countries in Latin America with an emphasis on the controlling influence of the state on political economy.[2] However, as well as in authoritarian societies corporatism can be found in countries with different political, economic, and cultural conditions such as Sweden, Switzerland, Holland, and other social democratic countries. In order to expand on its role, Schmitter divided corporatism into two categories: national corporatism and societal corporatism.[3] Based on the extent of governmental power over the country, societal corporatism was thus separated from the corporatism that had previously been linked to authoritarianism, thereby highlighting two types of relationship between governments and interest groups: interest group-dominated nations or nation-dominated interest groups.[4] Unlike traditional corporatism that was centered on the idea of authoritarianism, the formation of societal corporatism starts with the coming together of various groups of people with similar interests, each of which comes up with its representative to take part in the policy-making process of the country. This kind of corporatism is commonly found in socially democratic countries. Sweden, Demark, Norway, Holland, and other democratic European countries as such are examples based on societal corporatism.[5] However, China's dominant-party system and its communist-based society mean a political and economic social context that is very different from this idea of societal corporatism.

Viewed from the perspective of the model of state corporatism, the interactions between government and society are led by the government. As the policy-maker, the government tends to mediate between interest groups with specific aims. Indeed, the formation of interest groups in society is frequently manipulated by government and interest groups are commissioned by, as well as subordinate to, government for the propagation of its policies. According to Schmitter, based on the model of state corporatism, governments have their own objectives when it comes to cooperation with interest groups, in particular the maintenance of authority over the nation.[6] Governments will establish an interest group mediator according to policy needs, as well as including all relevant members within the system of governance. The commissioned interest mediator, therefore, possesses a government-granted monopoly, and can thus achieve national objectives through mandatory social cooperation. State corporatism of this type can frequently be found in authoritarian states and/or developing countries. Moreover, even when putting aside early studies focused on authoritarian states, there are still many discussions within academia today about the contemporary authoritarian-oriented countries, including Singapore, South Korea, Japan, and Taiwan, at least between the 1950s and 1980s. The perspective of state corporatism is used to discuss the interactions between governments and interest groups in such countries.[7] Not surprisingly, therefore, the approach is also frequently adopted to analyze the prevailing circumstances in China.[8] Describing the interactions between the Chinese Government and private corporations, Solinger pointed out that the state has gradually untied society following economic reform.[9] The government and corporations are now more interdependent, thereby blurring the boundary between state and society. Nevertheless, the main resources are still controlled by the state. The private corporations are required to establish a good relationship with the government if they are to gain access to resources. As Chinese scholars Liu,[10] and Sun,[11] have claimed, the relationship between the government and social groups, as well as the process of the transforming governance in China, both remain within the framework of state corporatism. Therefore, the focus of this study is to identify whether the Chinese Government has a specific policy or objective for elite football development as a means by which to enhance understanding of the role played by the Chinese government in this process. Put simply, is the government a passive arbitrator or a purposive dominator? Secondly, if the Chinese Government has specific goals for football development, what are the channels to achieve these goals? Does the Chinese Government have the power to lead society in this respect? Does society have leverage to negotiate with the government? Can these inquiries help us focus on the concept of state corporatism and observe whether society take orders from the government during these interactions? Or, have corporate forces gained their momentum such that the development of elite football in China is being operated differently?

With the concept of state corporatism in mind, this analysis draws upon an interrogation of empirical data from interviews conducted with 25 officials involved in various organizational roles within China's administrative system for elite football. Interviews were conducted with officials from organizations that included: the General Administration of Sport (GAS); the Chinese Football Association (CFA); the China Football Association Super League Company (CSLC); the Executive Bureau of CSL; CSL Club managers; Local football management centers. In addition, eight interviews were conducted with Chinese sports academics and journalists working in China and elsewhere. It was also possible for us to access high-ranking sport leaders' personal accounts from documents and articles, for example: (i) official websites, such as those of State Council (SC), Ministry of Education (MOE), Ministry of Finance (MOF), GAS, Chinese Olympic Committee (COC), CFA, and; (ii) databases, such as SPORTINFO.NET.CN and the China National Knowledge

Infrastructure (CNKI); and (iii) newspapers including *China Sport News, Sina Sport News, Titan Sport News, Sohu Sport News,* People's Daily Online and *Xinhuanet News.*

China's Strategies for Elite Football Development after the 2008 Beijing Olympics

The goal of elite football achievement for China hit rock bottom following the 2008 Beijing Olympics. The male national football team was knocked out in consecutive World Cup Asian preliminary contests in 2006, 2010, and 2014. By July 2009, the Chinese football team's ranking had reached a record low point (108th worldwide and 13th in Asia) according to the Fédération Internationale de Football Association (FIFA). Moreover, on 15 June 2013, the Chinese national team was beaten 1–5 by Thailand in a friendly match, a result that was mocked by the media and by fans as the '615 Massacre'. It had been one of the most humiliating days in the history of Chinese football and in order to prevent the further decline of Chinese elite football, several policies were proposed, aimed at halting the decline and gradually fulfilling the three World Cup dreams announced by the new leader, Xi Jing-Ping.

Establishment of the Control, Ethics and Disciplinary Committee of National Football Leagues (CEDCNFL)

According to the vice-director of the Sports Ethics and Integrity Risk Research Centre, Beijing Sports University, the Chinese Football Association Super League (CSL) has been struggling with issues of match-fixing, gambling, and gang manipulation since its formation. Although the Chinese Football Association (CFA) and Ministry of Public Security (MPS) co-founded a task force for 'anti-football gambling activities' in 2006, the outcomes were unsatisfactory. Furthermore, the scandal of high-level officials in the CFA collectively taking bribes was also exposed. In order to stop such deviant activities as match-fixing, gambling, and gang manipulation of football, seven departments in the State Council co-founded the CEDCNFL under the direction of the then vice-president, Xi Jing-Ping, after the 2008 Beijing Olympics.[12] This move was in accordance with the idea proposed by the executive vice-chairperson of the CFA, Chang Jian, in his 2014 CFA Work Report. CEDCNFL is led by GAS and composed of MPS, the Ministry of Civil Affairs (MCA), the Ministry of Justice (MJ), the People's Bank of China (PBC), State Administration of Taxation (SAT), and State Administration for Industry and Commerce (SAIC).[13]

Instructions to Entrepreneurs to Fund the CFA

The then vice-president, Xi, highly valued the development of Chinese football. Therefore, the then state councilor, Liu Yen-dong, assembled and hosted a conference for football reinvigoration on 28 January 2011. The president of Dalian Wanda Group (DWG), Wang Jian-Lin, was invited as the representative of the Chinese corporations. Liu suggested that the Chinese corporations should devote more effort to the development of football in China and this received a positive response from Wang who then carried out his promise to support Chinese football six months later. On 3 July 2011, both the initiation of 'European Training Camp for Chinese Football Stars of Hope' and the contract signing ceremony for 'Strategic Partnership between the CFA and the DWG' took place in the Beijing Institute of Technology (BIT). DWG provided 500 million RMB over three years to fully support the reinvigoration of Chinese football. One of the senior staff members in charge of the financial affairs of the CFA stated, with reference to the 500 million strategic partnership between DWG and CFA, that it would consist of six elements – selecting youths under 16 for training at top European football clubs, financing three national youth football leagues with athletes aged from 10 to 17, introducing world-class foreign head coaches to lead the national team without a salary cap, becoming the name sponsor for CSL, exploring and reforming the current system of assessment and rewarding for referees, and funding the national women's football team.[14]

In addition to Wang's DWG, the board chairperson of Evergrande Real Estate Group (EREG), Xu Jia-Ying, worked with Real Madrid Football Club (RMFC) in Spain to build the Evergrande Football School (EFS) and planned to spend 10 years widening the cultivation of youth football talent. EREG would donate 100 million RMB to the China Foundation for Poverty Alleviation (CFPA) annually for 10 years. Part of this donation would be used to finance those talented, yet financially disadvantaged, children so that they could have access to professional football training and coaching. This move is closely related to the preference of President Xi concerning football as well as the instructions of the Chinese Communist Party Politburo Standing Committee (CCPPSC).[15]

Establishing the National Youth Campus Football Leading Group Office (NYLGO)

According to a former official in the CFA School Football Office (SFO), SFO was initially co-founded by GAS and the Ministry of Education (MOE), under the instruction of the State Council, to provide training for more than 5000 principals and instructors as well as 800 level C and D coaches annually. The elite training centres started a trial run in 20 cities in 2014. GAS contributed sports lottery profits and increased investment from 40 million RMB in 2009 to 56 million RMB in 2013.[16] In order to gain more resources from the MOE, the responsibility of developing campus football was taken over from GAS to the MOE.[17] In 2015, the MOE worked with the National Development and Reform Commission (NDRC), the Ministry of Finance (MOF), the State Administration of Press, Publication, Radio, Film, and Television (SAPPRFT), GAS, and the Central Committee of the Communist Young League (CCCYL) to form the 'NYLGO' with the consent of the State Council. The MOE director leads the group, while Wang Deng-Feng, the head of the Division of Physical, Health and Arts Education (DPHAE) in the MOE, serves as the office chief; members of this office include officials from the relevant departments mentioned above.[18]

Raising the Profile and Status of Football in the National Games

The GAS director, Liu Peng, made football the focus in his report of the 2011 National Sports Minister Conference for the very first time. In the report, he asserted that 'the emphases of the Party and the state, the concerns of the political leaders, and the anticipation of the public about the development of football have surpassed the sport itself. We have to acknowledge it is our unshakable responsibility and our mission to help to develop football'.[19] GAS also emphasized the significance of football in the National Games because they have become a driving force to motivate local sport bureaus to develop the sport. Specifically, Under 18 matches were added to the games to sit alongside adult matches. The male and female football teams that had won first place were previously awarded only one medal respectively. However, the scoring system was altered so that a province/city team that secures first place will obtain three gold medals instead of one; this means that the provinces/cities where football has been best developed can now win as many as six gold medals. This alternation is intended to encourage more local governments to develop the sport.[20] In an interview with Xinhua News Agency, GAS deputy-director, Xiao Tien, suggested that 'the provincial governments and the Chinese People's Liberation Army (PLA) value football more since the new policies, such as three gold medals for first place and the addition of U18 matches were introduced. More teams were founded … and if we can persist, the shortage of talent reserves in football may be improved greatly'.[21]

Strengthening the 'Inviting In' and the 'Sending Out' Policy

The 'inviting in and sending out' policy involves government agencies (CFA and MOE) and business stakeholders (Wang from DWG and Xu from EREG). As for 'inviting in', the main purpose is to introduce high-level foreign experts to provide scaled training for Chinese coaches, referees, and instructors.[22] The CFA executive vice-chairperson, Chang Jian, pointed out in the 2014 *CFA Work Report* that 'systematic and scaled national football training has been available with the support of FIFA and AFC since 2004. For instance, training for professional coaches and instructors was provided together with levels A, B, and C coach training'. Furthermore, Chang Jian also suggested that 'level D coach training was made available in 2010 to gradually connect with the world of the professional, levels A, B, C, and D coach training systems. There were also improvements in the training of referees, of referee instructors, and of technical directors'. Nonetheless, the MOE also planned to hire 100 quality football coaches to deliver their training services at schools in 40 cities in order to fully promote campus football. During the interview with the XinHua News Agency, the head of DPHAE, MOE, Wang Deng-Feng, suggested that 'we would like to ask them to teach football in different schools with football features for one year. Our football coaches will work with and learn from them. They are like the academic advisors in graduate schools. We intend to conduct a one-year trial run to see the outcomes'. He also mentioned that 'the MOE planned to invite coaches from countries excelling in football such as Germany, Italy, Spain, France, and Argentina. The invitation can be issued either directly by the MOE or from local governments just as the cooperative model between Chengdu and Metz, France that has run for more than a decade'.[23] This is the first time that the Chinese Government has attempted to use the integration of foreign coaches into different schools as one of the 'stepping out' strategies.

The 'sending out' element refers to encouraging football clubs, corporations, and other social forces to select professional and young players to participate in training in countries excelling in football so as to aspire to play in their high-level professional leagues.[24] Under the direction of the Chinese leaders, in 2011, DWG started to sponsor the Chinese Football Stars of Hope Project. Shi Shue-Ching, the director of football affairs at DWG, said that 'the talent training program of the Chinese Football Stars of Hope is one of the crucial items in the strategic partnership between DWG and CFA. The purpose is to cultivate Chinese potential football stars and revitalize Chinese football. The reason why we chose Real Madrid Football Club (RMFC), Valencia Football Club (VFC), and Villarreal CF was not only because they are traditionally top teams in Primera división de Liga but also because they have the leading youth training systems in both Spain and Europe'.[25]

Taking Action on the Separation Between the Government and Football Associations

As for the scandals of CFA officials taking bribes and match-fixing in CSL, during his interview with XinHua News Agency GAS director, Liu Peng, argued, that 'CSL needs to be reformed, so as to change the situation that CFA is hosting while managing the games'. He emphasized that 'the government-led system of CFA had caused a lot of issues. The unreasonable system was also the hotbed for corruption. Reform is a must and we are initiating specific reforming measures'.[26] Immediately before the 2014 CFA convention, the GAS deputy-director, Cai Zhen-Hua, invited Wang from DWG and Xu from EREG to serve as the vice-chairpersons for the 10th CFA convention with the expectation of energizing CFA through the power of the corporations.[27] In fact, the formal reform policy was never confirmed until the passing of 'The Overall Reform Plan to Boost the Development of Football in China' (the Reform Plan) on the occasion of the 10th assembly of the Central Leading Group for Comprehensively Deepening Reforms hosted by Xi Jing-Ping on 27 February 2015.[28] After the Reform Plan was announced by the State Council, the GAS deputy-director and the CFA chairperson, Cai Zhen-Hua, pointed out at the press conference that 'the Reform Plan has addressed the issue of separation between the government and football associations. The purpose of rebuilding CFA is clear – to change the overlapping organizational structure of CFA and the Chinese Football Management Center (CFMC), GAS'.[29] In other words, 'CFA will disconnect from GAS and become autonomous in terms of its institutional setup, work planning, financial and salary management, human resources, and professional international communication'.[30] However, Cai also stressed that 'the disconnection between CFA and GAS does not mean that the government would give up the principle of leading by the Chinese Communist Party (CCP) and managing by laws.'[31] Such a contention came as no surprise because it is specified in the 9th article of the Reform Plan to 'enforce leadership by the Party, establish a sound Party structure in association football at all levels, follow the cadre and personnel policies of Party, and reinforce the ideological and political work as well as daily management of cadres. The party committees assigned by CFA will be led by the GAS Party group'.[32] This revealed that the Party-led principle of the CCP would persist no matter how the reform develops.

Emphasizing the Bellwether Role of Football in the Sports Industry

In order to reinforce the link between development of football and industry so as to provide powerful support for football, the State Council of China announced *Several Opinions of the State Council of the People's Republic of China, on Accelerating the Development of Sports Industry to Promote the Sport Consumption (The Opinions)* on 20 October 2014. In this document, it was emphasized that 'football should be viewed as one of the potential industries and be promoted both in depth and width. A long-term development and facility construction plan should be initiated to promote campus and social football'.[33] After the release of this document, one of the drafters, the GAS vice-director of the commercial affairs department, Chen En-Tang, pointed out the reasons why football was viewed as the entry point for sport industry. He mentioned that 'there are a great number of fans of football in China, yet they have been frustrated by the national teams' frequent losses in the international arena. Moreover, the achievements of national football teams also do not match the international status of China'.[34] Hence, Chen said 'the issues of football have attracted attention from all directions especially the public. Therefore *The Opinions* specifically proposed mid and long term development programs for football, hoping to actively promote football on campuses and in society'.[35]

Power Relations and Interactions Between Stakeholders

Since the 2008 Beijing Olympics, the main stakeholders within the development of Chinese elite football have been government officials and corporate owners. The government officials include president Xi Jing-Ping and corresponding officials from the State Council, the MOE, GAS, NDRC, MOF, CFA, local sport bureaus and football federations, while the most influential corporate owners are Wang from DWG and Chairperson Xu from EREG.

The Pursuit of Xi's Three Dreams for Chinese Elite Football

The leaders of the People's Republic of China have all been fond of football and made promises to promote the sport. Nonetheless, president Xi was the first and only leader who has made football development one of his major policies and has put continuous efforts towards this. Xi was on the Hui-Wen football team in high school and liked to watch football matches.[36] His affection for the sport did not end when he became the leader of China. In July 2008, the then vice-president, Xi, once entered the field of play and made several impressive kicks during a visit to Olympic football stadium and the Chinese female football team in Qinhuangdao. In fact, Xi also showed his well-honed skills on the field while visiting the headquarters of Gaelic Athletic Association in Dublin, Ireland during February 2012.[37] According to Chinese football academia, the then vice-president had expressed his dissatisfaction about the under-performing Chinese football team during and after the 2008 Beijing Olympics,[38] and commissioned the state councilor Liu Yan-Dong to exert his power.[39] Xi mentioned how he had enjoyed football during his visit to Bayer HealthCare in Germany on 12 October 2009. He noted that there were first-class football fans and a considerable market for football in China, yet the competitive level of Chinese football was relatively inferior and he wished the situation could be improved. He announced that 'we made a resolution after hosting the 2008 Olympics: it may take long, but we will be determined to develop Chinese football, for we had won gold medals in most other sports'.[40]

After these statements by Xi, Liu Yan-Dong, the councilor of Politburo and State Council, attended a workshop on 14 October 2009. Liu stated publicly that 'raising the profile of the Chinese football is significant for constructing an overall world sports power, boosting the healthy development of sport industry, satisfying the spiritual and cultural demands of the people, as well as enhancing the soft power of China'. Liu also suggested that 'the focus should start young. Talent should be cultivated through on-campus football activities. The social foundation of the sport of football should be built in order to improve and popularize football in China'.[41] According to the MOE deputy director, Liu Li-Ming:

> GAS and MOE issued *The Nationwide Notice for Activating On-Campus Youth Football Activities* on April 14th, 2009, so as to implement the instructions of central leaders. GAS and MOE

also co-hosted the initiation ceremony for this program in Qingdao on October 14th, 2009. A nationwide workshop for football affairs was held. Councilor Liu attended both the ceremony and workshop to deliver her speech.[42]

Councilor Liu also assembled another key football workshop on 28 January 2011. In addition, GAS director, Liu Peng, the assistant secretary general of State Council, Xiang Zhao-Lun, National Development and Reform commissioners, relevant officials from MOF and MOE, delegates from the corporations, together coaches and players from both the male and female national football teams were all assembled to progress in-depth discussions regarding the development and reform of Chinese football, the establishment of a youth training system, and regulations for professional leagues.[43] This workshop also announced and produced a draft of the official document of *Opinions of GAS and MOE on Improving Youth On-Campus Football Work*.[44] as well as the '500 million in three years' strategic partnership between DWA and CFA.[45]

On 4 July 2011, president Xi greeted guests from South Korea and was presented with a football signed by Park Ji-sung. Meanwhile, Xi publicly announced that his three dreams 'are "entering the World Cup", "hosting the World Cup", and "being World Cup champions"'.[46] Despite this, Xi's three dreams for football did not improve the development of Chinese football, with the Chinese national team being well beaten 1–5 by the Thai national team in Hefei on 15 June 2013. The well-known CCTV commentator, He Wei, even described this game as shameful.[47] According to Chinese scholars, the failure of the Chinese national team exerted a powerful influence on football in China more generally, reinforcing Xi's determination to initiate overall reform.[48] In order to alleviate the dissatisfaction felt by the leader of China, at the 10th CFA assembly held in 2014, the GAS deputy-director and CFA president, Cai Zhen-Hua, declared that 'we shall never forget how we lost to the Thai team by 1 to 5 last year … June 15th was a shameful day for Chinese football'.[49] Cai also stressed that 'the ancient aviators in China could make it to the sky and realize their flying dreams. I thus firmly believe we can fulfill our football dream as well'.[50] GAS director, Liu Peng also highlighted Xi's football dreams several times during his speech. He stressed that Liu Yan-dong had hosted many conferences about on-campus youth football and football workshops. Many other significant talks, guides, and orders were also delivered.[51] Furthermore, Liu Peng emphasized that 'the Party, State Council, and the public all deeply expect to see the improvement of football. Chinese sports now should use all the resources to the utmost to serve the public as well as to strive for the glory for China'.[52]

In addition to the efforts of GAS and CFA, Xi also gradually directed the responsibility of football promotion to the MOE. As an official from the CFA School Football Office noted, 'the lottery profits of 5.6 million per year from GAS are definitely not sufficient for the development of on-campus football. Therefore, the well-budgeted and resourced MOE should take the lead in the long-term development of on-campus football'.[53] The MOE has done so by forming the NYLGO under the direction of the Party and State Council. The MOE director, Yuan Gui-Ren, served as the leader of NYLGO, with MOE deputy director, Hao Ping, and GAS deputy director, Cai Zheng-Hua, as deputies. The office was set up in the MOE to process daily routines. Wang Deng-Feng, the head of the Physical, Health and Arts Education department of the MOE, serves as the office chief,[54] and was also appointed as the CFA vice-president charged with increasing the impact of the MOE on football.[55]

At a teleconference concerning on-campus football hosted by the councilor of the Politburo and State Council, Liu Yan-Dong, MOE director Yuan explained several points about the promotion of on-campus football, in particular the establishment of around 20,000 football teams featuring middle and primary schools as well as 200 quality high school football teams nationwide, the construction of around 30 on-campus football trial run regions by 2017, the organization of four level leagues for primary, middle, and high schools as well as universities in accordance with the national on-campus football competition program, and a training project for 6000 football coaches nationwide by 2015.[56] During the meeting, GAS director, Liu Peng, also initiated several important implementation strategies for MOE led by on-campus football: (1) to work with the MOE to arrange for the employment of veteran football players, students, and professionals as school coaches; (2) to establish a sound youth league from Under 9 to Under 22 and make connections between leagues at different levels; (3) to integrate the resources of GAS and MOE to construct a youth football training compound; (4) to provide more access for student football players to the reserved talent pool for the national team, professional football clubs, or to famous overseas clubs.[57]

During an interview with the Xinhua News Agency, Wang Deng-Feng stressed that the leading group was constituted by the MOE, NDRC, SAPPRFT, GAS, and CCCYL, with each agency having its own strengths. The main leaders are the MOE, GAS, and CCCYL, while the other three agencies provide support for such things as field design, financing, and press releases. 'The three main leaders now require an integrated plan and a specific division of labor. For instance, the training of coaches, referees, and teachers requires the efforts of CFA. This is a sound system of teamwork'.[58] The Reform Plan also underlines that:

> GAS shall advance policy studies and use its leadership to continuously promote the reform and development of football in China, assure the implementation of this plan, and establish the inter-departmental system of football development and reform, while the MOE shall fulfill its responsibilities of supervision over on-campus football activities.[59]

Chinese Leaders Appeal to Corporate Owners to Finance Chinese Football

In 1999, the DWG dropped out of the football arena as a result of dissatisfaction with the poor condition of football in China. In 2011, however, the president of DWG, Wang, decided to re-enter the industry with a three-year plan supported by 500 million RMB. Wang was invited to be the consultant for CFA during the 10th CFA convention held on 21 January 2014. He talked about this new position during an interview on CCTV's *Dialogue*, saying that he would continue to support CFA for three years having been selected as a consultant. He stressed that 'it's great to see Xi's passion for football, which will provide important support for Chinese football. People say I am only responding to the call of President Xi, but I think it is actually my honor to be involved'.[60] As a matter of fact, when he was asked in another interview why he had re-entered the domain of football, Wang calmly explained his three reasons, namely 'the leader's direction, social demand and persistent passion'.[61] In order to answer the appeal of President Xi, Wang not only introduced top coaches and sent out young players to countries excelling in football but also purchased a 20% share of Club Atlético de Madrid (CAM) for 4.5 million euro, officially becoming one of the shareholders on 21 January 2015. The investment in CAM was mainly to work with the program of 'Chinese Youth Football Player in Spain'. From the DWG perspective, Wang indicated that 'DWG is glad to contribute to the growth and development of CAM in Asia and would like to learn from their experiences in youth training for developing football in

China'.[62] According to the agreement, CAM would build a youth training centre for young Chinese players in Spain.[63] Wang also mediated with three noted corporations and the management of Infront Sports & Media (ISM) to successfully merge a 100% share of stock in ISM with DWG holding 68.2% of the shares to further help realize Xi's three dreams for Chinese football. At the contract-signing ceremony, Wang suggested that 'the merger with ISM would help realize Xi Jin-Ping's World Cup Dreams since the group possess tremendous marketing resources for football and on-ice sports'.[64] After taking over the business of ISM, since 2016, the DWG has further become a top-level sponsor partner of FIFA, which could be an advantage for China's bidding for World Cup events in the future.

Furthermore, the chairperson of EREG, Xu Jia-Yin, also works with RMFC to construct Evergrande Football School and there is also a 10-year plan to expand the cultivation of youth football talents. During those 10 years, EREG will donate 100 million to the China Foundation for Poverty Alleviation per annum. Part of this donation will be used to support talented, yet financially disadvantaged, children so that they can have the access to professional football training and coaching. This move is closely related to the preference of president Xi in relation to football as well as the direction of the Party.[65] In addition, Xu built up the 'Evergrande Model' for Chinese football, cultivating football talent to support the national team. Both have had considerable influence on China's football development.

The Chinese leader canvassed the opinions of five stakeholders – the current GAS deputy director and CFA chairperson, Cai Zhen-Hua; FIFA executive committee member and AFC vice-president, Zhang Ji-Long; Mr Wang from DWG; Mr Xu from EREG; and the so-called 'founding Father of CSL', Lang Xiao-Nong – to prepare the grand blueprint for football development in China. These five stakeholders represent administrative management, industrial management, international organizations, investors, and CSL management respectively.[66] Their views have been more or less documented in the 'Reform Plan'. As Wang Jian-Lin stated during his interview on *Dialogue* on CCTV, 'all the major leaders have acknowledged this issue, and therefore we have this football reform conference and the overall reform plan submitted by the State Council. We have found the "right medicine" to bring life back to Chinese football, namely the "Reform Plan" proposed by the Party leaders'.[67] As a matter of fact, the night before a visit to the United Kingdom, Xi assigned Liu Yan-Dong to attend the China–UK Football Development Forum in order to arrange exchange and cooperation on football with the UK. This was unsurprising and indeed the current GAS deputy director and the CFA chairperson, Cai Zhen-Hua, Mr Wang from DWG and Mr Xu from EREG also attended the meeting.[68] From this, we can tell much about the Chinese Government's appreciation of Mr Wang and Mr Xu, along with its ambition to reinvigorate and promote Chinese football to the world through resources provided by enterprises.

Conclusion

The developing strategies for elite football in China have been closely associated with the objectives of the Chinese leader, Xi Jin-Ping, in the wake of the 2008 Beijing Olympics. The focus of these strategies, managed by the chief of CFMC, GAS, has now been upgraded to be handled by state councilor, Liu Yan-Dong.[69] Due to the fact that elite football development involves various factors and aspects and is therefore complicated, and that the enormous amount of expense is unaffordable for the CFMC, the State Council has gradually taken over the responsibility to coordinate relevant departments and acquire more resources from private corporations and local governments, and, in time, to save elite football in China. With regard to China's management of a series of corruption scandals in football, the State Council has called its seven departments together and set up the CEDCNFL. The State Council also pledges to give the CFA more autonomy to allow professionals to build a system consistent with elite football development. Indeed, the State Council put forward the idea of the 'separation of government and football associations' in practice, so as to reduce the conflict of interests between the CFMC and professional football clubs. In addition, in response to the problem of a lack of football talent, aside from putting an emphasis on the importance of football at National Games, China is also dedicated to youth on-campus football, having the MOE replace the School Football Office in the CFA to lead the development of on-campus football. In order to gain more resources, senior officials in the State Council of China directly turned to the private corporations for patronage. These corporations have also cooperated with football clubs in Europe and South America so that the 'inviting in and sending out' policy could be reinforced. Moreover, the State Council published two official documents, namely *Several Opinions of the State Council of the People's Republic of China, on Accelerating the Development of Sports Industry to Promote the Sport Consumption* and the *Overall Reform Plan to Boost the Development of Football in China* in 2014 and 2015, respectively. Football has thus become the bellwether sport for the sports industry development in China.

As for power relations, the stakeholders involved are government officials and owners of private enterprises. In addition to Xi Jin-Ping, government officials include members of the State Council, MOE, GAS, NDRC, MOF, the CFA, local sports bureaus and local football federations. As for the entrepreneurs, Wang from DWG and Xu from EREG have been the most influential actors. However, the private enterprises have responded to the preferences of the government. Wang has sponsored the CFA, especially by introducing top trainers and sending out young players to countries excelling in football. Xu also built up the 'Evergrande model' for Chinese football, cultivating football reserved talents to support the national team. Both Wang and Xu have had a major influence on China's football development.

Viewed from the perspective of the model of state corporatism, the development of Chinese football after the 2008 Beijing Olympic Games has been dominated by the government and, in particular, the leader of the country, Xi Jing-Ping. The goals set by the government for Chinese football were also based on Xi's three World Cup dreams. As a consequence, in order to accomplish Xi's 'World Cup Dreams', the sport system, the education system, and even the industrial sector appear to have come to regard raising the level of elite football in China as an important task. However, those three systems also have conflicts of interest in reality and this is a crucial issue that cannot be ignored in relation to the future development of Chinese football. Last but not the least, the 'Party group' at all levels of the football associations in China, has played and will continue to play a key role in governing the development of the Chinese football.[70]

Notes

1. P.C. Schmitter and G. Lehmbruch (eds), *Trends Toward Corporatist Intermediation* (London: Sage, 1979).

2. J.M. Malloy, *Authoritarianism and Corporatism in Latin America* (Pittsburgh, PA: University of Pittsburgh Press, 1977); H.J. Wiarda, *Corporatism and National Development in Latin America* (Boulder, CO: Westview Press, 1981).
3. P.C. Schmitter, 'Still the Century of Corporatism?', *Review of Politics* 36 (1974), 85–131.
4. Howard J. Wiarda (ed.), *New Directions in Comparative Politics*, 3rd ed. (Boulder, CO: Westview Press, 2002).
5. M. Anthonsen, J. Lindvall, and U. Schmidt-Hansen, 'Social Democrats, Unions and Corporatism: Denmark and Sweden Compared', *Party Politics* 17, no. 1 (2011), 118–34; E. Heemskerk, R. Mokken, and M. Fennema, 'The Fading of the State: Corporate–Government Networks in the Netherlands', *International Journal of Comparative Sociology*, 53, no. 4 (2012), 253–74; A. Rolland, 'Reviewing Social Democratic Corporatism: Differentiation Theory and the Norwegian Labor Press', *Communication Review* 11, no. 2 (2008), 133–50.
6. Schmitter, 'Still the Century of Corporatism?'
7. J. Lee, 'A Comparative Analysis of Corporatist Policy-Making Coordination in Japan and Korea', *Korean Social Science Journal* 33, no. 1 (2004), 61–88; Tzong-Ruey Shen, 'The Transformation of Functions on the Labor Union in Taiwan', *Journal of Culture and Society* 12 (2001), 159–87; Tzu-Ting Huang, 'The Characteristic of Singapore's Social Welfare Policy: State and Social Groups Under State-Corporatism', *Review of Global Politics* 20 (2007), 111–50.
8. G. White, 'Chinese Trade Unions in the Transition from Socialism: Towards Corporatism or Civil Society?' *British Journal of Industrial Relations* 34, no. 3 (1996), 433–57; R.W. Scapens and C.L. Yang, 'Chinese Public Finance Framework: A Critical Analysis', *Financial Accountability & Management* 26, no. 2 (2010), 163–89; J. Unger, 'Chinese Associations, Civil Society, and State Corporatism: Disputed Terrain', in J. Unger (ed.), *Associations and the Chinese State: Contested Spaces* (New York: ME Sharpe Inc, 2008), 1–13; J. Unger and A. Chan, 'China, Corporatism, and the East Asian Model', *Australian Journal of Chinese Affairs* 33 (1995), 29–53. Hsin-Hsien Wang, 'Bringing Society Back In? A Theoretical Review on the Rise of Intermediary Organizations in China', *Journal of Social Sciences and Philosophy* 18, no. 2 (2006), 293–326; Wei-Ming Liu, 'Corporatism and the New Perspective on China's Political Transformation', *Theory and Reform* 4 (2005), 5–8.
9. D.J. Solinger, 'Urban Entrepreneurs and the State: The Merger of State and Society', in A.L. Rosenbaum (ed.), *State and Society in China: The Consequences of Reform* (Boulder, CO: Westview Press, 1992), 121–41.
10. Qian Liu, 'Corporatism and Chinese Studies: A Literary Survey', *Chinese Social Science Quarterly* 2 (2009), 75–93.
11. Pei-Dong Sun, 'Civil Society or Corporatism: Review of Studies on Emerge of Economic Community and the Transformation of the Relationship Between State and Society', *Social Sciences in Guangdong* 5 (2011), 218–24.
12. This is according to the vice director of Sports Ethics and Integrity Risk Research Center, Beijing Sports University, interviewed on 18 January 2014.
13. Jian Chang, *The 10th CFA convention Documents – The 10th CFA convention Work Report* (Beijing: Chinese Football Association, 2014), 26.
14. This is according to one of the senior staff members in charge of the financial affairs of the CFA, interviewed on 22 January 2014.
15. This is according to one of the senior staff members in the GAS, interviewed on 13 January 2015.
16. This is according to a former official A from CFA School Football Office, interviewed on 4 January 2014.
17. This is according to an official B from CFA School Football Office, interviewed on 15 January 2014.
18. Ministry of Education, PRC, 'Notice from the Ministry of Education on Forming "National On-Campus Youth Football Leading Group"', http://www.moe.edu.cn/publicfiles/business/htmlfiles/moe/s5972/201501/183357.html (accessed 16 January 2015).

19. Peng Liu, 'Talks from Director Liu Peng on National Sports Bureaus Assembling (full text)' (2011), http://www.sport.gov.cn/n16/n1077/n1392/n2590312/n2590332/2635182.html (accessed 16 January 2015).
20. This is according to official from Athletic Sport Department, GAS, interviewed on 21 January 2014.
21. Jing-Yu Wang and Zheng Li, 'Exclusive Interview with Xiao Tien: "One Champion Three Medals" Works on Boosting football in China', http://news.xinhuanet.com/sports/2013-09/12/c_125377062.htm (accessed 16 January 2013).
22. General Office of the State Council of PRC, 'Overall Reform Plan to Boost the Development of Football in China', http://www.sport.gov.cn/n16/n1077/n1227/6255814.html (accessed 16 January 2015); China Interactive Sports Technology Invention, '*Mr. Xi and Chinese Football Back in the Years*', http://politics.sports.cn/yw/2015/0228/91110.html (accessed 16 January 2015).
23. Bin Gong and Yong Wang, 'Exclusive Interview with Wang Deng-Fong: Construct New Football Schools in the in the football-featured school system', http://news.xinhuanet.com/sports/2015-03/04/c_127543708.htm (accessed 16 January 2015).
24. General Office of the State Council of PRC, 'Overall Reform Plan to Boost the Development of Football in China'; China Interactive Sports Technology Invention, 'Mr. Xi and Chinese Football Back in the Years', http://politics.sports.cn/yw/2015/0228/91110.html (accessed 17 January 2015).
25. Sina Sport, 'Shi Xue Ching Talls: Wanda Select Youths for Free Study in Spain' (2011), http://sports.sina.com.cn/j/2011-12-20/11175876137.shtml (accessed 17 January 2015).
26. Xiang-Fei Ma, 'Liu Peng: CFA Management and Operation Combined System Would Prolong the Reform of Football in China' (2010), http://www.chinadaily.com.cn/typd/2010-09/28/content_11356810.htm (accessed 17 January 2015).
27. This is according to one of the senior staff of the CFA, interviewed on 15 January 2015.
28. General Office of the State Council of PRC, 'Overall Reform Plan to Boost the Development of Football in China'; China Interactive Sports Technology Invention, 'Mr. Xi and Chinese Football Back in the Years', http://politics.sports.cn/yw/2015/0228/91110.html (accessed 17 January 2015).
29. Zheng-Hua Cai, 'Separation CFA from Administration Doesn't Equal to Ease on the Political Leading and Management', http://news.xinhuanet.com/sports/2015-03/16/c_127586695.htm (accessed 19 March 2015).
30. Ibid.
31. Ibid.
32. General Office of the State Council of PRC, 'Overall Reform Plan to Boost the Development of Football in China'; China Interactive Sports Technology Invention, 'Mr. Xi and Chinese Football Back in the Years', http://politics.sports.cn/yw/2015/0228/91110.html (accessed 20 March 2015).
33. State Council, PRC, 'Several Opinions of the State Council of the People's Republic of China, on Accelerating the Development of Sports Industry to Promote the Sport Consumption' (2014), http://www.gov.cn/zhengce/content/2014-10/20/content_9152.htm (accessed 20 January 2015).
34. Xinhua News, 'Deputy of Economic Department of GAS Considers the 'Opinions' as Highly Valuable and Practicable' (2014), http://www.sport.gov.cn/n16/n1077/n1227/5828703.html (accessed 20 January 2015).
35. Ibid.
36. Xiang Li, 'Chinese Leaders and Football: Xi Jin-Ping Wish for Winning the World Cup Champion' (2012), http://cnsoccer.titan24.com/2012-12-26/195942_4.html (accessed 20 January 2013).
37. Xinhua News, 'Xi Jin-Ping's Three Dreams of Football: Hosting and Winning World Cup' (2013), http://news.xinhuanet.com/sports/2013-06/06/c_124819008.htm (accessed 20 January 2015).

38. Hui Sheng and others, 'Xi Jin-Ping: Mr. Football at the Diplomatic Arena' (2014), http://politics.people.com.cn/BIG5/n/2014/0330/c1024-24772409.html (accessed 6 January 2015).
39. This is according to a professor from Beijing Sport University, interviewed on 1 July 2014.
40. Yen Lu, 'The Recent Concerns Expressed by Chinese Officials are Worth for Notice' (2009), http://www.chinanews.com/ty/ty-gnzq/news/2009/10-15/1912040.shtml (accessed 6 January 2015).
41. Yan-Dong Liu, 'Liu Yan-Dong: Find the Crux of Problem and Advance the Development of Football in China' (2009), http://www.chinanews.com/ty/news/2009/10-15/1911147.shtml (accessed 6 January 2015).
42. Li-Ming Liu, 'Ministry of Education Deputy: Advance the Comprehension and Mechanism of On-Campus Football', (2010), http://sports.qq.com/a/20101227/000736.htm (accessed 6 January 2015).
43. This is according to an assistant for deputy director at General Administration of Sport, interviewed on 15 July 2014.
44. General Administration of Sports and Ministry of Education, 'Opinions of GAS and MOE on improve youth on-campus football work' (2012), http://www.wanda.cn/2011/2011_0130/4784.html (accessed 6 January 2015).
45. Shue-Ching Shi and Hai-Yang Lu, 'President Wang Jian-Lin Participates in Football Work Conference', http://sports.sina.com.cn/c/2011-07-06/11285646169.shtml (accessed 6 January 2015).
46. Sina News, 'Xi Jin-Ping Proposed Three Wishes for Chinese Football: Participating, Hosting, and Winning World Cup', (2011), http://hunan.voc.com.cn/article/201306/201306161513127169.html (accessed 6 January 2015).
47. Cheng Kuo, 'National Team Dreadfully Lost to Thai Team by 1:5: Forced to Facing the Facts of Chinese Football', (2013), http://hunan.voc.com.cn/article/201306/201306161513127169.html (accessed 6 January 2015).
48. This is according to a professor from Beijing Sport University, interviewed on 1 July 2014.
49. Zhen-Hua Cai, *The 10th CFA convention Documents – The Talk on CFA convention* (Beijing: Chinese Football Association, 2014), 13.
50. Ibid., 20.
51. Peng Liu, *The 10th CFA convention Documents – The Talk on CFA convention* (Beijing: Chinese Football Association, 2014), 2.
52. Ibid., 9–10.
53. This is according to an official B from CFA School Football Office, interviewed on 15 January 2014.
54. Ministry of Education, PRC, 'Notice from the Ministry of Education on Forming "National On-campus Youth Football Leading Group"', http://www.moe.edu.cn/publicfiles/business/htmlfiles/moe/s5972/201501/183357.html (accessed 6 January 2015).
55. Chinese Football Association, *The 10th CFA convention Documents – The List for 10th CFA authorities* (Beijing: Chinese Football Association, 2014), 76.
56. Kuei-Ren Yuan, 'Effective Approaches to Promote and Lead to Breakthrough of On-campus Football' (2014), http://www.moe.edu.cn/publicfiles/business/htmlfiles/moe/moe_797/201412/179080.html (accessed 6 January 2015).
57. Peng Liu, 'Summary on the Talks Regarding National Youth On-Campus Football Works: Improve Professional Instructions and Establish Reserved Talents Cultivation System' (2014), http://www.moe.edu.cn/publicfiles/business/htmlfiles/moe/moe_797/201412/179080.html (accessed 6 January 2015).
58. Bin Gong and Yong Wang, 'Exclusive Interview with Wang Deng-Fong: Construct New Football Schools in the Football-Featured School System', http://news.xinhuanet.com/sports/2015-03/04/c_127543708.htm (accessed 6 July 2015).
59. General Office of the State Council of PRC, 'Overall Reform Plan to Boost the Development of Football in China'.

60. CCTV, '"Dialogue" Football in China: Analysis of the Current Status and Future of Football Reform', http://jingji.cntv.cn/2015/03/18/ARTI1426648722161960.shtml (accessed 6 July 2015).
61. Yu-Xuan Sun, 'Game of Power: Uncover the Veil of Football Power Figure, Wang Jian-Lin', http://sports.qq.com/a/20150213/045959.htm (accessed 6 July 2015).
62. Xinhua News, 'Wanda Group Purchases 20% stock and Officially Becomes the Stockholder of Royal Madrid Football Club', http://industry.sports.cn/news/others/2015/0401/96115.html (accessed 6 July 2015).
63. Nan Xiao, 'Wang Jian-Lin Purchases 20% Stock of Royal Madrid Football Club. A One Stone Two Birds Move', http://sports.people.com.cn/n/2015/0121/c22176-26422836.html (accessed 6 July 2015).
64. Bin Gong et al., 'Wang Jian-Lin: Merge of Ifot Group will Speed up the Application for Hosting World Cup', http://news.xinhuanet.com/sports/2015-02/10/c_127480519.htm (accessed 6 July 2015).
65. This is according to the secretary of the chairman of the CFA, interviewed on 13 January 2015.
66. Lei-Shi Jia, 'Central Government Consults Five Stakeholders Including Cai Jeng-Hua, Xu Jia-Yin and Wang Jian-Lin for Football Development (2014), http://sports.sina.com.cn/c/2014-09-29/07427351745.shtml (accessed 6 July 2015).
67. CCTV, '"Dialogue" Football in China'.
68. Chunyan Zhang and Chi Ma, 'London forum advances soccer hopes', http://europe.chinadaily.com.cn/world/2015-09/18/content_21920790.htm (accessed 6 July 2015).
69. CCTV, 'Vice premier to lead football reform team', http://english.cntv.cn/2015/05/01/VIDE1430428922901855.shtml (accessed 6 July 2015).
70. See also Yu-Wen Chen and others, 'The Chinese Government and the Globalization of Table Tennis: A Case Study in Local Responses to Sports Globalization', *The International Journal of the History of Sport* 32, no. 10 (2015), 1336–48; Tien-Chin Tan, 'Assessing the Sociology of Sport: On Globalisation and Sport Policy', *International Review for Sociology of Sport* 50, nos 4–5, (2015), 612–6; Tien-Chin Tan and Alan Bairner, 'Globalisation and Chinese Sport Policy: The Case of Elite Football in the People's Republic of China', *China Quarterly* 203 (September 2010), 581–600.

Disclosure Statement

No potential conflict of interest was reported by the authors.

Funding

This research was funded by the Ministry of Science and Technology in Taiwan (grant number NSC 102-2410-H-003 -136 - & MOST 105-2914-I-003-009-A1).

Index

Note: **Boldface** page numbers refer to tables & *italic* page numbers refer to figures. Page numbers followed by "n" refer to endnotes.

African Athletics Confederation 45, 46
African games 40
Agabani, Hassan 41, 42, 45
AGF *see* Asian Games Federation
Alford, Jim 49
All-China Olympic Trials 72
'all games, all nations' 4, 11
'ancient Greece' 99
Anson Road stadium 67, 71, 73
Antwerp Olympic Games (1920) 80, 86, 88
Asian Games 23, 115, 116; Indonesia in 21, 33–4
Asian Games Federation (AGF) 21, 22
Asian Tigers 113
Athens Olympic Games 81, 83, 99
athletic infrastructure 42, 46
athletics confederations 41
authoritarianism 148
Aw Boon Haw 62
Aw Kow 62

Bach, Thomas 32
Bairner, Alan 131, 143n37
Baker, N. 60, 71
Bandung Conference (1955) 22
'basic globalisation' 94, 105
Basuki Tjahaja Purnama 34
Beijing Institute of Technology (BIT) 150–1
Beijing Olympic Games (2008) 126, 130, 140, 147; China's preparation for 131; elite athletes for 134–5; elite football achievement after 150; opening ceremony of 99; performance of Chinese elite athletes in 139; political significance of 136; success of 137; *see also* Chinese Olympic discourse themes
Beijing Sport University 128
'Big Olympics' 82
BIT *see* Beijing Institute of Technology
BMA *see* British Military Administration

BORs *see* British Other Ranks
Bouchard Gérard 96
boycott, Olympic 48
Boyle, Danny 100
Brazilian Olympic Committee (COB) 85
Brazilian Olympic Movement 89
Brazil, Olympic Games in 79; Antwerp Olympic Games 80, 86, 88; Athens Olympic Games 81; athletes 79; Federal Capital 80; independence centennial anniversary 87; inhabitants 78; 'Olympic' expression 80–4; in 1910s and 1920 84–7; 1922 and 2016 Games 88–9; people's strengths 85; political consequences in early 1920s 87–8; press coverage 84–7; shooting in 86; song 78
BRICS 113
British Military Administration (BMA) 60, 61; immediate priorities of 64; memorandum 65; in 1945–1946 63–4; 208-day period of 64
British Other Ranks (BORs) 66
Brownell, Susan 141n1, 144n45
Brown, Elwood 89
Brundage, Avery 13, 40
Bryson, Hugh 62, 69
Burghley, David 40–2, 69, 70
Busan Asian Games (2002) 115

Cai Zhen-Hua 153, 155, 157, 160n29
CAM *see* Club Atlético de Madrid
Cambodia, role in GANEFO movement 25
campus football 148, 151
CCAO *see* Chief Civil Affairs Officer
CCP *see* Chinese Communist Party
CCPPSC *see* Chinese Communist Party Politburo Standing Committee
CEDCNFL *see* Control, Ethics and Disciplinary Committee of National Football Leagues
CFA *see* Chinese Football Association
CFA Work Report (2014) 152
CFMC *see* Chinese Football Management Center
CFPA *see* China Foundation for Poverty Alleviation

INDEX

Chang Jian 150, 152
Chen En-Tang 153–4
Chief Civil Affairs Officer (CCAO) 63
China: administrative system 149; athletic 65; dominant-party system 148; Indonesia's attitude towards 21–2; national soccer team 73; sporting community 60, 61; support of GANEFO 23–4; 'two Chinas' issue 22, 25; *see also* football, in China
'China Dream' concept 137, 138, 140
China Foundation for Poverty Alleviation (CFPA) 151
China National Amateur Athletic Federation (CNAAF) 72
China National Games 73
China–UK Football Development Forum 157
Chinese Communist Party (CCP) 153
Chinese Communist Party Politburo Standing Committee (CCPPSC) 151
Chinese Communist Revolution (1949) 60
Chinese elite sport system 125, 140; Chinese Olympic movement and 129–32; extrinsic functions of Olympics 128–31; Olympic performance 135; policy documents and speeches **127**; research question 126–8; *see also* Beijing Olympic Games (2008); Chinese Olympic discourse themes
Chinese Football Association (CFA) 150–1, 153
Chinese Football Management Center (CFMC) 153
Chinese Football Stars of Hope Project 152
Chinese national team 150, 155
Chinese Olympic Committee (COC) 126, 134
Chinese Olympic discourse themes 128, 140; extrinsic functions 128–31; nationalism and patriotism in 131–3; *1994 Plan* 138; post-2008 136–9; socialism in 133–6; *2001 Plan* 138; *2011 summary* 138
Chinese Olympic dream, realization of 132
Chinese Olympic movement 129–30, 132
Chinese Swimming Club (CSC) 66
CIOA *see* Committee for International Olympic Aid
'Citius, Altius, Fortius' slogan 10
Club Atlético de Madrid (CAM) 156
Clube Olimpico Guanabarense 83
CNAAF *see* China National Amateur Athletic Federation
COB *see* Brazilian Olympic Committee
COC *see* Chinese Olympic Committee
Collins, Randall 113, 122n23
Committee for International Olympic Aid (CIOA) 39
Communist Party of China (CPC) 129, 135, 142n26, 143n44, 144n50
'complex globalisation' 94
'consumer culture' 101
continental athletic events 41

Control, Ethics and Disciplinary Committee of National Football Leagues (CEDCNFL) 150
Cool Runnings (Turteltaub) 111
corporatism 148–9, 158
Correio da Manhã 84
Corri, Ernesto 84
Coubertin, Pierre de 9, 10, 85, 88, 93, 97
CPC *see* Communist Party of China
cross-culturalism 95
Crown Colony of Singapore 66, 69
CSC *see* Chinese Swimming Club
cultural exchange, of social media 94, 103–4
cultural politics 113–14
'culture', concept of 94–5

DAGI *see* Dewan Asian Games Indonesia
Dalian Wanda Group (DWG) 150–1
Dayan, Daniel 97
decolonialization 41
'deep mining' process 103
Defence National League 87
Democratic Revolutions of 1848 8
Deng Xiaoping 132
Departemen Olahraga (DEPORA) 23
de Souza, Jocelyn 73
Dewan Asian Games Indonesia (DAGI) 21
Dewan Olahraga Republik Indonesia (DORI) 23, 26
Diack, Lamine 45, 46, 48, 49, 51
DORI *see* Dewan Olahraga Republik Indonesia
Douyin Xiong 129, 130, 141n8, 142n24
Dubai International 44–5
Dumont, Santos 85
DWG *see* Dalian Wanda Group

East Asian financial crisis 117
Edstrom, Sigfried 69
Elias, Norbert 61
Eliot, T.S. 94
English public schools 9
'era of Olympic dominance, the' 98
EREG *see* Evergrande Real Estate Group
European Clubhouses 62
Evergrande Model 157
Evergrande Real Estate Group (EREG) 151, 157
expression, Olympic 80–4

Facebook 101, 102
Fairclough, Norman 126, 142n17, 142n20; CDA framework 127; order of discourse 128
Farhi, Paul 111, 122n11
Fédération Internationale de Football Association (FIFA) 53, 150
FIFA World Cup Finals 109, 110, 115, 116, 118
flag, Olympic 11
football, in China: administration system 148; Beijing Olympics (2008) 147, 150; campus 148; Control, Ethics and Disciplinary Committee of

INDEX

National Football Leagues 150; development and reform of 155; development strategies 150; Evergrande Model 157; government and football associations 153; 'inviting in and sending out' policy 152–3; National Games, profile and status of 151–2; National Youth Campus Football Leading Group Office 151; professionalization of 147; reinvigoration of 151; and sports industry, bellwether role of 153–4; *see also* Xi Jinping
Fourth Asian Games 21–3, 26
Francis, Amadeo 43, 45, 50
French Revolution 8
Friese, Hermann 84

Gaelic Athletic Association 154
Games of the New Emerging Forces (GANEFO) 1; Cambodia's role in 25; China's support of 23–4; Federation *(musjawarah)* 24–5; foundation of 21; legacy of 26; Sukarno's policy 22, 25
Games of the Newly Emerging Forces (GANEFO) 40
Games of the XXXI Olympiad 1
GANEFO *see* Games of the New Emerging Forces; Games of the Newly Emerging Forces
'Ganyang Malaysia' 28
GAS *see* General Administration of Sport
Gazeta de Petrópolis 81, 82
General Administration of Sport (GAS) 149, 151; Beijing Olympic Games 129, 130, 134, 139, 142n25
Gilmour, Andrew 69, 71
Gilmour, Oswald 62, 64
'Girl from Ipanema, The' 78–80
Girls' Sports Club (GSC) 67
globalization 41; concept of 94; context of 94–6; Olympic Games in 103–4
Glovini, Octavio 84
Goh Hood Kiat 69, 72
Greek Olympic Games 82
GSC *see* Girls' Sports Club
Guiding Theory and Principle 137

Hamengku Buwono IX (Sultan of Yogyakarta) 26, 29
Herb, Guntram 131, 143n36
He Wei 155
He Zhenliang 134
Holder, Frederick W. 41, 43
Holt, John 40, 41, 43
Horne, John 121n1
Hua Li 136
Hui-Wen football team 154
Hu Jintao 126, 134, 139, 141n11, 142n15, 143n41, 144n54, 145n63, 147

IAAF *see* International Association of Athletics Federations

Independent Olympic Athletes (IOA): advent of 3; Coubertin's assignments 10; delegation constitution 3–7, 15; in Olympic Games 6–7; Olympic Truce ideal 6
Indonesia 19–20; in Asian Games 21, 33–4, *34*; attitude towards Taiwan 21–2, 25; in bidding process 33; and Cambodia 25; confrontation policy 25; cooperation 33–4; dispute over Olympic rings 29–30, *31*, 32–3; Games of the New Emerging Forces 20–5; interest in hosting sporting events 33; and International Olympic Committee 21, 22, 30, 32; Komite Olympiade Indonesia 22; Ministry of Youth and Sports Affairs 29–30; *Orde Baru* (New Order) government 27; Persatuan Olahraga Republik Indonesia 22; politicization of sport 21–2; Southeast Asian Games 25–9; Southeast Asian Peninsular Games 27; Sports Council of the Republic of Indonesia 23, 26; Sultan Hamengku Buwono IX 26
Indonesian Olympic Committee *see* Komite Olympiade Indonesia
Indonesian Sports Association 22
Industrial Revolution 8
Infront Sports & Media (ISM) 157
'Inspire a Generation,' London Games motto 99
intercultural exchange, of social media 94, 105
inter-culturalism 95–6
interest group-dominated nations 148
Interim Brazilian Olympic Committee 85
International Association of Athletics Federations (IAAF) 39; African member federations 41; budget 41, 43–4, **48**, 49; Burghley, David 40, 42; decolonialization 41; developing countries 41–2; Development Committee 43, 44, 49; development courses **46**; Diack, Lamine 46–7; Dubai International's sponsorship 44–5; expenditures **45**; extended development initiatives 48–51; financial resources 41; financial support 40, 46; globalization 41, 42; Holder, Frederick W. 41; Holt, John 40; income 49; member federations 40–4; Olympic Solidarity 46; Paulen, Adriaan 42–3; potential development aid program 40–1; shares of increased income 44–8; Technical Aid Program 41–3; Western training philosophy 42; world cup development fund 44–5
International Journal of the History of Sport, The 1
International Olympic Committee (IOC) 2, 40, 69, 110, 118; African games 40; in Brazil 84; Brundage, Avery 13, 40; capitalism 13–14; contracts with sponsoring companies 13; Coubertin, Pierre de 9, 10, 93; determination of 98; dispute over Olympic rings 29–30, *31*, 32–3; as global corporation 12–14; Indonesia and 21, 22; as international institution 7–12; internationalism 10–11; legitimacy of 12; mass media and broadcasting rights 13; members of 5;

INDEX

National Olympic Committees and 4; Olympic flag, creation of 11; peace and prosperity 9–11; PRC relationship with 126, 129; television rights sales 49; toward conflicts and political issues 14, 15; and United Nations 6
international Olympic movement 88, 129, 130, 140
'inviting in and sending out' policy 152–3
IOA *see* Independent Olympic Athletes
IOC *see* International Olympic Committee
Island Club 62
ISM *see* Infront Sports & Media

Jakarta 24, 28
Jalan Besar stadium 67, 71
Japanese occupation 61, 63, 64
Joko Widodo 32
Jornal do Brasil 81, 85, 91n45
Juguo Tizhi 134, 137, 139, 140, 144n55

Kallang Plain 71
Kaplan, David 131, 143n36
Katz, Elihu 97
Kenya, Olympic Games (1996) 50
Khomenkov, Leonid 47, 49
Kim, Yuna 118, 119
Kirsch, August 47, 50, 51
KOGOR *see* Komite Gerakan Olahraga
KOI *see* Komite Olympiade Indonesia
Komite Gerakan Olahraga (KOGOR) 21
Komite Olahraga Nasional Indonesia (KONI) 26, 29, 30, 32
Komite Olympiade Indonesia (KOI) 22, 29, 30, 32
KONI *see* Komite Olahraga Nasional Indonesia
Korea 118; Asian Games (2014) 116
Korea Democratic Party (2011) 148
Korean Peninsula 117
Korean War 117

laissez-faire colonial approach 60, 61
Lang Xiao-Nong 157
Latin American Olympic Games (1922) 87–8
Lehmbruch, G. 148
Liu Changchun 126
Liu Li-Ming 154
Liu Peng 151, 153, 155
Liu Yan-Dong 150, 154, 155, 157
London Olympic Games 60, 68, 85, 99–101
Los Angeles Olympic Games (1984) 49

Mabbott, Chappelet 4
Malayan Chinese Amateur Athletic Federation 62
Malayan Chinese Organising Committee 73
Malayan Civil Service 61
Malayan People's Anti-Japanese Army (MPAJA) 65
Malayan Planning Unit (MPU) 63

Malaysia, Southeast Asian Peninsular Games 28
male national football team 150
Maynooth University 1
McKerron, Patrick A.B. 59, 64
Melbourne Games (1956) 97
Melbourne Summer Olympic Games 74
Meyer, Micheal Meyer 126
Ministry of Education (MOE) 151, 152
Ministry of Public Security (MPS) 150
Ministry of Youth and Sports Affairs 29–30
Modern Era Olympics in 1896 88
MOE *see* Ministry of Education
Mount Emily Swimming Pool 66
MPAJA *see* Malayan People's Anti-Japanese Army
MPS *see* Ministry of Public Security
MPU *see* Malayan Planning Unit
Mukora, Charles 45
multiculturalism 60, 95
Munich Olympic Games (1972) 41
Municipal Commissioners 66, 71
Museum Monas 25

NAAFIs *see* Navy, Army, Air Force Institutes
Nally, Patrick 45
national corporatism 148
National Games, profile and status of football in 151–2
nationalism, Olympic discourse 131–3
nationality 72–3
National Olympic Committees (NOCs) 3, 40; and International Olympic Committee 4; recognition of 5–7
National Playing Fields Association 72
National Shooting Federation 86
National Shooting Stand (1899) 86
National Sports Minister Conference (2011) 151
National Youth Campus Football Leading Group Office (NYLGO) 151
nation-dominated interest groups 148
Nations and Nationalism 131
Navy, Army, Air Force Institutes (NAAFIs) 66
Nebiolo, Primo 44, 52, 53; election 48; financial resources 47; insecure financial situation 45; leadership 49–51; Olympic Solidarity 44, 46; Technical Aid Program 43
New Emerging Forces (NEFOs) 21
'new Greece' 99
NOCs *see* National Olympic Committees
Non-Aligned Movement 19, 20, 22, 24
NYLGO *see* National Youth Campus Football Leading Group Office

OCA *see* Olympic Council of Asia
Old Established Forces (OLDEFOs) 21, 22
'Olympic Cirque' 83
Olympic Council of Asia (OCA) 20, 30, 33–4
Olympic Glory Plan 126, 129, 134, 137, 142n25

INDEX

Olympic media development: Athens 2004 99; Beijing 2008 99; 'the era of Olympic dominance' 98; function of 96; London 2012 99–100; 'Satellite Television before the Internet' (1968–1988) 98; television before satellites (1936–1964) 97; 'TV age of sports' 97
Olympic Movement 10, 60, 70, 104
Olympic rings, Indonesia's dispute over 29–30, *31*, 32–3
'Olympics in Conflict: From GANEFO to the Rio Olympics' 1
Olympic Solidarity 39, 40, 44, **46**, 49
Olympic Truce ideal 5–6
O Malho journalist *86*, 87
on-campus football competition 156
'One World, One Dream', Beijing Games motto of 99
O Paiz 80, 81
opening ceremony: Athens Olympic Games (2004) 99; Beijing Olympic Games (2008) 99; content of 101; London Olympic Games (2012) 99–100; as 'mega-events' and 'media-events' 100
Opinions of GAS and MOE on Improving Youth On - Campus Football Work 155
Opinions on Further Strengthening and Improving the Ideological Education of National Teams, The 135
orientalism 119
Overseas Chinese *(hua qiao)*: community 60, 61, 70; population 60

Pagden, Hugh 65
Pan-American Games (2007) 79
Pan-Malayan sports federation 68
Papaioannou, Dimitris 99
Paralympics 126
Paranhos, Raul 85
Paris Conference 80
Paris Grand Prix 81
Paris Olympic Games (1900) 84
Park Ji-sung 155
Pastore, Salvador 84
patriotism, Olympic discourse 131–3
Paulen, Adriaan 42–3
Peng Liu 132–3, 137, 141n9, 144n47, 145n60
People's Liberation Army (PLA) 152
People's Republic of China (PRC) 126, 129, 130, 141n7, 143n43, 147; accomplishment of 137; socialist character of 131, 133
Peran Olahraga Nasional (PON) 22
Persatuan Olahraga Republik Indonesia (PORI) 22
PLA *see* People's Liberation Army
PON *see* Peran Olahraga Nasional
PORI *see* Persatuan Olahraga Republik Indonesia
post-2008 Olympic discourse 136–9
PRC *see* People's Republic of China

pre-2008 Chinese Olympic discourse 128; extrinsic functions 128–31; nationalism and patriotism in 131–3; socialism in 133–6
process-oriented methodology 61
process-sociology approach 61
Provisory Brazilian Olympic Committee 85
Pyeongchang's 'Dream Program' initiative 121
Pyeongchang Winter Olympic 110, 112, 119–21

Race Course Golf Club 62
rationing system 66
RDCs *see* regional development centers
Red Army 133
Reform Plan 153, 156, 157
regional development centers (RDCs) 39–40
rehabilitation process 63
Republic of China 72
requisitioning 65
Rio de Janeiro 1; Latin American Olympic Games in 80; newspaper 80–2; Olympic Games (2016) 89; Paris Conference 80; population 83; social and intellectual elite 80
Roche, Maurice 94, 97
Rome Olympics (1960) 13

SAAA *see* Singapore Amateur Athletic Association
SAFA *see* Singapore Amateur Football Association
Saint Louis Olympic Games (1904) 84
'Satellite Television before the Internet' (1968–1988) 98
SCASF *see* Singapore Chinese Amateur Sports Federation
SCC *see* Singapore Cricket Club
Schmitter, P.C. 148, 149
School Football Office (SFO) 151
scoring system 152
SCRC *see* Singapore Chinese Recreation Club
SEA Games *see* Southeast Asian Games
SEAP Games *see* Southeast Asian Peninsular Games
Second World War, decolonialization 40
'sending out' element 152
SFO *see* School Football Office
Shi Shue-Ching 152
Sinatra, Frank 78, 79
Singapore Amateur Athletic Association (SAAA) 69
Singapore Amateur Football Association (SAFA) 67
Singapore Amateur Swimming Association (SASA) 67–8
Singapore Chinese Amateur Sports Federation (SCASF) 62, 72–3
Singapore Chinese Recreation Club (SCRC) 66
Singapore Cricket Club (SCC) 62, 64, 66, 67

INDEX

Singapore Olympic and Sports Council (SOSC) 62, 68–71, 73
Singapore Recreation Club (SRC) 67
Singapore sport (1945–1948): Anson Road Stadium 67; Baker, N. 60, 71; Crown Colony of 66, 69; de-requisitioning and revival 66–7; framework for analysis 61–3; international relationship 60; Jalan Besar Stadium 67; and Malaya 68–9; nationality 72–3; overview of 59–60; rehabilitation process 63; requisitioning 65; Singapore Amateur Swimming Association 67–8; Singapore Olympic and Sports Council 68–71; stadiums and playing fields 71–2; Valberg, Lloyd 71, 73; Young Men's Christian Association 64, 67–8
Singapore Swimming Club (SSC) 65, 66, 68
Sir, Jozsef 41, 43–4, 46, 49
snow sports 111
Sochi Winter Olympics 126
socialism, Olympic discourse 133–6
social media: characteristics of 104; commercial feature of 97; cultural exchange 94, 95, 103–4; 'culture', concept of 94–6; events 97; Facebook 101, 102; feature of 93–4; forms of 101; globalization, concept of 94–6; intercultural exchange 94; for Olympic Movement 96; organization of Olympic Games 96–8; platforms 103; sponsors on 102; in twenty-first century 93; Twitter 102; *see also* Olympic media development
social rehabilitation 71
'social rising' 8
Socialympics 94, 101, 102
societal corporatism 148, 149
Socio-Political Process 98
SOSC *see* Singapore Olympic and Sports Council
Southeast Asian Games 25–9; *gotong royong*, concept of 28; Srivijaya 29
Southeast Asian Peninsular (SEAP) Games 27, 27–8
South Korea 120; cultural politics 117–18; FIFA World Cup 115, 116; international sport competitions 114–15; sports mega-events in 114–16; Western cultural imperialism 119; world system theory 113; *see also* Pyeongchang Winter Olympic; Winter Olympic Games (2018)
Soviet sport authorities 47
sponsoring companies, contracts with 13
sport, importance of 9
'sporting countries' 11
'Sport Power' 137–40
Sports Council of the Republic of Indonesia 23, 26
sports for peace, Coubertin's notion of 9
sports-media complex 97
SRC *see* Singapore Recreation Club
Srivijaya 29

SSC *see* Singapore Swimming Club
state corporatism model 148, 149
Straits Chinese Football Association league 65
Strickland, Edward 69
Suharto 26
Sukarno 19, 24; 'Bandung spirit' 22; concept of museum 26; 'Founder and Honorary President' 23; Games of the New Emerging Forces 22, 25; ideology and nation-building policy 21; *konfrontasi* policy 25, 36n28; Third Worldist policy 21
'Sukseskan GANEFO Ganjang Malaysia' 25
Summer Asian Games (1986) 114
Summer Olympic Games 110, 111, 114, 118
'Swifter, Higher, Stronger', Olympic moto 103
Syonan Sports Association 69

Taiwan, Indonesia's attitude towards 21–2, 25
Tanglin Club 66
Technical Aid Program 41–3
Thailand, SEAP Games Federation 28
theory-driven empirical study 61
Third Worldist policy 20–1
'Top-Tier Athletes Program' 29–30
traditional media 102
Turnbull, C.M. 64
Turteltaub, John 111
'TV age of sports' 97
Twitter 101, 102
'two-China' issue 126, 129

Union of Soviet Socialist Republics (USSR) 47
United Nations (UN) 3, 22, 117; and International Olympic Committee 6
USSR *see* Union of Soviet Socialist Republics
utopic integrated education 82

Valberg, Lloyd 71, 73
Vietnam, bidding process 33

Wallerstein, Immanuel 112, 122n22
Wang Deng-Feng 151, 152, 155
Wang Jian-Lin 150, 151, 157
'Welcome Home', Athens Games motto of 99
white athletes, Western countries 110–12
Winter Olympic Games (2018) 109, 112, 114, 119; Asian Games (2014) 116; bidding campaigns 110; cultural politics 112–14; empowerment 118–20; global economy 112–14; periphery 112; of Pyeongchang 110; racial inequality 122n13; semi-peripheral

INDEX

countries 113; South Korean cultural politics and 117–18; sports mega-events 114–16; Western white competitors in 110–12; *see also* South Korea
Wodak, Ruth 126
world systems theory 112

Xiang Zhao-Lun 155
Xiao Tien 152
Xi Jinping 126, 138, 148, 153, 154; dreams for Chinese elite football 154–7; visit to Sochi 137
XinHua News Agency 152, 153

Xuanjian Ma 130
Xu Jia-Yin 157
XVIII Asian Games 33–4, *34*

Young Men's Christian Association (YMCA) 64, 67
Yuan Gui-Ren 155
Yuan Weimin 132, 133, 143n42

Zhang Ji-Long 157
Zhang Yimou 99
Zhou Enlai 126
zones of prestige 112–14